VOICES FROM
THE ARCTIC
CONVOYS

VOICES FROM THE ARCTIC CONVOYS

PETER C. BROWN

FONTHILL

Learn more about Fonthill Media. Join our mailing list to
find out about our latest titles and special offers at:
www.fonthillmedia.com

Fonthill Media Limited
Fonthill Media LLC
www.fonthillmedia.com
office@fonthillmedia.com

First published in the United Kingdom and the United States of America 2014

British Library Cataloguing in Publication Data:
A catalogue record for this book is available from the British Library

ISBN 978-1-78155-284-1

Typeset in 10pt on 13pt Sabon LT Std
Printed and bound in England

Contents

Introduction

Following the German invasion of the Soviet Union through Operation *Barbarossa* in June 1941, the Russians were forced into a precarious position—they were ill-prepared for the might of the German army, and the Russian army had all but collapsed under the onslaught. Moscow was nearly reached and Leningrad was surrounded. The British Prime Minister, Winston Churchill, promised to supply Stalin 'at all costs', knowing that, had Russia fallen, the full weight of the Nazi machinery would have been directed at the West, and so on 12 July, 1941, the Soviet Union and Great Britain signed the treaty on 'mutual assistance' against Germany, and in August, Allied convoys commenced running. Over four million tons of supplies were delivered to the Russians, including tanks, aircraft, trucks, tractors, railway engines, ammunition, and raw materials.

The Arctic route around occupied Norway was the shortest and most direct route to carry supplies from Great Britain and America to the Soviet ports, though it was also the most dangerous. The gruelling weather conditions; severe cold, storms, fog, ice floes, waves so large that they tore at the ship's armour plating, and strong currents making navigation difficult to maintain convoy cohesion while under the constant threat of attack from above and below from German air, submarine and surface forces. Many considered that no ships at all would get through.

At the start, the convoys usually ran from Hvalfjord, Iceland, to Archangel in the summer months when the ice permitted, and then shifted south as the pack ice increased and terminated at Murmansk. After September 1942, they assembled and sailed from Loch Ewe in Scotland.

The convoys ran in two series, following the first convoy, which was un-numbered but code-named 'Dervish'; the first series was numbered PQ for outbound convoys, and QP for homebound, and ran twice monthly from September 1941, but were interrupted in the summer of 1942 after the disaster of PQ-17, and again in the autumn after the final convoy of the series, PQ-18, due to lengthening daylight hours, and continued preparations for Operation 'Torch', the name given to the Allied invasion of French North Africa in November 1942.

The second series of convoys, numbered JW for outbound convoys, and RA for homebound, ran from December 1942 until the end of the war, though with two major interruptions in the summer of 1943 and again in the summer of 1944. Outbound and homebound convoys were planned to run simultaneously; a close escort accompanied the merchant ships to port, remaining there to make the subsequent return trip with the next convoy. In addition, a covering force of heavy surface units was also provided to guard against sorties by German surface ships. These would accompany the outbound convoy to a cross-over point, meeting and then conducting the homebound convoy back, while the close escort finished the voyage with its charges.

The convoys—which Winston Churchill once called 'the worst journey in the world'—played a crucial role to the Allied War effort in the overall victory of the Second World War. A total of seventy eight convoys made the perilous journey to and from orth Russia, carrying four million tons of supplies for use by Soviet forces fighting against the German Army on the Eastern Front, and thousands of British and Allied merchant and naval seamen lost their lives during the four year campaign. Eighty-five out of the 1,400 merchant vessels and sixteen Royal Navy warships were lost. The Allied seamen showed true heroism in their long and perilous sea passages in convoys, being constantly attacked by enemy forces in the appalling weather conditions of the Arctic. The bravery of these men and women who unsparingly fought for the Victory will be always remembered and respected.

This collection of stories from the Allied seamen who endured the long and perilous journeys, comes from personal interviews and letters, and along with photographs provides a first-hand—and often graphic—insight into life on the Arctic convoys.

Acknowledgments

I am grateful to the many people who have helped me in gathering material, and kindly given me permission to use photographs and text, in particular: Dean Boettger, *Royal Canadian Navy History & Heritage;* Kathryn Bradley, *Lowestoft Journal*; Paul Britton, *Manchester Evening News*; Jacky Brookes, *Russian Arctic Convoy Museum Project*; Philip Bulman; Iris Burgess; Lynda Brunning; Charles 'Charlie' Chaplin; Andrew Choong, *Curator of Historic Photographs & Ships Plans, National Maritime Museum, Greenwich*; Brian Coates, *Halifax Courier*; Kathleen Daveney; Brian H. Donohoe, MP for Central Ayrshire; Patricia Hartley; Rosemary Heddle; Graham Hutt; Chris Jones; George Laverick, Hon. Secretary, Tyne Branch (RNA); Kris Lockyear; Samantha Mair; Sigita Minate; Alf Muffett, Curator, *RNPSA Museum*; Barbara Mumford; Peter Nicol; Sally Pilkinton; Rebecca Ricks, *Plymouth Evening Herald*; Julie Robinson; Brian Sandom; John Thorne; Monica Turnbull, *Sunderland Echo*; Fred Wadley; Alistair Wilson; Ian Wilson; Michael Wright; and *The National Archives*.

Donald Sydney Allen
HMS *Ledbury*

I was born on 9 October 1922, at Streatham, London, the son of Sydney Alfred and Elsie Dorothy Allen, and had a younger sister.

After sitting the Civil Service Entry Examination at King Edward Buildings, off Liverpool Street, I was told that I had passed and would be assessed as Clerical Grade Three. In August 1939, with war being a distinct possibility, I was sent to the Royal Engineers records office in Chatham.

It must have dawned on someone in the Ministry of Defence that Chatham would not be a safe place for army records should war be declared, and so we were soon shipped down to Brighton, where it so happened that my mother had taken a house to be near one of her sisters. It was nice to be back home with the tlc my mother could provide, but this did not last long because after the retreat at Dunkirk in 1940, Brighton was considered unsafe and the office was transferred to Radcliffe, in Salford, Lancashire.

I was billeted in the nearby town of Whitby, where I joined the St John Ambulance Brigade and a local emergency rescue service, where I was issued with a pair of blue overalls and a tin hat. During an air raid on Piccadilly, Manchester, we were sent there to help in the rescue of people from demolished buildings. Most of the buildings were on fire, and I found my first dead body; a young woman of about thirty. There were five of us in the team and we dealt with some forty casualties that night.

By 1941, at the age of seventeen-and-a-half, I was getting tired of office life and decided to volunteer for the Royal Navy. I was duly accepted and sent to the training establishment HMS *Raleigh*, Torpoint, Devon.

Following basic training as a seaman I was drafted to Portsmouth barracks to undertake training in RDF (Radio Direction Finding—later to be called Radar). It was here that I met Reg Gowing, who also lived in Brighton, and we discovered that by buying a two shillings workman's return ticket to Portsmouth, we could go home every other night.

Since 'Pompey', as Portsmouth was known, was full of sailors there were always a few who would like a night in Brighton. I should point out that the train left Brighton at six o'clock in the morning and was due to arrive in Portsmouth at eight o'clock, which was the time we were due back in barracks. More often than not we were late but were able to avoid being charged as Reg's uncle was in the Regulating office where we handed in and collected the railway tickets.

This went on for some three months when I thought that enough is enough; let's volunteer for a ship. Reg wasn't too keen on this idea, but I managed to talk him round. We went to see the DO (Divisional Officer), who must have thought we were mad, but said he would see what he could do. As we came away, Reg said, 'Well, we'll be alright for another three months'. How wrong can you be? The next day they piped 'Ordinary Seamen Allen and Gowing to report to the Drafting office'. There we met the DO who said, 'I found you a ship, lads. She's a brand new Hunt-class destroyer called *Ledbury* and is in Thornycroft's yard in Southampton. If you hurry, you might be in time for the commissioning'.

We arrived at the gangway in time to see the commissioning pennant being hoisted. This was 27 January 1942, and this would be our ship for the rest of the war until she paid off in Sheerness, in June 1945.

My action station on HMS *Ledbury* (L90) was in the '291' Radar office (The type 291 Radar had a hand-steered antenna) just in front of the funnel and above the galley. Reg was on the bridge to relay my messages to the Captain (Lieutenant Commander Roger Percival Hill, DSO, DSC).

We were sent to the Home Fleet base at Scapa Flow to work up the ship's company to an effective fighting force. 'Action Stations' were called at six o'clock in the morning until we could close up (batten-down the hatches) in under one minute. Then it was out to sea to escort the Battle Fleet on exercise, shooting at the tug towing the target (and nearly sinking her in the process) until the Captain was able to announce to the C-in-C (Commander-in-Chief) that the ship was ready for deployment.

Donald Allen in uniform. (*Courtesy of Rosemary Heddle*)

Our first assignment was to escort the Fleet Oiler *Black Ranger* off Jan Mayen Island in the Arctic. Destroyers from the Russian convoy would come and take on fuel while we stood guard against submarine attacks. This was a mundane task that lasted for two weeks before we would return to our buoy at Scapa, and enjoy the mail from home until the next trip.

We did four of these trips with the *Black Ranger* and *Grey Ranger*, and fortunately didn't lose either of them. We were then given the task of joining the big boys as close escort on our first Arctic convoy—PQ-17, which was bound for Archangel.

PQ-17 turned out to be one of the biggest blunders in Naval history, when the First Sea Lord, believing that the German Battleship *Tirpitz* had put to sea, decided to scatter the convoy. Up to this time we had only lost one merchant ship when we received the signal from the escort commander to strike, which meant 'follow me'. So we joined forces with two cruisers, HMS *London* (69) and HMS *Norfolk* (78), steaming at twenty-four knots to engage what we thought would be the enemy. In the meantime, we were picking up signals from stricken merchant ships; 'am being attacked by air', 'have been torpedoed', 'am sinking SOS', etc. By

Donald Allen with a poppy wreath. (*Courtesy of Rosemary Heddle*)

the time we realised that the *Tirpitz* had merely changed berths, it was too late to go back, and out of thirty five merchant vessels, only fifteen made it to Russia; the rest were lost to the U-boats and the Luftwaffe. We had to take oil from the *London*, and the Admiral ordered a marine band to play to us while this was taking place. The first tune they played was Colonel Bogey, which summed up our sentiments exactly.

Back home, HMS *Ledbury* went for a boiler clean at Rosyth. The whole crew was feeling low, and Reg and I decided to take the long journey south for four days leave. It was at a dance that Reg met a girl called Sylvia, who would later become his bride. Wanting to escort her home in the blackout, she declined, saying she was with a friend. Undaunted, Reg said, 'Well that's no problem. I too have a friend', whereupon I was introduced to Joan Moreton, and escorted her to her home in Beaconfield Road, and from then we corresponded to one another regularly by letter.

On our return to Rosyth, we were sent to Malta as close escort to the convoy on Operation 'Pedestal', to relieve the siege of Malta. The convoy was met with continuous attacks by Axis forces of surface vessels and submarines, and out of the fourteen merchant ships that made up the convoy, only five arrived at the destination.

HMS *Ledbury* returned to Grimsby for a refit in August 1942, and a long well-earned leave for her crew. Following the refit, we were sent back to Scapa Flow

HMS *Ledbury*. (*Author's Collection*)

for one last convoy to Russia before being sent out to the Mediterranean for the Allied Landings in Sicily and Salerno. I have to this day the greatest respect for the merchant navy and for the sacrifices they made; only one in four survived the war.

Rosemary Heddle, Donald's daughter:

Our father, Donald Allen, penned the above notes himself sometime during the last decade so the information could be passed on to us, his children, grandchildren, and great grandchildren, after his death. To my knowledge, he went on the Arctic Convoy journey at least five times. He would break down in tears frequently if he tried to tell us very much as to what happened during those terrible years.

I do know that their ships were covered feet deep in ice, and that the conditions were so dreadful that they worked and slept in their duffle coats. That was all they had and it was the only way they could try to keep warm. Rum became a favourite tipple and probably helped to keep them sane!

Donald was a very compassionate man; my Godfather, Reg Gowing, who sadly died a long time ago, used to tell me how heroic our father was. At one time a seaman lay on the deck with part of his head hanging off, and it was our father who stayed and comforted that man until he finally died in his arms.

Donald became chairman of the 'North Russia Club' some years ago. It finally disbanded after more and more of those brave men died of old age, and there were simply not enough members left to keep it going. The money left from the club was gifted to the Royal National Lifeboat Institution, who purchased and named a boat called *Northern Light* (D705). The naming ceremony took place on 29 October 2008.

Other clubs Donald belonged to were the 'George Cross Island' (where he remained an active member until his death), the 'Italy Star' and the local 'Royal Naval Association Club' in Ashford, where he enjoyed social evenings amongst friends.

Our father, who was dearly loved by his family, sadly died in hospital whilst on holiday in Suffolk with me on 12 August 2011.

Rosemary Heddle, June 2013.

Russell Bennett
SS *Induna*

Russell Harrison Bennett was a young Canadian who was serving on the SS *Ballot,* which had sailed from New York to Iceland to meet convoy PQ-12 to Murmansk, but had missed it and so sailed in convoy PQ-13. When she arrived in Iceland she had no armament of any sort, so the British put two Maritime Gunners aboard her with one very old machine gun. It was a Lewis gun, one that had left over from the First World War; at that time it was all that the British Merchant ships carried as armament.

The *Ballot* was to undertake the voyage to Russia, and the ice in the winter forced the convoys to take a course that took them very near to the north cape of Norway, and right into the range of the German forces; Junkers Ju-88 bombers, and the waiting U-boats which were homed-in by Focke-Wulf long range aircraft.

After leaving Iceland, PQ-13 struck very bad weather, causing the ships to get badly scattered, and when the weather moderated and cleared a little, the long range enemy planes found the ships, and homed in on the destroyers, but these were beaten off by the escort ship HMS *Trinidad*. Then the Junkers bombers and the high level Focke-Wulfs began bombing.

The *Ballot* suffered near misses from a dive bomb attack by a Ju-88, and she lost steam, causing her to drop astern of the convoy. This was in the Barents Sea (referred to by the sailors of the time as 'The Devil's Ballroom'), about 120 miles north of Russia.

Her crew of sixteen abandoned her, and they were picked up by the Whaler *Silja* (FY301), which was on passage to be turned over to the Russians. Three of these set out, but one was sunk and one turned over with the ice.

A few ships went north to get near the ice and the SS *Induna* got stuck. The other ships went on but the *Silja* stayed with the *Induna*. As she was a small ship with limited room, the men from the *Ballot* walked over the ice onto the *Induna*. The Silja then ran out of fuel; her crew had been burning everything to keep her going, so the *Induna* took her in tow, but at around 2200 hrs the tow broke and the two ships parted. The captain searched for the drifting ship until 0400 hrs, but then could spare no more time, as they would have to make a run for Murmansk.

At first light the following morning (30 March), the *Induna* was struck by a torpedo in the No. 5 hold, right under the aviation sprite, and the explosion threw barbed wire from the hold onto the top of the deck cargo of petrol drums, which in turn, ignited and exploded, turning the deck into a burning mess. The Mate ordered us to our boat stations, and a few people started to run through the fire while some on the stern jumped into the sea out of the way of the heat and flames. The last man through was one of the men from the *Ballot*, he had only a short coat and trousers on, but he had no shoes, and his feet were ripped open by the barbs; he left footsteps of blood on the ice from his badly cut feet, and he was on fire.

The Mate lowered the lifeboat to deck level, and ordered us to get into it. At this point the burning man was rolled into the boat, and we set about beating out the fire on him.

Once the boat was lowered into the sea, we had to see that the boat did not smash up with the heavy swell, and we were ordered to row round to take the rest of crew off, but another torpedo sank her before we got alongside.

It was then that we saw how badly burnt the poor soul was. There was a spare coat and blanket in the boat, and we threw these over him as best that we could. He was sitting upright on the seat, with the seas and spray breaking over him, and he sat like that for the four days we were adrift.

I had a carton of Players cigarettes in my pocket, and asked if anybody wanted one, they had better see to themselves. A while later this young man asked if he could have a cigarette, and it was that I saw his hands were burnt and bent. No way could he hold a cigarette so I lit one and put it into his mouth. He took a draw and moved his head when I had to take it out. We got by like this, and he seemed happy to do it that way, and over the next four days his mouth developed crack lines and scabs from the cold and the burns.

All day and all night, we took turns in bailing the boat out so that the water kept down. At night we snuggled near each other and got low down, out of the cold. We dozed and it was only when the water covered our feet again that we had to start baling out again.

To think of the pain that poor man was in; how many times had the barbed wire stabbed him, and his badly burned feet were in freezing cold water. Yet he never moaned. Not once.

At dusk on the fourth day land was sighted, and the young man asked if we could turn the boat so that he could see it. We did this, and he then told us to put an oar in his hands, that he could rock his body to help us get there. He still wanted to help. His hands had become swollen to twice their normal size; his fingers were drawn bent with the cold, and his knuckles were burst and covered with scabs.

A while later we were spotted by a ship of the Russian Navy. We were all picked up, and a rope was lowered for the young man, but I don't know how they managed to get him out of the lifeboat and onto their vessel.

I was on the bridge when I was called by one of the Russian crew, a lady. She was having difficulty with the cabin boy, a lad named Anderson, another American who was around seventeen years old. She could not lay him down; he was frozen bent, and I helped her to get his jacket off. I cut it up the back. He was black to way up above the waist, and when she saw this she told me to leave him.

When we were down below in the nice warm cabin, they opened a bottle of vodka. One of the crew poured himself a small drink in a cup, and then poured me a large one, and then for the rest of us. We had about three each. We hadn't eaten for four days and it went straight down to our feet.

Once again, I was called by the lady crew member, and taken to a bunk to see the young man who had suffered such injuries. He got himself half way up and put out his hand as far as he could for me to hold, and said the words I can never forget: 'We made it kid'. I was then taken away by someone, but before I went I saw the eyes of the crew lady who was looking after him, and they were damp, and full of sadness and pity, for I think that she knew he had very little chance. That was the last I saw of him. His hands were more like paws; bent and burnt as were his arms. His head was one big scab, and what his feet were like I do not know.

We arrived in Murmansk the next morning, and were taken to School Number One, where we were put into beds. I slept, but was woken to be told that the young cabin boy had died. I drifted off the sleep again. When I woke up again, they told me that 'the Canadian' had also died. How he suffered no one will ever know, but he never moaned. He was a truly wonderful man, one who it was a privilege to have known, and to be able to speak about. He is now in the keeping of the Russian people. Please say a prayer for him. I do every day.

Most of the sixteen who left the SS *Ballot* died at the sinking of the SS *Induna*, or in the boats; those who did not die lost limbs. However, the *Ballot got to Murmansk and then back to America.*

Austin Byrne, 20 June 2013.

George Billing
HMS *Nabob*

I was born in Canterbury, Kent, on 16 January, 1925, and since the age of ten had wanted to join the Navy, and at the age of sixteen, went with a college friend of mine, Douglas Tulloch, and we both passed the entrance examination. We both also passed the medical, but when it came to the eyesight test, Doug passed the colour test, but I failed it.

After taking it again, I was told that I had a slight red/green imbalance, and therefore couldn't go to the Conway Training Ship with my friend.

When I was due to be called up, I volunteered ten days before my eighteenth birthday. I was accepted by the Navy, but had to be a Writer (the naval equivalent of a clerk) instead of an Able Seaman. Just to be in the Navy was small compensation for what I had originally wanted—to be in the Navy as a career. Doug ended the war as a Lieutenant-Commander; I was demobbed in September 1946 as a Writer.

So there I was on my first day; sitting in a room at Chatham (HMS *Pembroke*) with about sixty other guys, all dressed in civvies. The Officer at front told us, 'You are going to be given a fifty page booklet containing 100 questions. You have half an hour to answer as many questions as you can. Are you ready? Begin.'
I opened the book to find all the questions were such things as:

Question 1: A Lion, An Elephant, A Chimpanzee, A Whale. Which is the odd one out?
Question 2: Which is lighter? A ton of feathers or a ton of coal?

The questions got progressively harder, but were all requiring just a one or two word answers. The problem was that my father was a school headmaster, and he used to get these things as part of his job, and we used to do puzzles like these all the time at meal times. Result!

I took my booklet up to the officer after twenty five minutes and said, 'I have finished, Sir.' He replied, 'You have still got five minutes to go. 'No Sir, I've done them all.' I replied. He then said, 'You can't have, no-one ever finishes all of them'. He then left to get a Senior Officer from the next room. He then quizzed me

HMS *Nabob* Ship's Office Personnel on 12 August 1944. (Back left to right): Chief PO Jean Potvin, Commander Charles Dillon, Lieutenant C. A. Parks, Writer George Billing. (Front left to right): Writer Arthur Clarke, Writer James Clements, Leading Writer Willard Keith, Leading Writer Merlin Kealey. (*Courtesy of George Billing*)

closely, and stupid eighteen year old me told him why I had done them all. Result? He turned and walked away.

My first training was in a big old house in Victoria Street in Liverpool, where about two dozen of us got kitted out with 'fore & aft' rig, which is the normal bell bottomed trousers, and top with square collar and lanyard round your neck. For about six weeks we attended Liverpool University, which consisted of the normal University Tutorials, but coupled with marching drills with Rifles, and practising being out in front issuing marching orders in a loud authoritative voice. Also during this time, we carried out target shooting practice at an indoor Firing Range, where I finished equal First with one other guy.

I was then posted to HMS *Royal Arthur*, which was the Butlin's camp at Skegness, and where my uniform was changed to 'square rig'; jacket, trousers, white shirt and tie, and peaked cap. The training, as far as I can remember, was mainly physical stuff; kitted route marches, early morning exercises to build up physique, and the odd classroom stuff. I am not sure how long we were there, but I suspect it was only a couple of weeks. Highgate School was next and concerned specifically learning about Ship's Office routines. This was a very demanding study involving the full gamut of Personnel Records, and methods of controlling data and knowing the pay rates and changes when due. This course was attended by about twenty potential Commissioned Officers in the Paymaster Ranks. At the end of the three week (approx.) course, I believe only two made the grade—obviously I wasn't one of them, so it was back Chatham, where at the shore establishment HMS *President V*, I awaited appointments.

Two days later, a tannoy message was broadcast: 'Writer needed to volunteer for appointment to HMS *Saker*'. On the basis of having being told many a time 'never volunteer for anything', I ignored it. Then someone said, 'you are the only Writer on the base, go for it'. So I did. It turned out that HMS *Saker* was a shore-based office of the Royal Navy in New York. There I worked for about five months, and got into a lot of trouble by staying up at all hours in the bright lights of New York, in contrast to the black-out of London, so I was billeted in the Brooklyn Navy Yard to keep me away from 'temptation'.

It was after being in Brooklyn for two weeks that I was appointed to join the British Escort Carrier HMS *Nabob* (D77), which was berthed close by, to look after the Pay and Records of the Fleet Air Arm personnel on the ship.

HMS *Nabob* was loaned to the Canadian Government by the Royal Navy, because Canada had no aircraft carriers or a Fleet Air Arm, and had no intention

HMS *Nabob* in Dry Dock in Rosyth showing the damage to the ship by the torpedo. Note the clothing hanging in the Air Service Crew's sleeping quarters, which indicates the size of the hole. (*Courtesy of George Billing*)

of doing so. The Admiralty told the Canadian Government that it was essential that their Navy must comply. It was then that the decision was made to loan HMS *Nabob* to Canada to be crewed by Canadians, and that the Admiralty would provide the Fleet Air Arm personnel to service and fly the aircraft. Because the crew were paid in Canadian Dollars, and the Fleet Air Arm personnel in Pounds, Shillings and Pence, that I was appointed to handle the Records and Pay, as the Canadians didn't fancy trying to figure out the complexities of Sterling.

The aircraft on board were Grumman Avengers (which were the US Navy's principal bombers), fitted with torpedoes and depth charges, and the support fighter aircraft were Grumman Wildcats. These were normally catapulted from the flight deck, as the deck was too short to fly off normally. At 'Action Stations', everyone had a job to do, and my job was in the ammunition locker beside the Bofors Gun Turret on the Starboard side. The locker was immediately behind the gun, with a waist-high delivery hatch, an Able Seaman and I passed clips of five shells through the hatch to a member of the gun crew on the other side of the hatchway. Easy, eh?

The day-to-day living was typically American, in that the seaman's mess deck was fitted out with a typical American-type servery, i.e., there were ice-cream dispensers on the bar, and the main meal food was served on American style metal trays, and the food was of a similar nature, chicken/turkey, peas and potatoes, were the norm, rather than the exception. Mostly everything was in tins, and the store room was adjacent to the dining area; this was most severely damaged and the two storemen were killed when the *Nabob* was struck by a torpedo.

'Operation Goodwood' was a plan for a series of three-stage attacks on the German battleship *Tirpitz* in the Altenfjord between 21 and 28 August 1944. We were a big force under the overall command of Admiral Sir Henry Moore aboard HMS *Duke of York* (17), which was divided into two separate fleets but in close visual contact.

Force 1 comprised the *Duke of York* and Fleet Carriers HMS *Indefatigable* (10), *Formidable* (67), and *Furious* (47), with the cruisers HMS *Berwick* (65), *Devonshire* (39) and *Kent* (54), and the destroyers HMS *Myngs* (R06), *Kempenfelt* (R03), *Vigilant* (R93), *Zambesi* (R66), and the Canadian HMCS *Sioux* (R64). Force 2 comprised HMS *Nabob* and *Trumpeter* (D09), the destroyers HMS *Virago* (R75), *Verulam* (R28), *Scourge* (G01), and the Canadian HMCS *Algonquin* (R17), with the frigates HMS *Bickerton* (K466), *Aylmer* (K463), *Bligh* (K467), *Keats* (K482) and *Kempthorne* (K483).

The force covered the Russian convoy (JW-59) of 33 ships that had left Loch Ewe, Scotland, on 15 August, and it was planned that the Avengers from the escort carriers fly attacks on German airfields on 20 August, and lay mines before attacking the *Tirpitz*. However, bad weather prevented the attack from going ahead, and it was while the task force was withdrawing, that in the late afternoon of 22 August, submarine U-354 encountered them northwest of the North Cape in the Barents Sea, and attacked. A single acoustic torpedo struck the *Nabob* in

George Billing, aged 88, wearing his campaign medals. (*Courtesy of George Billing*)

HMS *Nabob*. (*Canadian Forces Photo, Courtesy of the Shearwater Aviation Museum*)

the starboard side, causing a thirty-two foot hole below the water line, abaft the engine room, and within minutes she was listing to starboard and was fifteen feet down at the stern, with sixteen of her crew missing.

She was prevented from sinking by the brilliant shoring up of the transverse bulkhead with timbers by the damage control team. This team were mostly Canadian Lumberjacks, and their handling of the bulging metal was masterly. Most of the crew that were not required to handle the damaged ship were transferred to two of the accompanying fleet; HMCS *Algonquin* and HMS *Kempthorne*. HMS *Bickerton* was lost during the operation, and HMS *Nabob* limped home on her own engines and just a skeleton crew on board including the captain, Horatio Nelson Lay, a number of necessary officers and engine personnel to keep the engines running, and defend against any further submarine strikes.

She arrived for emergency repairs at Scapa Flow on 27 August, and then sailed to Rosyth where she entered dry-dock. When the ship was finally emptied of water, the rest of the Canadians were sent back to Canada, and I was promoted to Acting Leading Writer (unpaid) so that myself, and a Leading Storesman, could complete the decommissioning of HMS *Nabob*. A Captain S. N. Harrison-Wallace was appointed to Chatham to oversee the finalisation of the process. On completion some three or four weeks later, the Leading Storesman left the ship at 1000 hrs; the captain left at 1400 hrs by taxi, and I finally saluted the quarterdeck at 1630 hrs to return to Chatham, again as a Writer, to await my next appointment.

I joined the 15th Minesweeper Flotilla on the lead ship HMS *Fraserburgh* (J124), on which I was designated the Writer for the captain in his capacity as MS15 (which was what he was known as) being responsible for the five minesweepers and two Danlayers. My Action Station was loader for the starboard Lewis Gun, the Gunner AB being the trained gunner for the gun.

A funny story regarding this was that my action station was as loader for the AB Gunner on the Starboard Lewis Gun, which was almost immediately below the bridge. Don't ask me why, but we were given a practice shoot for our guns one day a short distance from shore.

The practice consisted of a bi-plane dragging a cigar-shaped drogue some distance behind it, and at a height that would ensure that it didn't get hit by any wayward marksmen. It circled *Fraserburgh* the first time, and all of our anti-aircraft guns were firing at the drogue, nobody was getting even close. My Lewis gunner was banging away and getting nowhere near, every fifth bullet in the magazine was incendiary so you could see how far out he was. Me, getting itchy, asked him if he minded if I had a go. He reluctantly said, 'OK', so I duly took hold of the gun and, as the plane came back round, I lined up through the sights and fired. I looked at the tracers and they were way short, so I ignored the sight, and angled the gun up considerably higher and fired again.

Suddenly there was a voice from the Bridge above (it was the First Lieutenant) 'Who's on the Lewis Gun?' I thought, Oh hell, I'm in for it now. I said, 'It's Writer

Billing sir.' 'Stay where you are', said the Lieutenant. Next, the captain said, 'From now on, you are the Gunner and the AB is your loader, Right?'

I never actually ever got to fire the gun again. I gather that the pilot of the plane was in radio contact with our bridge, and his drogue was getting shredded, and he could see where the fire was coming from.

The war ended while I was serving on board the *Fraserburgh*, and so I was demobbed from there. I married my girlfriend, who was a WAAF who served at an Air Force Base in Lincolnshire, in March 1947, and had three children; two girls and a boy. We separated in late 1969 and with a job to go to in advertising, I emigrated to New Zealand, and intended to stay single, but I met a lady at a dance in 1970, who I married and we had had two sons, and subsequently, I have two grandsons.

I am currently a member of the Convoys Club, and also a member of the Royal New Zealand Naval Association. I have three WW2 Medals, plus three Medals from the Russians, which were presented by the Russian Ambassadors in New Zealand.

This next bit is another of life's funnies. As a job, after the war, I got into Advertising, and me being me, I studied at night school to learn as much as I could about Advertising. I finally, after two years of hard work, passed all the examinations, and became a Diploma Member of the Institute of Advertising, and a Member of the Communications Advertising and Marketing Foundation, in July 1957. Anyway, I was promoted to Executive of Ogilvy & Mather Advertising Company, (Presented with a key to the executive toilets. Wow!!), The company had their own Library, and one morning I wanted to take a book on a certain aspect of Marketing with me to a Client Meeting. I rang our Library to ask if they had it. A man rang me back and said 'Yes, sir we do have it and I will send it up.' I said, 'Don't bother, I'll pick it up on my way out', to which he replied, 'Very good sir, I'll have it ready for you.' So, on my way down, I called into our Library, and the man came towards me with the book, handed it to me, and said, 'No trouble, sir.' The man? It was MS15, and he didn't recognise me. I always thought it was a small world, but that really confirmed it for me!!!

I have had a wonderful life, full of a lot of amazing things. I never had a 'youth' like the teenagers of today, I was fourteen-and-three-quarters when war was declared, and twenty-one-and-three-quarters when it ended. I lived in Sidcup back then, 'Bomb Alley' as it was called. You grew up very quickly, and too many didn't get to enjoy getting old. That's the problem of getting old; you have too many memories that nobody else can share.

George Billing, 2 July 2013.

Orston Bulman
SS *Empire Baffin*

I was born in Sunderland on 21 November, 1918, and have lived in Sunderland all my life; I wouldn't want to live anywhere else. I finished my schooling at the age of fourteen and started work as a delivery boy, but got the sack after I got the bicycle wheels caught in the tram lines and wrecked it. After that I worked in the stores of an engineering company until I was sixteen, when I started my engineering apprenticeship. The company closed down and I was transferred to J. L. Thompson's Shipyard and finished my apprenticeship there in November 1939.

I received my call up papers and decided I wanted to join the RAF, but while I waited for the papers to come through, I was approached by an uncle who was Chief Engineer on a ship, and said that he wanted a Fourth Engineer for his ship, and asked if I would like to join it—which I did, and went to sea with the SS *Scorton* of the Chapman's Shipping Line of Newcastle.

Two weeks later, my parents wrote and told me that the Military Police had arrived up at the house to ask why I hadn't turned up at Speke aerodrome to train in camp. Apparently they went back to the house three times to make sure I wasn't still at home, and then it was dropped and I never heard anything more.

The *Scorton* left loaded with coal from South Shields and discharged it in Ireland, and then we went down to South Africa to bring grain back to the UK. Our second voyage was to America, and we formed a convoy at Loch Ewe, on the west coast of Scotland, and we sailed north to Greenland. We got caught in a force ten gale, with sixty foot waves. It was like climbing up the side of a mountain. We were light ship (no cargo on board), and most of the time the propeller was out of the water, with the ship pitching, and we started taking waves over the stern of the ship.

The convoy had all been dispersed by then, and the captain decided to turn around and face into the storm, and as the ship turned, a wave hit us, and turned us, and I never thought the ship would come back up again. It was that low you could have walked along the bulkhead, but right itself she did and for three days

British Steam Merchant *Aelybryn*. (*Orston Bulman*)

we faced the waves; the engine going at full speed, but it seemed like we were stood still until the gale abated, and we could turn round again. We received a message to go to Port Saint John in Canada, where the convoy reformed, and we went down to New York and loaded up with munitions to bring to the UK.

I was Third Engineer on the *Aelybryn* in May 1941; we were light ship and sailed to Loch Ewe where a convoy (OB-318) of about forty ships formed, and we sailed north, off Greenland, and I could see the icebergs, but we had to go that far north to get away from the submarines. We were the 'coffin ship'; we were in the last row of ships in the convoy, and it meant that if any ship was torpedoed, we had to stop and pick the crew up. But about five days out, a submarine pack caught us, and it happened. A ship was torpedoed, and we stopped to pick up the crew, after which time we were miles behind the convoy. A ship's boiler is designed to work under a certain pressure, and has safety valves which, if the pressure is exceeded, lifts and blows the pressure off. We screwed the safety valves down, to give us an extra couple of knots so we could rejoin the convoy. In the ship's engine room, there is a tunnel in which the shaft from the engine to the propeller, and there is a water tight door to this tunnel.

It was around 0400 hrs on 10 May, and I had just been along the tunnel, checking the bearings on the shaft, and had just got back to the engine room and was about to close the water tight door when there was a hell of a bang. We had been torpedoed. It had hit the stern of the ship, which took the rudder, propeller and most of the back end of the ship off. As the ship lurched under the impact, I was thrown across the engine room, but managed to hold onto a hand rail. All the water and the cordite came into the engine room; it was becoming thick with fumes, and the engine, with the drive shaft smashed, instead of doing eighty revolutions per minute, was now doing around 300. I darted into my cabin, which was next to the engine room, grabbed my uniform (I was in my working overalls), and went up onto the deck.

It was pitch black, and there was a twenty-foot swell. We had two ship's crews for one set of four lifeboats, and as the other crew had only been picked up the previous afternoon, no allocation was made for them with regards to the lifeboats, and there was a mad rush. However, both crews got in. I remember that we had an Indian crew, and they came along with their suitcases, and they were chucking them into the lifeboats, and we were chucking them into the sea.

The ship was still afloat when we left it, and we managed to keep pretty much together. Around ten hours later, in daylight, there was no sign of the ship, and we were picked up by a converted fishing trawler, which took us to Reykjavík. There were crews there from Norway, Sweden, Canada, and America. The British crews were put into an army transit camp, while the other nationalities were put up in hotels and were given clothing, and money to spend. After about a week, we were put aboard a passenger boat along with a lot of soldiers and military and naval people who were being transported back to the UK.

When I got back to Sunderland, I found that my parents hadn't been told that I had been picked up; that I had gone down with the ship, and they were shocked to see me. It was a good day. However, there was a letter from the ship owners waiting for me at home, in which they told me that my contract with the shipping company was completed when the ship was torpedoed, and that my salary stopped on that day, and to receive any money due to me, I had to go and apply to the unemployment benefit office.

I had a few days 'Survivors' Leave', and then I joined a ship called the SS *Empire Eve,* which was a CAM (Catapult Armed Merchant) ship, going from Sunderland to New York to bring back munitions and engineering equipment to the UK. We had a rocket-assisted Hurricane aircraft on the catapult rails. Fortunately, this wasn't needed; the fact is that once the aircraft has been launched, it can't come back, and so the pilot has to run it out of fuel, and then ditch it in the sea, and hope to get picked up.

I did two trips on that ship, and then in April 1942, I joined the 6,978-ton cargo ship SS *Empire Baffin* as Second Engineering Officer.

Convoy PQ-16

This voyage began on 17 April 1942 at Teesport, Yorkshire, where the *Empire*

Baffin was being loaded with war materials—guns, ammunition, crated aeroplanes, petrol, high octane aviation fuel, transport vehicles, and she had tanks on the deck. We sailed to Loch Ewe and then on to Hvalfjord, Iceland, where we joined the main convoy of thirty-six ships en route to Russia.

We were used as bait to try and draw the German pocket battleships out of Sweden, and were joined by our main fleet of battleships. Four days into the journey, it was thought that a German cruiser was at sea to intercept the convoy, but this information proved to be wrong and the battleships returned to Scapa Flow, leaving us with an escort of destroyers and corvettes, and a converted anti-aircraft Merchant ship which carried the convoy commodore.

It was less than a day after the main fleet had left us that the convoy was found by a cruising four-engine Focke-Wulf FW-200 Condor which, keeping out of the range of our guns, relayed our position and course to German headquarters. That evening the German bombers arrived and with twenty hours of daylight the attacks continued around the clock, and we were also informed that a number of German submarines were closing in, which continued to harass us. The German's tactics changed so that half a dozen aircraft would come towards us in a group, and the ship's guns would be firing at them, while other aircraft came down out of the sun to attack the convoy; they were very hard to see.

We had a Merchantman in the convoy that had been specially built for anti-aircraft protection, and she saved us. She put up such a barrage of steel into the air that the German aircraft veered off, unable to get at us. It was the submarines that did the damage. The ship in the next column to us was the first to receive a direct hit. She was carrying petrol and spare ammunition, and exploded in a terrible blast, disappearing under the surface in a few seconds with no survivors. The raids continued for five days with seven ships being sunk and a number of others being damaged; the ship behind us had two hatch derricks blown onto the bridge, killing the bridge personnel.

I was on watch in the engine room when we were straddled by a stick of bombs which seemed to lift the ship out of the water, throwing me across the engine room. I hit my head on an engine column and lost consciousness for a few seconds. When I opened my eyes the engine was still running but the room was full of coal dust and scalding steam from broken water gauge glasses. With other engineers we were able to close the valves.

Further examination revealed damage to the propeller drive shaft bearings and stern gland leakage. Repairs by all hands commenced immediately as we had to keep our station in the convoy to avoid being torpedoed by waiting U-boats—a number of which had attempted to infiltrate the convoy and had sunk two ships at the rear.

As well as the attacks by Junkers Ju-88 bombers we were now being attacked by torpedo carrying aircraft which, as they flew in just above sea level, below the depression limit of our anti-aircraft guns to effectively fire at them. When their torpedoes were dropped, the most we could do was to alter course to avoid them.

With the continuous raids, the threat of being torpedoed and seeing other ships sunk; the sight of bombs dropping and knowing you had nowhere to run and hoping if you were hit that you would have time to launch the lifeboats, we were grateful when Russian aircraft arrived to give us some protection.

We arrived at Murmansk, and after docking were boarded by Russian soldiers who, despite our protestations, dismounted our guns and took our ammunition, and remounted them on the roof of a nearby warehouse. We soon discovered why when a raid by Junkers Ju-87 'Stuka' dive-bombers took place which demolished a section of the quayside. Our remounted guns protected our ship as the cargo was being unloaded.

We were not allowed ashore, and there were armed guards at the end of the gangway to ensure that we stayed on board our ship, but we could see that on the railway line that was about fifty yards away from where we were docked, and all day and every day, a cattle truck would be taking hundreds and hundreds of wounded Russian soldiers away from the front.

After two weeks, we joined a returning convoy from Archangel to the UK, and apart from two ships being torpedoed, we arrived at the River Tyne where we took a few days leave.

Back to sea again to another convoy and more torpedoes and stress—it went on and on. There were no atheists on board; everyone said a little prayer when we sailed.

On the Russian convoys, we were all paid five pounds a month 'danger money'; the Americans got the equivalent of forty dollars a day. After that convoy, I had a week's leave, and then I went to Swansea to join the tanker *Empire Dickens* as Second Engineer. We departed for Milford Haven on 26 August 1942, from where she sailed the next day to join convoy ON-125, which departed from Liverpool on 28 August for Galveston, Texas, where we loaded up (along with two converted whalers) with 100 Octane fuel for use with high compression engines.

We left Texas on 18 October with convoy HX-212, and once into the Atlantic we were attacked by submarines, and two other tankers were hit in the same night. Tankers have separate compartments for their load, and don't sink straight away. The torpedoes hit a compartment which exploded, and the flames shot up into the sky and the sea around the ship was alight. You could see it for miles. But they remained afloat, and each tank exploded in turn until finally, the whole ship blew apart. There were no survivors from either of those ships. It's a terrible thing seeing a tanker going up in flames. There were eighty-odd men who lost their lives in about ten minutes.

We were now the only tanker in the convoy and had to get to our destination, and we were surrounded by cargo ships. The submarines were trying to get us, and were sinking the cargo ships either side of us, and a destroyer would come in alongside until another cargo ship took its place. We eventually got to Avonmouth,

Somerset, which was reached by detaching from the Convoy at the Belfast Lough on 1 November, and joining convoy BB-232, and discharged our cargo.

I stayed on board the *Dickens* (the food was good, and there was no telling what the food would be like on another vessel) and the next journey was to Curaçao, Netherlands, where we loaded with 100 Octane again, bound for the UK. We were told that there were submarines waiting outside Curaçao for us to sail, and they had sowed mines. We were fitted with Paravanes, which came out from the bow, and fanned out with the movement of the ship. The tension of the towing cable would cut the wires of any submerged mines, and they would float off. We caught two of these, and after the mines surfaced, they were exploded by rifle fire from the men on one of the destroyers. Our escort ships kept the submarines at bay, and we got home safely, and discharged at Avonmouth.

I left the ship then and joined the SS *Starstone*, an oil-fired cargo ship, which was loaded with munitions for the British troops in Italy, and left Manchester on 11 May, 1943. After discharging at Italy, we went Light ship to the Mauritius to load up with sugar. I left the deep sea and went to work on coastal shipping carrying coal from the north east to the Thames and under the bridges to Wandsworth Gas Works. It was rough work with six watches, and doing your own greasing. When loaded the ship had very little freeboard and in any kind of sea acted like a submarine—you needed a strong stomach. But while the ship was being loaded each time I was able to get time at home.

I stuck this life for two years and then swallowed the anchor and came ashore to work as an Engineering Surveyor until I retired.

Orston Bulman, June 2013.

David E. Cottrell
HMS *Swift*

I was born in Bristol, and it was an influence from my mother that I joined the Navy, describing it as the 'best place for me'.

I did my basic training at HMS *Raleigh*, the shore training establishment near Torpoint, Cornwall, and was then sent to HMS *Drake* in Devonport, Plymouth, where I waited for a ship.

I was sent to Gibraltar to join HMS *Hartland*, but through an accident (I fell from one boat to another and broke a leg) I never did, and so returned to England where after convalescing I joined HMS *Swift*.

HMS *Swift* (G46), an S-class destroyer, was commissioned in December 1943, and later sailed north to carry out her running-in trials. These trials were conducted in and around the Hebrides and Tobermory. When the trials finished at the end of December, we were then assigned to the 23rd Destroyer Flotilla based in Scapa Flow. It was intended for us to join Convoy JW-55B, but due to engine trouble caused by over activity throughout the running-in trials we missed that convoy—which was the one in which the flotilla took part in the sinking of the *Scharnhorst*.

So in January 1944 the *Swift* joined Convoy JW-56B, which comprised of seventeen Merchant ships and an escort of three minesweepers, three corvettes, one sloop and three destroyers, and left Loch Ewe on 22 January for the port of Murmansk.

On 26 January we were joined by another five destroyers, and two days later another eight destroyers and we were shadowed by three cruisers.

En route, many rapid signals were sent to the American merchant ship *Henry Lomb* which had drifted astern of the convoy and had to return hurriedly because enemy aircraft had been sighted and fifteen U-boats had been detected on course for the convoy.

Life aboard HMS *Swift* up to this moment had been quite pleasant, and it now looked that the action was about to start; attack from above and below.

The enemy made a series of attacks throughout the whole journey, all the way up to Murmansk. Subsequently, seven destroyers were sunk and four more were

Going for the Mail at Scapa Flow. (*Courtesy of David E. Cottrell*)

damaged, and four Merchant ships were sunk and six more were damaged. The enemy lost several aircraft but only one submarine; U-314.

The whole of this trip was fast and furious, and we didn't see much of our ts because we spent nearly all our time at our action stations. We could only catch up on our sleep between action and it was bitterly cold with ice and snow.

The convoy arrived in the Kola Inlet on 30 January where we dropped anchor within sight of Murmansk. While we waited for the return convoy, we were constantly dive-bombed by German Junkers Ju-87s 'Stukas', and Murmansk was in flames most of the time.

The return convoy was RA-56 which sailed from the Kola Inlet on 3 February. A larger convoy than the last, it consisted of thirty-nine merchant ships, and an escort of nine minesweepers, seven corvettes, one sloop, nineteen destroyers, and three cruisers.

Although this convoy was shadowed by U-boats and the Luftwaffe, no intercepts took place due to heavy seas with waves over a hundred feet high, and with ice and snow. One minute we were on top of the waves looking down into a valley, and the next we were in the valley looking up to the mountainous waves above us. Yet despite the movement and bad weather, it gave us ample time to catch up on our sleep.

We all arrived safely in Loch Ewe on 10 February. The destroyers returned to Scapa Flow while we awaited orders to join our next convoy.

In Scapa Flow, posing for this photo to send home. (*Courtesy of David E. Cottrell*)

In the meantime, because I was very experienced in cinema technique, I would go ashore and collect a cinema projector along with a number of films, and would put on a show for the crew.

On 11 February we were assigned, with a number of destroyers of our flotilla, and the Fleet aircraft carrier HMS *Furious* (47), to attack enemy coastal shipping off the Norwegian coast and into a fjord where we were bombarded from both sides. Although we had sunk a number of coastal merchant ships, we did not encounter any German war ships, and so returned safely to Scapa Flow.

On 15 February we were urgently assigned to go and search around the coast of Norway for the British submarine HMS *Stubborn* (P238), which had been very badly damaged by German escort ships after a failed attack on a German convoy off Foldfjord, and was disabled upon the surface. When we eventually found the submarine, we took her in tow and proceeded back towards Scapa Flow. We were constantly attacked by enemy aircraft, but we beat them off and got back safely.

Our ship was refuelled and restocked with ammunition, and on 20 February, we formed part of Convoy JW-57, which consisted of forty-five merchant ships, six corvettes, seventeen destroyers, one cruiser, an escort aircraft carrier and three smaller vessels used as rescue boats. This was the largest convoy ever sent to Russia.

Due to the difficulty of detecting U-boats in Arctic waters it was very necessary to have aircraft spot the submerged U-boats and it was essential to have a cruiser protect the carrier.

Fourteen U-boats operating in two Wolf packs attacked the convoy throughout the trip, and although the Luftwaffe was also present, these were dealt with by the Wildcat fighters that were launched from the carrier.

On 24 February, U-713 and U-601 were sunk; I was the Gun Layer on 'Y' gun on HMS *Swift*, and on action stations the following day, when we were some two hundred miles off Nordkapp, off the coast of Norway, the shout went out, "Torpedo!" with a bearing, and one of two Gnat torpedoes fired from U-990 passed across our bow, missing us by inches and hit the Milne-class destroyer HMS *Mahratta* (G23), which immediately blew up and sank. Sadly there were only sixteen survivors from the compliment of two hundred.

There were no Merchant ships lost, and the *Mahratta* was the only loss on that convoy which arrived at the Kola Inlet on 28 February. We had run very low on fuel due to the greater amount of activity on the way, and went to Polyarny to refuel. We went alongside the wooden jetty and as it was going to take many hours to refuel and have repairs made to the damage we had sustained, the captain told us we could have a run ashore for just two hours of each watch. A gangplank was lowered but before any of us could descend it, two Russian armed guards, who were stood at the bottom, crossed their rifles across the gangplank, ordering "Nyet!"—"No!" so we didn't get a run ashore.

We didn't stay very long in the Kola Inlet; the previous convoy had been unloaded and was ready to return. We were all very glad to be leaving because

HMS *Swift*, January 1944. (*Commons Licence*)

being anchored so close to Murmansk we were sitting targets for the German dive-bombers.

We joined Convoy RA-57 on 2 March, which consisted of thirty-three merchant ships, one cruiser, and along with two escort aircraft carriers, had seven minesweepers, four corvettes, and sixteen destroyers.

For the first two days of the convoy the weather was so bad that aircraft could not take off from the carriers, so the Russian aircraft kept the U–boats at bay, and that meant we could get some rest.

Then on 4 March, the convoy was attacked. U-703 torpedoed the merchant ship *Empire Tourist*, which sank almost immediately, and then the Fairey Swordfish of 816 Naval Air Squadron, launched from the escort carrier HMS *Chaser* (D32) damaged U-472 which was later sunk by destroyers. On the following day, U-366 was sunk by rockets from a Swordfish aircraft, and many enemy aircraft were destroyed, and on 6 March, U-973 was sunk (with three survivors of the crew being picked up by HMS *Boadicea*) and two other U-boats were damaged. We were attacked all the way back but apart from the loss of one Merchant ship, and several damaged, the convoy reached Loch Ewe otherwise intact on 10 March.

After a well-earned rest in Scapa Flow, we were afforded a leave in one of the islands; Kirkwall. We were to have several leaves there, and it was nice to taste good beer again.

We left Scapa Flow on 3 April to escort the aircraft carriers *Furious* and *Victorious*, and several Woolworth Carriers (Merchant ships that had been converted into Aircraft Carriers) of the Fleet Air Arm to attack the *Tirpitz* in Altenfjord.

After the Swordfish aircraft had taken off, small German patrol boats tried to attack us but the destroyers beat them off. Unfortunately not all of our aircraft returned; HMS *Furious* stayed behind with us for quite some time, but when it was realised that no more aircraft were coming back, we returned to Scapa Flow.

We enjoyed another leave in Kirkwall while HMS *Swift* was refuelled and stocked up with supplies, but she wasn't assigned to any more arctic convoys; her next assignment was a supporting role in the D-Day Landings, where she ended her short life; being mined and sunk off Sword Beach.

David E. Cottrell, 25 May 2013.

Stan Douglas
HMS *Javelin*

I was born in North Ormesby, near Middlesborough, North Riding of Yorkshire, in 1922.

I was eighteen when my brother arrived home safely from Dunkirk serving with the Green Howards. 'Stan', he said, 'the bloody Germans are on the way, the Army is in disarray, this is serious trouble'. My mind was made up that day, and I joined the Royal Navy and was sent to HMS *Victory* in Portsmouth.

My first two years were spent aboard minesweepers in the Mediterranean including the Hunt-class HMS *Bagshot* (J57) which was based at Alexandria. The British Army had been pushed back to the border of Egypt following the capture of Tobruk by Axis forces, and a difficult situation developed. We remained in Alex, which was under siege, from 1 June until 25 October 1942. Talk about HMS Hardship! One had to experience it. This vital port was not entirely blitzed as Rommel needed it as much as the Allies—for his own offensive plans towards Cairo, but he kept the pressure on. Our presence was rewarded by witnessing the opening barrage on display by Montgomery's Eighth Army.

After the victory of El-Alamein, the theatre of war changed dramatically. I was drafted to Malta to join the more modern Halcyon-class minesweeper HMS *Speedy* (J17). Malta had so far withstood the siege but Port Valetta was in a shambles. We made St Paul's Bay our anchorage, and this enabled the sweepers to make a fast exit for the continuous work of keeping the harbour approaches clear. It was a never-ending task; aircraft from the nearby Italian bases being a constant threat. Operation 'Torch' altered the scene. The allied landings in North Africa brought the winds of change that swept us back to the UK in September 1943.

In December 1943, I was drafted to the J-Class destroyer HMS *Javelin* (F61), and after working up trials, sailed to join the Home Fleet at Scapa Flow for convoy work escorting the Fleet, and patrolling off Norway and Iceland. The reason behind this arduous task was that the German battleship *Tirpitz* was anchored in the Norwegian port of Narvik, and posed a constant threat to the shipping lanes to the Atlantic. This priority was not an easy task, but a necessary one. We would leave Scapa for a patrol which lasted about twelve days at a time, and our endurance was tested to the limit. The most urgent need was to refuel, etc, which brought a welcome respite.

In March and April 1944, we joined Operation 'Tungsten', together with HMS *Victorious* and four escort carriers for a Fleet Air Arm attack on the German battleship *Tirpitz*. On the second attack, the *Javelin* was in a position to retrieve any downed pilots. This mission coincided with escorting convoy JW-58, and this took time and effort which resulted in us running out of fuel, but brought us into the 'Land of the Midnight Sun'; a most rewarding experience. The ship was covered in a mantle of snow and looked dramatic and dangerous. Stationary inside the Arctic Circle, we waited for an escort carrier to arrive and refuel us, and then we then left for Scapa Flow.

Upon our return, the late King George VI paid a visit to the Home Fleet. This was a rare occasion, but the buzz on the mess deck was that we had been earmarked for the upcoming allied invasion of Europe; Operation 'Overlord'.

In June we left Scapa Flow to join the Fleet for the planned invasion of Normandy as part of the 10th Destroyer Flotilla on what would be more commonly known as D-Day—Tuesday, 6 June 1944.

HMS *Javelin*. (*Author's Collection*)

Afterthoughts

The *Javelin* joined other ships with a mission to escort the Merchant ships getting vital supplies to the Russian port of Murmansk as well as keeping the German battleship *Tirpitz* anchored in a Norwegian fjord. Kept there she couldn't harass shipping lanes in the Atlantic. The ships were away from Scapa Flow for about twelve days at a time, either patrolling the seas off Norway and Iceland or guarding those convoys, often unseen. But! There was the other enemy—the weather. Icy arctic winds froze water on the decks and whipped up massive waves in the North Sea.

While the bigger, and heavily laden, cargo ships ploughed through the waves, the crews on board a light weight destroyer such as *Javelin* endured a living hell. Only two words describe the experience—'hellish' for the living conditions and 'atrocious' for the weather. These nightmarish conditions had to be endured.

Accommodation was bare necessities for the ratings and reasonable comfort for the officers. The living space was cramped, noisy with fans and auxiliary machinery. Free movement was impeded by ammunition hoists and chutes leading to upper deck gun positions. There was a total lack of privacy and it was impossible to avoid constant contact.

The crew in their hammocks had to endure being bumped by other swaying hammocks as well as mess mates moving through the congested living areas. Space was further eroded by wet oilskins and sodden duffle coats hanging in smelly bundles. Mess tables were secured parallel to the ship's side with a single padded seat on one side.

These foetid spaces, running with condensation, where water mixed with rotting food, broken crockery and dirty clothing became more horrifying as the ship pitched and writhed in the freezing arctic gales which produced terrifying and mountainous seas. Conditions became even worse when day succeeded day so that when harbour was eventually reached, like the austere and isolated Fleet base at Scapa Flow, a morning of intense activity was needed to clean the filth, vomit and debris from the mess decks.

Another problem occurred when great seas swept the iron clad waist and quarterdeck, smashing boats, ripping out fittings and armaments. For several days it was impossible for men to move either forward or aft. Relieving engine and boiler room watchkeepers every four hours meant crazy dashes along wave swept, ice covered decks. Added to the baptism of fire in wartime you were tested in the bitterly cold, incessant gales and the tremendous seas that swept into the Arctic with the immense, immeasurable force of the North Atlantic behind them.

We had no doubts about our survival as a fighting unit, always aware that the next departure to sea or even the current stay in harbour could end in sudden death.

We regarded the congested, comfortless, mess deck and primitive conditions as an oasis of comradeship and security within the context of an endless and merciless war.

Stan Douglas, Napier, New Zealand, 20 July 2013.

Alf 'Chick' Fowler
HMS *Sheffield*

At the end of the summer of 1941, I went to the recruitment office at Romford to join the RAF. At the interview, I was asked where I was educated, and I replied,

'Hamstel Lane in Southend, sir.'

'Hamstel Lane? What's that?'

'A Junior School, sir.'

'Oh, so where did you go from there then?'

'I went to Wentworth Road School, sir'

'What was that—a grammar school?'

'No, sir. A general education school'

'Oh,' he said, 'You're not of a high educational standard then.'

'By what standard, sir?' I asked.

'You're not grammar school or college or private school'

'No, sir.'

'Oh, we don't take people like you', he said, and he turned me down.

He must have seen by my face that I was disappointed and said, Look, I can see you are disappointed, but don't be discouraged, lad. If you are interested in flying, the recruitment office for the Fleet Air Arm is upstairs. If you like, I'll give them a ring, and you can go and have a word with them.

I thought well I'm here, I might as well. So he made a phone call and told me they would see me right away, and to go and see a sergeant in the Royal Marines.

So upstairs I went and this sergeant started talking about the Royal Navy and at the end of it I told him that I didn't particularly want to join the Royal Navy but I wouldn't mind the Fleet Air Arm.

'That could be arranged', he said, 'if you join the Royal Navy, you can get a transfer at any time to another department.'

I was as green as grass.

I joined up, and the sergeant told me that if I was interested in mechanics, to go into the Engine Room branch, and so that was what I did, thinking that I would transfer to the FAA and go flying—which never materialised of course.

Alf 'chick' Fowler with shipmate Jack
Scrimshaw on HMS *Sheffield*, 6 March 1943.
(*Courtesy of Alf Fowler*)

Chipping ice off the forward boiler room fan intake on convoy JW-51 in 1942. (*Courtesy of Alf Fowler*)

About two weeks later I received my call papers up for the army, so I phoned them and said that I had already signed up for the Royal Navy, and was just waiting for my papers.

These arrived about a week later, and had to report to the same place I had signed up at on 22 September. I arrived there and so did four others, and we and all picked up rail passes to take us to Malvern in to commence six weeks of Naval training at the Naval Establishment HMS *Duke*.

After the initial training and kitting out, the medical examination and other important aspects of naval traditions, we all passed out and waited to be deployed to the main naval bases before being drafted to a ship. This was HMS *Pembroke*, the shore establishment at Chatham, Kent, which would be my home naval base until I was drafted to a sea-going ship.

Entry was via the dockyard. St. George's Church was on the right and the Police Office was on the left. This is where one reported to when leaving or returning to the barracks. From there the long road took us past the Commodores House, and opposite that was the Ward Room—the accommodation for the officers (you were not allowed to walk on the pavement alongside the building and if you did the duty Petty Officer would blow a whistle and you were in the rattle). The main barracks were situated on the right hand side further along the road, and each barrack block (there were five) was three storeys high and was named after famous names in naval history. In my case, this was the Anson block, which would be my home until I would be drafted onto a sea-going ship.

Opposite the barrack blocks were the Parade Ground, Captain's House and NAAFI Canteen. Adjoining that was the Drill Shed which housed the Drafting Office among others. At the end of that building was the swimming pool, which was used not only for out-of-hours pleasure but one in which non-swimmers were taught to swim; something of a must.

Further along the road were the Writers School and a corner section that was used for Gunnery Training. Apart from the Officer's Quarters and the Ward Room, this was the only other part of the barracks that was landscaped.

We had to go through the joining routine, which involved a visit to all the offices in turn that one had to deal with where someone would take down details about me and then file them away; the Victualling Office, the Drafting Office, the Sick Bay, and most importantly, the Pay Office (as a Stoker Second Class I drew three shillings a day) before being allocated one of the barrack rooms.

I was able to get home many times over the months I was stationed there. Sadly, the time ran out, and between lessons at the school on St Mary's Island and the runs ashore, in April 1942 over the Tannoy came the call, 'Stokers Fowler (and many others) report to the Drafting office'. I had been given my first ship.

I reported to do the drafting routine with the other ratings. This was the exact opposite of the joining routine and is a sort of booking-in process, and the next morning, routine completed, and with bag & hammock, we had a roll call and

HMS *Sheffield* in Arctic waters on convoy JW-51 in 1942 (a). (*Courtesy of Alf Fowler*)

HMS *Sheffield* in Arctic waters on convoy JW-51 in 1942 (b). (*Courtesy of Alf Fowler*)

HMS *Sheffield* in Arctic waters on convoy JW-51 in 1942 (c). (*Courtesy of Alf Fowler*)

HMS *Sheffield* in Arctic waters on convoy JW-51 in 1942 (d). (*Courtesy of Alf Fowler*)

HMS Sheffield having problems retrieving the Walrus in 1942. (*Courtesy of Alf Fowler*)

The funeral of Stoker Spong on HMS *Sheffield* in November 1942. (*Courtesy of Alf Fowler*)

were then detailed which coach to catch to Chatham station as we were all going to the same ship and a new crew.

The train journey from Chatham took the best part of the day as the Southampton-class light cruiser HMS *Sheffield* (C24) was berthed at a place called Hebburn, on the River Tyne (She had been under repair there after hitting a mine off Iceland on 3 March). It may well have been a special train but delays were the order of the day, and we arrived late in the afternoon, dirty, tired, and hungry.

Our bags and hammocks were loaded into a lorry while we were marched into the dockyard where, to my amazement, amid what seemed to be the biggest scrap metal yard I had ever seen (pipes, valves, engine parts, electric cables, all dumped in heaps with a winding path leading to a gangway here and there), and tied up alongside was the *Sheffield*, which was to be my home for the next three and a half years.

HMS *Sheffield* was known throughout the fleet as The 'Shiny Sheff' because of her bright and shiny appearance. This was due to the fact that she had been adopted by the City of Sheffield, the Stainless Steel City of the world, and they donated all the normal steel parts of a ship with Stainless steel, hence her nickname. But to see her at the moment, she was no Shiny Sheff—far from it in fact, but within a month she was a ship to be proud of and it remained that way for me for all the years I spent aboard her.

The first thing to be done was the joining routine, and this completed, it was off to the Chief Stokers Office to be allocated a Mess. His name was Pritchard, and I am glad to say that over the years, we got on okay. As a new crew member, and a real sprog, I had to learn my way about the ship, which was no easy task as she was a 10,000 tonner; 500 feet long and 65 feet wide.

Below decks she carried fuel, water, stores and ammunition as well as the two boiler rooms. Accommodation for the ships' company was divided up into port and starboard sides, with some mess decks for the Engine Room branch being forward and some amidships—this was a precautionary measure in case of damage to the ship at any time, and avoided the risk of losing the whole Engine Room branch in one go. The same thing applied to other branches aboard; seamen, writers, cooks and Royal Marines.

The space on the mess deck I had to hang my hammock up in was eighteen inches wide. The hooks and bars were fixed at specific distances apart, and we were slung head to feet to allow the maximum number of hammocks to be crammed in.

We had heating too; square panels of metal faced the deck at intervals, and behind these were steam pipes, and behind these were fans that pushed through warm air. In the winter, these kept the deck just about warm. Conversely, in the hot weather, by shutting off the steam but leaving the fans on kept it cool.

We were now ready for sea—my first voyage with the Royal Navy!

We moved out of Hebburn on 20 July with the band playing and the people of the town waving farewell—a moving experience and one that will repeat itself many times in the next four years. The journey took us to Iceland, where we

Captain Clarke, Sir Stafford Cripps, and Commander Searle on board HMS *Sheffield c.* 1942. (*Courtesy of Alf Fowler*)

HMS *Sheffield* off Reykavick, Iceland. (*Courtesy of Alf Fowler*)

joined other ships that would escort the convoys to Russia.

Our role was to cover the area between the Norwegian coast and the Arctic Circle. The actual convoy of Merchant ships mustered at Loch Ewe, ready for the escorts of Corvettes and Destroyers to guard them out on the Murmansk run. The cruisers and battleships kept a sharp look out for German ships; the *Scharnhorst*, *Admiral Hipper*, and others.

The Engine Room department used a twenty-four-hour system which was divided into four-hour shifts—watches (except the 'dog watches' which were the first and last shift and were of two hours duration). A bell was rung every half hour, and the total number of bells in a watch (except the dog watch) is therefore eight. Eight bells announced the end of a watch. One bell announces that half a watch has passed, and so on to its end.

When you were off-watch in the engine room, you were given another job to do, which was usually damage control. In other words, if you were in certain positions where you were above the water line, you would man the pumps and things like that.

When the convoy moved off, we steered a bit further north as we had on board, stores and, believe it or not, Husky dogs. These were landed on Spitzbergen, Bear Island, just across the Arctic Circle and some 100 miles short of the North Pole. It was this that gave me the title of 'An Honourable Bluenose'. A similar title was

Iceland 1943. (*Courtesy of Alf Fowler*)

Iceland 1943. (*Courtesy of Alf Fowler*)

Iceland 1943. (*Courtesy of Alf Fowler*)

given to one who crosses the equator. I still have it and it hangs on a wall at home.

Arrival in Spitzbergen: the dogs and equipment were unloaded, and before we departed there was a chance to see the Aurora Borealis—a sight never to be forgotten, and one that is very difficult to describe to anyone. It was also an indication to me that to stand on deck in the Arctic was not to be done again without a duffle coat and gloves as one just literally froze on the spot. I was told that the seamen who remained on deck to do their work were subject to this every day, and often for all day. The conditions were, in a word, atrocious.

After seeing the convoy into a safety zone, we returned to Iceland, escorting the convoy PQ-17 which had been badly mauled by the German forces on their outward journey; Prime Minister Winston Churchill later referred to it as 'One of the most melancholy naval episodes in the whole of the war.'

Our return to Scapa Flow via Iceland was greeted by a quick re-fuel and taking stores aboard in readiness for our next job.

It was now October and we were ordered down to Clyde. We anchored off Greenock and commenced exercises at Sea for several days with a couple of destroyers. Late one evening we went for a night exercise but didn't return to Greenock, but tied up at Belfast, Northern Ireland.

The next evening, just as it got dark, we embarked some 700 American troops, called the Sea Bees, and once on board, we sailed. Where to? We had no idea. In conversation with our now overcrowded new shipmates, we discovered that they were all experts in their own field of dock operations, and some were train drivers

HMS *Sheffield* in the Great Storm of February 1943. (*Courtesy of Alf Fowler*)

and crane operators—all rather puzzling. We found out also that many of them were actually English. Our ship's company was 700 officers and men, and the addition of another 700 men was disastrous in terms of accommodation.

For the next week or so we were at sea and on one occasion, one of the seamen said that he thought we were going round in circles because the sun was never in the same place at a certain time as it should be. All became clear when the rock of Gibraltar came into view; an unmistakable indication that we were about to enter the Mediterranean.

In the early hours of the following morning, two destroyers, HMS *Malcolm* (D19) and HMS *Broke* (D83), came alongside and the Sea Bees were off loaded onto them; these were to be part of the amphibious assault on the port of Algiers in Operation 'Torch'—the North African Landings which took place on 8 November 1942.

The following day we escorted a Troop ship along the coast to put more troops ashore at that part of the coast further along than Algiers. An urgent recall to the UK saw us harrying back to Portsmouth at full speed, and then on to Scapa Flow for yet another convoy to Russia.

The usual things occurred, the odd contact with an enemy ship and several submarines, but no real close clash. It was, as ever, bitterly cold and the ship was covered in ice. The upper deck seamen were busy chipping the ice from anywhere it seemed to be getting thick. It was imperative that the ice was cleared as soon as possible for the simple reason that too much ice over the superstructure and guns would make to ship top heavy and could cause it to capsize. This has been known to be the cause of loss for some of the smaller ships in convoys; it didn't take much to overturn them.

We were all most grateful to the good ladies of the City of Sheffield for the gloves, socks and balaclavas that they had sent us, all of which had been hand-knitted by the various ladies groups in the city.

The convoy to Murmansk was a successful one until we returned to Scapa Flow. On our way back we picked up ships on our RDF (Radio Direction Finding—the forerunner of Radar).

All battleships had an escort of destroyers so it appeared that these two destroyers, in the conditions they found themselves, must have believed that the object they saw in the mist and gloom was the ship they were supposed to be escorting (I understood later that we had been mistaken for the *Admiral Hipper*), and so swung into position, one each side of the Sheffield.

A recognition signal was flashed from them and it was then realised that they were enemy ships. Quick action had to be taken and (I was later told) the Chief Yeoman, Tiny Fuller, flashed the same signal back to them which gave us time to act. The order went out 'Stand By to Ram', but 'A' turret had already turned and opened fire on the *Friedrich Eckoldt*, a Type 1934 A-class destroyer (Z16), which sank with all hands. The second German vessel had moved away rapidly and was not engaged.

HMS *Sheffield* in the Great Storm of February 1943. (*Courtesy of Alf Fowler*)

Commander St Leger Searle and Captain Clark, HMS *Sheffield*. (*Courtesy of Alf Fowler*)

HMS *Sheffield*. (*Courtesy of Alf Fowler*)

HMS *Sheffield* in rough Seas off Iceland in 1943. (*Courtesy of Alf Fowler*)

It was many years after that, as a mature person, I realised that I had been part of something that meant the lives of over 200 sailors had been lost and the families of those men had suffered a great loss too. But that was a time of war, and if she had just been damaged and stayed afloat, we would have tried to rescue as many survivors as we could. Such is the rule of the seas—something that does not happen with any other fighting unit in wartime.

As it happened it was my lucky day. I was in my action station at the time in a defence station in the cable locker and if you have ever seen what happens to a ship that has rammed another, I would not be sitting her scribing this!

After this incident we made our way towards Iceland but encountered the most savage storm of all time. High winds and enormous waves, some forty feet high, which caused quite a lot of damage to the superstructure and one mighty wave crashed down onto 'A' turret with such force that it severed the four-inch plating like it was eggshell. Several men in the turret were injured; one sustaining a broken leg. Damage to the rest of the ship was the same. With the storm so big, we had to heave-to and it took us four days to reach Iceland where by then we were all thinking about a spot of leave as soon as we got back to Scapa Flow.

It didn't turn out like that, though. Once we had arrived, workmen came aboard and started to repair the ship there and then. The first signs of unrest appeared next day when it was discovered that the portable air compressor was missing and believed to have been thrown overboard during the night. The Captain made it very clear that he was angry at the actions of a few and so placed Royal Marine Sentries on duty while the repairs were carried out. It did, however, give the ship's diver a chance to earn his corn as he was detailed to go overboard and recover the compressor.

Alfred Fowler, 4 June 2013.

Charles Harris
Chief Petty Officer, 2nd Hand,
HMS *Shera*

Charles Harris (known as Charlie) was born in Lowestoft on 28 April, 1921, the son of Charles and Florence. He was a fisherman before war broke out, and when called up, did his six weeks basic training at Sparrows Nest (HMS *Europa*); headquarters for the Royal Naval Patrol Service.

In the first week of January 1942, Charlie marched along the quay at Milford Haven to join his first wartime ship in the RNPS. What a sight that met him. HMS *Shera* (FY1724) was listing twenty degrees to port and Charlie felt that ancient forlorn feeling that mariners get with unlucky ships, and had a bad feeling about her. This old Norwegian Whaler, which was built by Smiths Dock Company, Ltd, at South Bank-on-Tees, UK, in 1929, had been taken over by the British Admiralty in 1940, and used as an auxiliary minesweeper. She had seen better days chasing whales than in the rough and cold seas of the North Atlantic.

Charlie's omens were justified. Having completed trials outside of Milford Haven, the *Shera* was heading back into Haven. Charlie was on the forecastle at Harbour stations, lined up on the forward part of the ship. He could see there was a trawler, the ST *Eveline* (FD12), dead ahead of them and the skipper (Temporary Lieutenant William Edward Bulmer, RNR) was not slowing down. Despite being an Able Seaman, Charlie had recently obtained his Mate's ticket and knew about seamanship. He then took the precaution of moving everyone back, and he was right to do so.

The *Shera* slammed into the anchored trawler and holed her. Charlie shouted up to keep going forward to hold the sinking vessel up, but despite this she sank taking the chief engineer with her. He had gone back below to get his wallet but didn't get back in time. It was the first of many lives this whaler would take.

After this, the *Shera* went to Greenock to be fitted with an anti-aircraft gun and undergo a stability test. However, there was no testing carried out to see if the ship was sound from the collision with the *Eveline*, and she then proceeded to Iceland.

En route, the ship had to call into the neutral Faroe Islands overnight due to heavy seas, and Charlie remembered seeing many of the locals coming down and stare at the ship as she bobbed at her anchor. She then proceeded to Iceland where her bad luck struck again.

Eight or nine of the crew came out in some kind of a rash, and had to be put ashore, Charlie being one of them. They were put in a Nissen hut where, although under army supervision, the soldiers would slide their food and drink through a gap in the door to minimise the risk of catching the mystery rash.

Charlie and the rest of his sick shipmates rested for five days in the hut, which was surrounded by snow and only had one small stove heater for warmth. During this time, the *Shera* had been to Seyoisfjorour, and had returned to pick up the sick seamen, whether they were fully recovered or not.

On 4 March the ship left Iceland and its safe anchorage for the last time. She was tasked, along with another Whaler, the MS *Svega* (FY294), to meet up with the Allied Arctic Convoy PQ-12, which had left Reykjavik, Norway, on 1 March, and consisted of sixteen ships with a close escort comprised of the minesweeper HMS *Gossamer* (J63) and five whalers, heading for the Russian port of Murmansk.
The crew of the *Shera*, however, had not been issued with cold weather clothing and had to rely on the clothes they had brought with them for warmth in the cold waters of the Barents Sea.

The ship had a crew of thirty; her captain was a former Merchant Navy officer and didn't take well to the routines of the Navy as on the way up to Russia, the crew had no practices; they didn't practice lifeboat drills, action stations, or what to do in an emergency.

On the eighth evening of the passage, the two whalers steaming together still had not met up with the convoy. Through both the dog watches (1600 hrs—1800 hrs and 1800 hrs—2000 hrs) Charlie and his watch, on their own initiative,

Charles Harris, Chief Petty Officer, 2nd Hand. (*Courtesy of Alf Muffett, RNPSA Museum*)

had spent their time clearing the ice that had been building up on her decks and rigging. The cold weather was taking its toll and the build up of ice was to be disastrous.

Charlie was asleep in his bunk on the forecastle locker (forward part of the ship) when the bunk above him collapsed on top of him, which was immediately followed by the ship's alarms sounding.

The ship lurched over and then turned on her port side. Without orders, everyone scrabbled for the hatch. As Charlie exited the hatch he was met by a scene of chaos and he saw a man struggling, and with one arm he pulled the man up onto the ship's side (he admits he was stronger in those days). He saw HMS *Svega* lower a boat and thought this was his chance. He was the last to jump into the water before the *Shera* fully sank. He looked back to see the ship's bow sticking straight up out of the water, and then slipped stern first beneath the waves.

Charlie couldn't quite remember how many men were in the water but he knew that everybody in the forecastle locker got out. He saw one man, a Cornish seaman who had been in the Patrol Service since the start of the war, swimming backwards, with the youngest member of the crew linked in his arms; the youngster being a weak swimmer. Charlie found a cork lifejacket and, hooking it under his arm, swam towards the boat from the *Svega*. He knew he was a good swimmer and believed it was the continuous physical effort that kept him alive, but he said that he could feel himself freezing to death; the feeling slipping away from his fingers and toes.

He was the first to be picked up by the small rescue boat, and a seaman in the boat took off his jumper and gave it to him. By this time he had survived an unbelievable twenty minutes in the water. Instead of putting the jumper on, Charlie wrapped it around his feet, as they were so cold they were freezing to the wooden bottom of the boat.

They picked up another four members of the crew; the Officers Steward, the First Lieutenant (who was a Norwegian and who was sitting on top of the wheelhouse which had broken away from the ship and was floating in the water), the wireless operator, and another crew member who he did not know. The unknown shipmate and the wireless operator did not survive. A total of just three men survived from a crew of thirty.

Charlie was slipping in and out of consciousness, but he remembers waking up to find a stoker slapping his feet, causing incredible pain but it was this action that he believes saved his feet from frostbite and at the age of ninety two was still able to climb the steps to the RNSPA museum.

The *Svega* arrived in Polyarny roughly four days later and Charlie was taken by ambulance to a Russian hospital. Despite the language barrier, they were good to him and gave him souvenirs like a small Russian badge of the Red Star and Sickle.

Four or five days later he was put on board the cruiser HMS *Kenya* and sent home. Throughout the voyage he was in the sick bay but remembers the captain's tannoy announcements about a possible sighting of the *Tirpitz* although this turned out to be a false alarm.

After disembarking at Scapa Flow Charlie was taken to a hospital in Aberdeen to be medically examined, as even the medical experts believed that he should not be alive.

On 27 April 1942, the day before his twenty-first birthday, Charlie walked through the door of his mother's house in Fleetwood for fourteen days sick leave and to the warmth and love of his waiting family.

Charlie returned to naval duties at RNPS headquarters at the Sparrows Nest, Lowestoft, where he was promoted to Chief Petty Officer, 2nd Hand. He was demobbed in the spring of 1946, and remains active at the Sparrows Nest as National Vice-Chairman of the RNPA Association and Museum.

Alf Muffet, RNPSA, June 2013.

Note: The Sailing Trawler *Eveline* (FD12) was subsequently salvaged and returned to service.

Frederick Humble
HMS *Bulldog*

I was born in Devonport, Devon, the son of Frederick James and Anne Humble, on 20 December 1923. I had two sisters; Doreen, who served in the ATS (Auxiliary Territorial Service), and Betty, who joined the WAAF (Women's Auxiliary Air Force).

My father was a musician with the Royal Marine Band on the British aircraft carrier HMS *Courageous* (50), but did not survive her sinking after she was attacked by U-29 while on anti-submarine patrol at the Western Approaches (Southwest of Ireland), on 17 September 1939. He was 41 years old. The ship sank within fifteen minutes with the loss of 519 men (including her commander, Captain W T Makeig-Jones) from the compliment of 1,260 which included the airmen of 811 and 822 Squadrons (Fleet Air Arm), and their Fairey Swordfish aircraft.

I went to Royal Hospital School at Holbrook, near Ipswich, for four years, and after joining the Royal Navy, I was first sent to HMS *St Vincent*, and then on to HMS *St George*, both of which were shore establishments at Gosport. At the outbreak of war on 3 September 1939, I was sent to the signal training camp HMS *Impregnable* to await a draft to a sea-going ship.

I joined the King George V-class battleship HMS *Prince of Wales* (53) on 15 February 1941, and in late May, while still not fully operational, she was sent into action with the German battleship *Bismarck* and received significant damage from heavy gunfire. Following repairs, the *Prince of Wales* carried Prime Minister Winston Churchill across the Atlantic to Newfoundland where, on 9-12 August, he joined the US President, Franklin D Roosevelt, for the Atlantic Charter conference.

Following her return to British waters, the *Prince of Wales* went to the Mediterranean, and then to the Far East with the battle cruiser HMS *Repulse* to counter the swiftly developing Japanese threat in the region, arriving there on 2 December 1941.

On 10 December, as part of Force Z, the *Prince of Wales* was dispatched to investigate reports of Japanese landing forces at Kuantan, Singapore, where she

HMS *Bulldog* in 1930. (*Author's Collection*)

was struck on the port side by torpedoes from Japanese aircraft, wrecking the outer propeller shaft and causing the ship to take on a heavy list. Six aircraft from this wave attacked *Prince of Wales*, with four of their torpedoes hitting the ship, causing flooding. Finally, a thousand-pound (500 kg) bomb hit the catapult deck, penetrated through to the main deck and exploded, tearing a gash in the port side of the hull. At 1315 hrs, the order was given to abandon ship, and at 1320 hrs, the *Prince of Wales* sank. Vice-Admiral Tom Phillips and Captain John Leach were among the 327 fatalities.

I was picked up by HMS *Vampire*, and it became obvious there was no more we could do. I was drafted along with others to an Indian cargo ship, and we were put ashore in Lanka Barracks. After a short time there, another Able Seaman named Baxter and I joined HMS *Hoxa* on 19 December. She was a coal burning Minesweeper based at Colombo, which had a mix of Scottish and Welsh crew, and the second in command was Danish. I was with her until October 1943, when I joined the light cruiser HMS *Durban* (D99), which was returning to the UK. On board, I saw Commander Williams who was one of my instructional officers at the Royal Hospital School that I attended. We arrived home, and I went back to HMS *Drake*, from where I was given twenty-eight days leave.

I then joined HMS *Defiance* to qualify as a Seaman Torpedo Man, and on 3 November 1944, was drafted to the destroyer HMS *Bulldog* (H91), on which I stayed until 30 April 1945.

Frederick Humble.

During this period we were on arctic convoy duty. These journeys would take fourteen days to reach Russia, and we were regularly under attack from aircraft and submarines. Food became scarce, and the weather was that bad it was frightening; you would have to wear goggles because if your tear duct went and your eyes watered it would just freeze. It was actually more terrifying than my experience on the *Prince of Wales*.

During my twenty-two years of service, I took various courses for a higher rating and finishing up as a CPO (Chief Petty Officer). Following my service, I was selected for Naval Careers Service, which I did for a further fifteen years, bringing the number of years I spent with the Royal Navy to thirty eight, retiring as Chief Petty Officer Electrician.

Pam Humble, 31 July 2013.

Frank Jones
HMS *Belfast*

Frank Bertram David Jones was born in the village of Breeding, West Sussex, on 15 December 1926, the son of Bertram Arthur and Eva Lilly Jones (née Hacker, from Ebbw Vale, Wales).

We lived on a dairy and produce farm just outside of Steyning, West Sussex, where we grew wheat, barley, hay, sugarbeet, and winter green feed for the cows and pigs.

I attended Steyning Church School until the age of thirteen, and then went on to Steyning Grammar School. I was a Boy Scout at Beeding, and also a Sea Cadet at the training ship at Shoreham, West Sussex. I left school five days after my sixteenth birthday, and on 20 December 1942, I volunteered for the Navy.

I was subsequently called up on 8 January 1943, and sent to the shore establishment HMS *Royal Arthur* at Ingoldmells, near Skegness, where we were kitted out with uniforms, tin hat, and gas mask, and two weeks of parade drill. Following this, we were sent to HMS *Iron Duke*, at Portsmouth, in March 1943 for more training and gunnery drill with the .38 calibre revolver, the Sten submachine gun, and the .303 Lee-Enfield Rifle. We had to prove that we were able to operate all of these arms, prior to being posted. I was then sent to Whale Island at Portsmouth for more gunnery training; the six-inch, four-inch, the 40 mm Bofors gun, and the 20mm Oerlikon Anti-aircraft guns, and after that I was given fourteen days leave. Upon my return in July 1943, I had to report the Naval Officer at Rosyth where I met another midshipman, and he took me out to the Southampton-class heavy cruiser HMS *Belfast* (C35), which had moved down from the Firth of Forth. In August, the *Belfast* was in port at Scapa Flow, north of Scotland, where I was signed on as an 'A1' (captain of the crew) of a Bofors gun.

Then in December, we escorted a convoy from Loch Ewe, Scotland, to the Kola Inlet, Russia, and on the way back from Murmansk on 26 December, met up with the German battle cruiser *Scharnhorst*, which was flying the flag of Rear Admiral Eric Bey, and had departed Langfjord, Norway, on Christmas Day with a screen of five large 'Z' class destroyers, and was attempting to locate and destroy the convoys of

HMS *Belfast*. (*Author's Collection*)

ships of JW-55A; eighteen merchants and twenty five escorts which had left Loch Ewe on 12 December, and JW-55B; nineteen heavily laden ships with thirty three escorts that had left Loch Ewe on 20 December, both bound for the Kola Inlet, Russia.

After a short fight, the *Scharnhorst* turned away from us and we lost contact. Some time later, we picked her up again after being sighted by the cruiser HMS *Sheffield* (C35), and with HMS *Norfolk* (78), went after her. Hit by gunfire from the Norfolk's eight-inch guns, the *Scharnhorst* turned and proceeded to go to her home port.

In what would become known as the 'Battle of the North Cape', the *Scharnhorst* was then caught at around midday between the three cruisers and the King George V-class battleship HMS *Duke of York* (17) and after some hard shooting, and being torpedoed by the *Duke of York*, the German battleship sank. During the battle, the *Norfolk* was hit and the *Sheffield* suffered damage.

HMS *Belfast* was refuelled at the Kola Inlet, and then left for the UK, arriving at Scapa to refuel again, and replenish her ammunition and stores on 31 December. On 10 January 1944, we sailed to Rosyth, where we were granted leave.

In February, we resumed our Arctic convoy duties, and then sailed with the covering force for Operation 'Tungsten'—the big attempt to sink the German Battleship *Tirpitz* with an air strike, on 3 March 1944; the date being set after the aircraft carrier HMS *Victorious* had completed her post-refit trials. Two waves of twenty one Barracuda torpedo dive-bombers took off from six carriers and caused lot of damage to the *Tirpitz*, including a 1,600 lb (726kg) bomb which hit the bows but failed to explode, but she stayed afloat.

Frank with his grandson. (*Courtesy of Frank Jones*)

HMS *Belfast* was made headquarters ship of Bombardment Force 'E', flying the flag of Rear-Admiral Frederick Dalrymple-Hamilton, and was to support the Normandy Landings by British and Canadian forces in the Gold and Juno Beach sectors. On 2 June, she left the River Clyde for her bombardment areas.

Winston Churchill had announced his intention to go to sea with the fleet, and witness the invasion from HMS *Belfast*, but it was opposed by the Supreme Allied Commander, General Dwight D Eisenhower, and the First Sea Lord, Sir Andrew Cunningham, and so prevented him from going. The *Belfast* spent the next five weeks shelling in support of the troops, and then returned to South Shields for a complete overhaul and around two week's leave for her crew.

Upon my return to the ship, she carried out her sea trials and retraining prior to going out to the Pacific, and by the time she got there, the fighting was just about over. After that we were given R&R (rest and recuperation), which took us to Australia and then New Zealand, and on 26 December, 1945, I returned to England on the aircraft carrier HMS *Indefatigable* (R10). In September 1948, I moved to live in New Zealand.

Frank Jones, 21 July 2013.

Chris King
HMS *Bluebell*

I was born in Dorset, England, on 3 October 1922, coming from a farming family. My father died just after I was born, so my mother had to find work and raise three children, me and an older brother and sister.

During the war, my sister worked at night in the ARP Control Room at the local Town Hall. My brother, who had joined the Territorials in 1938, transferred to the RAF and became a Flying Instructor, teaching basic flying on Tiger Moths. He then arranged a transfer to Bomber Command but was killed with his crew when their Wellington bomber crashed on take-off during night flying exercises.

I was employed in a Bournemouth law office both before and after the war, and moved out to New Zealand in April 1957 with my wife (an ex-WRNS) and two small boys. We settled in North Canterbury and increased our family by another son.

Although I joined the LDV (or Home Guard), in 1940, it seemed clear to me that as an active healthy young man I should do something more to help Britain's war effort—hence my volunteering for the Royal Navy. I had been a Sea Scout and also a dinghy sailor out towards the Isle of Wight and back on the odd occasion when we lived at Christchurch on the English South Coast, so joining the Navy seemed my obvious choice.

In September 1941, I enquired at the Royal Naval Recruiting Office in Southampton about enrolment in the Navy. By 6 December, following the 'acceptance trials' and training as a communications rating at HMS *Royal Arthur*, a peacetime holiday camp at Skegness, I found myself, a fully-fledged part of 'the Andrew' heading for Liverpool to join the Flower-class Corvette HMS *Bluebell* (K80) as a Coder.

The corvettes were built to relieve the bigger destroyers so that they could go off into the deep sea, and the idea was that the corvettes would do coastal patrols around England. It was soon realised, however, that they were very short of ships to escort the convoys, and there were enough of these smaller ships, which were wonderful sea boats, to go into the blue water, as it was called. The one drawback

Chris King in 1945.

with a corvette was that if they encountered a U-boat on the surface, it was always quicker to manoeuvre, so it was pretty hard trying to chase it. If the U-boat was submerged, we had the edge over them in speed, and were able to attack them, but even then our top speed was seventeen or perhaps eighteen knots, and then the funnel would start to glow red.

I had enquired in Barracks as to what sort of warship the *Bluebell* was but the men who could probably best tell me were already out there in the murky Atlantic, or wherever, cursing the rolling and pitching corvettes and all those who had designed them. At the dockside I hesitated, as the Marine driver threw my bag and hammock out of the van, and a slight sense of panic set in. This surely must be the boat to take me out to the warship, I thought, but then I saw the board with 'BLUEBELL' stencilled on it, facing the gangway, and the Marine said, 'This is it, Jack. Good luck, you'll need it' then jumped in his van and drove away.

Although at first everything and everyone seemed so strange, but I came to discover that the ninety crew on board were a closely knit bunch whose lives were in each other's hands with everyone playing some part in getting the ship to whatever destination their Lordships at the Admiralty might decide to send us, and back again. There were plenty of occasions for arguments with some almost coming to blows, but generally things worked out quite well. They had to on a ship only 203 feet long, and with a crew of ninety which was double the compliment it was designed for.

I learned that some time before I joined her, HMS *Bluebell* had been escorting a convoy, for which there were only three escorts, and terrible devastation was caused by attacks from U-boats, and the *Bluebell* picked up something like 200 survivors. It was very trying accommodating them and her own crew, but she got them all back safely to Glasgow.

The most unpleasant part of the convoys was that you were not supposed to stop to pick up people; there were designated rescue ships that would try go and pick up any men in the sea.

On the initiative of our Navigating Officer and the Skipper, I was recommended as a CW (Commission and Warrant) candidate, and papers to chart my progress while at sea were started for me. This meant that I did various sea-going duties unrelated to my coding duties, and this tended to upset the watch-keeping by the other two coders if I wasn't available. One extra duty was taking the ship's wheel, a large heavy wooden-spoked wheel which took some strength to counter the yawing of the ship and stay on course. The Quartermaster would ask permission of the OOW (Officer of the Watch) on the bridge for me to take the wheel, and then suddenly it was my responsibility to hold the ship's course, which was not always very easy. It was not good to see the compass bearing getting away from you especially as the OOW on the bridge was watching the same compass readings. Zigzagging could be tiring work, so the Quartermaster was always glad when I accepted his offer to take the helm. I also had a variety of seaman's duties to tackle.

Sometimes too, the OOW would call for me to come up on the bridge. He was probably glad of the company, and apart from instructing me in the art of conning the ship, navigation and general convoy procedures, we would talk of many other matters of home and the future, after the war. I do well remember one

HMS *Bluebell* 1940. (*Author's Collection*)

occasion when we were tucked away in a small bay below Murmansk, awaiting orders, the skipper decided to take our ship's boat away for a sail. He knew I had been a 'week-end sailor' and so ordered me to go along as crew. It was the most boring sailing I had ever done. Apart from being very cold, and wrapped up in oilskins, I just had to sit up near the bow ready to change the boom round from one side of the mast to the other (dipping lugsail design). A captain isn't the best company for an ordinary rating, and our skipper was a rather nervous man of few words. We soon discovered there was not enough wind to blow a feather away. In fact, although we had made a little progress upstream, we were soon drifting back, past the *Bluebell*. The First Lieutenant turned on the tannoy speaker and soon the voice of Scotsman Sir Harry Lauder, singing 'Keep right on to the end of the road', came wafting over the water to us. The skipper was not at all amused and ordered me to take the sail down, and then we both rowed the boat back to the ship. The skipper went straight to his cabin leaving me to get the boat inboard, with the help of the duty watch and generally tidy up all the gear. Altogether a miserable episode for what was meant to be a 'make and mend day', when although you were supposed to make or mend your clothes, as in Nelson's day, you could actually just lie in your bunk and read or dream of home.

My first trip on HMS *Bluebell* (which would be my home for almost three years) was from Liverpool to Gibraltar, just skirting the Bay of Biscay, escorting a convoy of merchant ships, travelling at an average speed of about seven knots. Then a few days in Gibraltar, shore leave, warnings not to drink the local brew, evenings at the many nightclubs and the realisation that everyone, while prepared to do everything for the good of the ship at sea, was intent on making the most of any shore leave, including rolling back to the ship, sufficiently drunk, and causing whatever mayhem a crowd of sailors could cause in the town.

Although all this may seem pretty gross behaviour now, I must emphasise that our lives, especially at sea, were in many ways completely unnatural, more particularly to us civilian or HO (Hostilities Only) ratings. We were cramped up in a very small ship for days, weeks, or sometimes months, rolling and pitching, trying to stay in our bunks by jamming feet and arms into each corner, while buckets and kettles, anything that could break free, slid from one side of the sleeping quarters to the other.

The watch-keeping routine at night: just as one got to sleep there would be a shake on the shoulder and then, dragging on extra clothes, oilskins, sea boots, and a towel tucked in round the neck to keep the water out, it was up the ladder and out onto the deck, forcing open the heavy watertight door, pitch black, blowing half a gale and the noise of the sea and wind hitting the ship with probably a good dose of spray to really wake you up. Then up the ladder to the wheelhouse, again a tricky manoeuvre, and inside, to be greeted by whomever was on the wheel. With just the dim green light of the compass and, looking through the front wheelhouse windows, you could just make out the ship's bow, lifting and then falling away into deep white foam followed by a cascade of water rushing over the ship. You soon got used to planting your feet firmly apart or leaning against the roll of the ship to stop from sliding.

The experience of the sea's motion was completely foreign to me of course, but it was a case of survival and getting used to it all. Fortunately I soon found my sea-legs and, praise be, never once felt the least bit sea-sick, in fact the rougher it got, the more my appetite increased! For those that did succumb it must have been a wretched time and it affected officers and ratings alike, even the older three-badge sailors who could never have served on a corvette in the Great War. The author who wrote, 'they (the Flowers) would roll on wet grass' was so right.

Sometimes, during a quiet night watch, the Telegraphist and Coder would talk of home, our next convoy operation, or the last, or next, run ashore. Sometimes the four hour watches seemed to last forever and it was always good, in the morning watch (0400 hrs to 0800 hrs) to see the light sky appearing and the shapes of the merchant ships over to one side of us. The weather and seas were not always bad and sometimes in the Mediterranean, it was a real joy to come out at night on to the upper deck, with a clear sky and calm sea, or cruising along in the daytime, watching the deep blue sea creaming alongside.

We did have an extensive refit in South Shields, near Newcastle, before going on our first Russian convoy. More armaments were added, the foc'sle was lengthened to give an extended cover of decking nearly half way along the ship which was supposedly to keep the inside dry. The bridge was completely uncovered and widened to give better all-round visibility and ASDICS were fitted. Later, the bows were strengthened to cope with the Arctic ice. After sea trials and the compulsory working up of both ship and crew at Tobermory, on the Isle of Mull, we felt very much endeared to our newly furbished ship.

Of the many convoys in the Atlantic, the Mediterranean, and up above the Arctic circle to Murmansk and Archangel, and of the enemy attacks by air and sea, there are already good and detailed records in many books. We had our fair share on the *Bluebell* and it was always so good to come steaming up the Mersey and see the Liver Building with the statuesque birds on their towers waiting to greet us. The Roebuck pub had adopted the crew and most would head straight there first night ashore, except for those lucky crew members getting seven days leave.

The first arctic convoy I was on was at the start of September 1942, which was PQ-18, the last of the PQ/QP series, and one of the biggest—around forty eight ships, counting the auxiliaries and contingents, and it was this size because of the debacle of PQ-17—yet despite its very heavy and very close escort of battleships and cruisers, it was the most heavily attacked; thirteen ships would be lost. HMS *Malcolm* (D19) was our escort leader, and I remember standing on the deck and counting the torpedo bombers as they flew in over the horizon, and when I got to something like twenty two, I stopped counting because they were still coming. We tried to keep as far away from the Norwegian coast as possible, but the ice barrier tended to push us in (this was winter), and this was where attacks were launched against the convoys.

The pattern seemed to be that a formation of high level Junkers Ju-88 bombers would drop a few bombs which really didn't do any damage to the convoy at all, and then the Junkers Ju-87 dive bombers with screamers fitted, would come down, drawing the anti-aircraft fire from the ships, and then the torpedo bombers would move in at sea level.

I must say that despite what had happened to PQ-17, and the fact that the Germans having had experience in attacking the convoys for a year, we never concerned ourselves with what might be likely to happen to us on this convoy. We knew it was probably going to be very unpleasant, but I think we accepted our fate, I suppose; it was a case of we are here, let's go. It's not like there was a choice not to go. We were young, and 'buoyed' up in some ways, and if ever we saw a plane shot down everybody cheered, and I remember seeing a submarine destroyed on one occasion, and we all cheered and shouted, and then that ship was torpedoed by a U-boat, and I guess that the submarine crew stood up and cheered.

The most frightening time was when we were attacked. I remember Dennis Glover, the New Zealand author, who took part in one of the convoys, said that it was very frightening, and that nobody should dismiss that. We did attack a U-boat, and it was quite an exhilarating experience; the ship moving at top speed across the area it had been sighted in, firing off our depth charges in a pattern, and keeping moving so we didn't blow our own stern off. We didn't get any confirmation of a hit but it still made us feel like we were fighting back, but we did shoot down a torpedo bomber, which was moving between the convoy ships at low level.

The average speed of the convoy was about seven knots, which enabled us to zig-zag away from our convoy station at around twice that speed, in and out between the ships, but when the sea was calm, we seemed to be just wallowing at convoy speed. The ships would be oil tankers, munitions ships, ships carrying railway engines on the deck, others with trucks, and all manner of raw materials, and they would be stretched out for miles and covered a huge area, and with clear skies could be seen from miles away by the Luftwaffe. I used to wonder why we couldn't step on it a bit.

I don't think I have ever felt so cold in my life. The temperature was well below freezing, and we all wore a lot of clothing; we had very heavy leather sea boots and long stockings that the ladies had knitted for us, and then our thick woollen jerseys under our overalls, which were the dress of the day, and we used to put on our heavy great coats over them, and sometimes an oil skin on top of that. We'd wear a scarf and always had a towel around our necks as well to stop the water getting in. I had a Russian hat that someone had given to me, which I wore with the flaps down, but even though we were well protected it didn't really make that much difference in the bitter cold. We'd all be issued a tot of neat rum every day, which was always nice to have, especially if you were on duty on the deck somewhere.

In the worst of the weather, a lot of our time on the trip would be spent keeping the deck, the rails, the guns, and the bridge, clear of ice build-up because the possibility of rolling over for being too top heavy was always there. It wasn't very comfortable trip at all, going all the way to Russia in something as small as a corvette. Although these ships were built in the style of an Icelandic trawler, they used to ship the seas over the bow, and the Barents Sea is noted for its rough sea, so the water swept right over the ship right up onto the bridge. Despite the refit which kept the mess decks and sleeping quarters slightly drier, the inside was always wet and dripping with condensation because of the metal sides, and she would roll and pitch and toss.

To say that the waves were sixty feet high is no exaggeration, and as strange as it may sound, but despite it being a great deal more uncomfortable from our point of view, we were quite pleased when the sea was like that because it meant it was too rough for an attack by enemy submarines or aircraft, and we were left alone.

The main part of the convoy went to Murmansk while we escorted a part of it to Archangel, which was almost completely iced up. We stayed there for a couple of months, and although we spent time ashore there, we felt we were being treated with some suspicion by the Russians, and I suppose to a degree, we were suspicious of them as well. They would post guards at many of the gangways on the quayside, but that was the state of the war at the time. On one occasion, I know that the mail that was bought up for us on a Catalina flying boat, was held up, and they wouldn't release the mail to the ships there, and Winston Churchill actually had to write to Josef Stalin and said that if the mail wasn't released to the sailors, the convoys would stop. We soon received our mail.

During our long stay there, we played ice hockey, having been lent the gear by some of the soldiers, and we went to the theatre. We couldn't work out why, after one performance, the crowd booed very loudly, as it seemed pretty good to us, but we found out that it was their way of acknowledging a great performance, rather than applauding. In Archangel, we went to the local cinema, and two of us went to the stockade, where we met some of the local people, and were able to converse by way of signing. There was curiosity on both sides, and it was a very interesting and quite an exciting stay.

We came back around Christmas time, and just after Christmas went out with one of the 'JW' convoys, which was the code given to the second series of convoys to Russia.

This one took us to Murmansk, and we were up there for May Day; at that time of year the weather was much better, although it was still an uncomfortable trip for the smaller ships like ourselves. We received a signal to say that two Russian destroyers would be coming out to help the escort to the Kola Inlet, which they did, taking station at various times.

Unfortunately, tragedy struck on the return journey. It was a very rough sea, and although the same two destroyers left with us to escort the convoy, they were very low on fuel. One turned back, but the captain of the second ship, because of the conditions, kept going with us until he really had to turn back because of the fuel situation, and in turning, the ship capsized, and I don't think there were any survivors from that.

Finally, in the middle of September 1943, while we were in Gibraltar, after a convoy to Malta and back, a signal arrived stating that I was to be relieved and sent back to the UK for my CW posting to HMS *King Alfred*, the Royal Navy Officers' training school at Hove, Sussex. My relief duly arrived and I headed back to England by fast destroyer. It was on my 21st birthday, after a week at *King Alfred*, when, although my signal and navigation tests were apparently okay, and my fingernails spotlessly clean, I received the thumbs down from the reviewing board and returned to active service, slightly crestfallen.

Fortunately for me, my unsuccessful spell at HMS *King Alfred* meant that I was not on board on 17 February 1945, when the *Bluebell* was torpedoed by U-711 while coming out of Murmansk. She blew up immediately; her depth charges had been set for shallow detonation as she was about to fire them, and as she began to sink, they all went off. One minute she was there, the next she was virtually gone. There was only one survivor, and not the man who had relieved me in Gibraltar.

A passing destroyer, HMS *Zest* (R02), threw him (Petty Officer Holmes) a life raft, and then went off to chase the U-boat, returning about three quarters of an hour later. They found him still clinging to the raft, and pulled him on board, where the surgeon who attended to him said that if he had managed to climb into the raft, he would probably have frozen to death. He survived because of his heavy clothing, and the Gulf Stream, which goes all the way around the world, had warmed the water enough for him.

There were about fifteen men, like myself, who had been posted from the ship at various times and survived the sinking of the *Bluebell*, and we had a very emotional meeting in 1993 at a Flower Class Corvette reunion in the UK.

My naval career then continued with a spell on a Landing Ship Dock (HMS *Eastway*), taking part in the Normandy and Southern France invasions, a short trip to Bremerhaven and Hamburg as part of the liaison staff on a Free French Frigate, the *Croix de Lorraine*. And then after some enjoyable months working in the Admiralty 'citadel' in London, living ashore and able to enjoy the sights and sounds of London, I was finally released under naval class 'A' in April 1946.

I don't think that I adjusted back to civilian life very quickly. I was with a law firm in England, and like me, a lot of them had been away in the same way, and it was such a different atmosphere. Most of us had become heavy smokers as well, probably because in the Navy we used to get duty free cigarettes, and a lot of people didn't know what we had experienced, and we didn't want to say too much about it. It was hard to get along with people again and make some friendships, and it was usually the men we found we could associate with, having lived with men of the same age as ourselves for the last five years.

Having said that, I found a very nice girl by the name of Jan Verco, who was a Meteorologist, or 'Met Wren', in the WRNS, and we got married in July 1947, and we left the UK for New Zealand in April 1957.

It has been quite difficult trying to express in words what those sea-going years were really like. I regarded them as 'unnatural' because I think no-one, however bad or for whatever reason, deserves to go through the conditions experienced, for such continuous periods, and I'm thinking of the gales and the seas. The various actions, the attacks, came and went, but the sea, the storms and gales, could be so relentless, tossing a little ship like the *Bluebell* around without mercy, like, as a former skipper had said, 'a cork' bobbing on the water. But the five years were a mind broadening experience for which I must be grateful. And I shall never ever forget those men, lost at sea, who I served with during my *Bluebell* years.

I have maintained a connection with the sea, and the Navy, and for the last sixteen years have been National President of the Russian Convoy Club in New Zealand. Our Chief of Navy, Rear Admiral Jack Steer, recently wrote, 'We are all part of the greater naval family . . . past and present sailors. Once you are part of this family you never leave it.' I believe this is so true.

Chris King, National President of the Russian Convoy Club of New Zealand, 3 July 2013.

Frank Luxford
HMS *Nigeria*

Frank Leonard Luxford was born in Holly Park Road, Friern Barnet, Middlesex, on 15 July, 1920, the son of George William and Minnie May Luxford (née Humphery), and lived at 9 Albemarle Road, East Barnet, Hertfordshire. His two older brothers, Harold and Tom, joined the army, while Frank, who had been working as a Butcher's Cutter at his local Co-operative since leaving school, joined the Royal Navy. He was twenty years old and wanted to be a signalman, and the only way for him to achieve this was to sign on as a cook, and work his way up.

Frank began a six day training course on 14 November 1940 at HMS *Royal Arthur*, the shore establishment at Ingoldmells, near Skegness, Lincolnshire, which had been a Butlin's holiday camp until it was commissioned in 1939. Following the course, he was cooking for the troops until 20 March 1941, when he was transferred to HMS *Pembroke*, another shore establishment, at Chatham, Kent to begin his training to be a signalman. He passed with flying colours, mostly ninety five per cent scores, and was then transferred as Ordinary Signalman to his first ocean going ship, the Crown Colony-class light cruiser HMS *Nigeria* (60), on 2 May. This would be his home until 31 January 1943, and during this time he saw action in the home waters and off the Scandinavian coast, and also took further exams and achieved the rank of Signalman.

Frank took a very active and conscientious roll in his duties while on board HMS *Nigeria*. This positive approach lasted throughout the duration of the war, whether he was seeing action in turbulent waters or back at the shore establishments being examined or just waiting for his ship to be repaired, the thought of being alive to live a normal life at the end of the war was enough for him to 'keep his head above water', and resilient to the end.

On 28 June 1941, HMS *Nigeria*, in company with HMS *Tartar* (F43), HMS *Bedouin* (F67), and HMS *Jupiter* (F85), intercepted in thick fog, the German weather ship *Lauenburg* (which was used in the early part of the war to provide weather reports for German shipping, particularly the U-boats), which was picked up through the use of HF/DF (High Frequency Detection Finding), north east of Jan Meyen Island, Norway.

Frank Luxford age 20. (*Courtesy of Peter Luxford*)

The crew of the *Lauenburg* abandoned the ship in two lifeboats after they were fired upon, allowing the British to board her, and acquired various valuable codebooks and parts of an Enigma machine. This was only a few weeks after HMS *Bulldog* (H91) had captured the first complete Enigma machine from the German submarine U-110 while escorting convoy OB-318 off Iceland, on 9 May.

In July 1941, HMS *Nigeria* was the flagship of 'Force K', commanded by Rear Admiral Philip Louis Vian. Force K made two expeditions from Scapa Flow, Scotland, to Spitzbergen, Norway; firstly to assess the situation there in preparation for the convoys to Russia, and then, in August, to escort Canadian troops and a team of demolition experts on the troopship *Empress of Australia* as part of Operation 'Gauntlet', the task of which was to evacuate Norwegian and Soviet personnel from the archipelago and destroy coalmines and fuel stocks that might be of use to the enemy. They also visited Bear Island and destroyed a German weather station.

On their return journey, the *Nigeria* and HMS *Aurora* (12) were diverted from the task force to intercept a German troop transport, and during this action the German artillery training ship *Bremse* drew the *Nigeria* and *Aurora* away from the transports so they could escape, but she was sunk when rammed by *Nigeria* and cut in half; the *Nigeria* suffering serious damage to her bow in the process.

On her return to Britain, she was sent to Newcastle for repairs, following which she was assigned to operate in the Mediterranean. Frank was on board her when she, as the flagship of the close escort group, commanded by Admiral Harold Burrough, participated in escorting a convoy bound for Malta on Operation 'Pedestal'.

However, on 12 August 1942, the *Nigeria* was torpedoed and damaged by the Italian submarine *Axum* north of Bizerta, Tunisia; one of three ships that were hit by a single salvo of four torpedoes. HMS *Cairo* (D87) was sunk and the oil tanker SS *Ohio* was damaged.

Above left: Frank at his post ready to send messages to other vessels by Morse Code. (*Courtesy of Peter Luxford*)

Above right: Brothers Harold, Tom and Frank Luxford. (*Courtesy of Peter Luxford*)

The *Ohio* reached Malta but as so badly damaged she had to be scuttled in order to off load her cargo. Admiral Burrough transferred his flag to the destroyer HMS *Ashanti* (F51), and the *Nigeria* managed to make it back to Gibraltar escorted by three destroyers. 'I was off duty at the time when we were torpedoed; I was lying on deck getting a bit of shut-eye with another sailor next to me, when all of a sudden we were hit by shrapnel from the torpedo, I suffered burns and minor injuries, whilst the sailor next to me died from his wounds. There but for the grace of God, go I.'

HMS *Nigeria* was sent from there to the United States for repairs, which took nine months to complete. While the crew of the Nigeria were waiting for their ship to be repaired, before going back to face more action in the war, they were billeted with families in Georgia. Frank was with Mr and Mrs J. L. Palmer, in Camilla, Georgia.

Frank then went to the British Depot Ship HMS *Wolfe* at Holy Loch, Scotland, on 1 February 1943, and then on 11 April, went back to the shore base HMS *Pembroke* prior to being posted to the escort aircraft carrier HMS *Nairana* (D05) on 26 November. He referred to this ship as 'One of the finest aircraft carriers afloat'.

By now, Frank had gained the position of Acting Leading Signalman, VS3 (Visual Signalman 3rd Grade) after passing more exams, and would have taken his turn on watch from the bridge of the *Nairana*, helping the aircraft take-off and land safely on the deck: 'I would see the returning planes coming in to land, and in some cases the plane would clip the bridge with its wing and spin the plane across the bow of the boat and end up in the drink.' On 26 May 1944, the Royal Navy Sea Hurricanes of 835 Naval Air Squadron took off and claimed the destruction of three long-range Junkers Ju-290s in defence of a convoy.

The Russian convoy missions, in my opinion, were amongst the worst missions of the war; the conditions the sailors had to endure sailing from England up to Murmansk in the Kola inlet Russia were indescribable. The mountainous seas throwing water all over the decks and by the time it had landed on deck it was ice. My father had told me about sailors losing the skin on their gloveless hands when reaching out for something to hold on to on deck when seas where high.

While still with the *Nairana*, and negotiating the arctic waters, Frank earned himself the title he had wanted to achieve—that of 'Acting Yeoman Signalman, VS2'. He had also been in charge of the 'Mess' bills between March 1944 and February 1945; these were monies paid by the ratings for various reasons.

The ship had its own magazine *Nairana Speaks*, edited by Leading Coder P. C. Hornby, a copy of which was found in Frank's memorabilia suitcase; Volume 1, Number 3: Spring 1945. It is very informative, and even has a 'Pin-Up Girl' competition, where you had to draw a pretty girl in a revealing position, which incidentally was won on this occasion by Petty Officer Walter. A bit of light hearted relief from the atrocities happening around them, no doubt. Other articles in the magazine included 'The Blitzing of Stikipantz'—more light relief maybe? Puzzle Corner, Radio Review, Current Affairs, and much more.

Frank left the ship on 21 May 1945, and returned to the shore establishment HMS *Pembroke*, and although it was the end of the war, it was not quite the end of Frank's life at sea. He was posted to HMS *Queen* on 12 August for a

Frank seen at top row, 2nd in from the left, with fellow shipmates and officers on board HMS *Nigeria*, around the time of his 21st birthday. (*Courtesy of Peter Luxford*)

HMS *Nigeria* (*Courtesy of Kris Lockyear*)

period of three days; I can only assume it was to bring some of our troops back home.

After returning to Chatham, Frank spent five months until he was demobbed on 14 March 1946. He was ready for a calmer life, returning to a civilian roll that was to be, thank goodness, for the rest of his life. Together with his two brothers, Harold and Tom, he re-kindled the four-generation-old family business of Stained Glass, designing and creating church windows, here in Great Britain and abroad. They didn't want to lose the traditional ancient craft, where unfortunately so many of the ancient crafts these days have been lost. So with their knowledge, passion and artistic skills of Stained Glass making, along with the financial help of their war gratuities, all three brothers formed a prosperous and thriving business. They all married and had children. Frank, and Eileen his wife, had two daughters, Yvonne and Rona, and a son Peter (me).

Frank's love for the sea never dwindled, he bought himself a Vagabond dingy and taught Yvonne how to sail. Then it was my turn at the helm, regretably the passion wasn't there, I was more interested in 'planes' than 'mains'. Frank thought if I joined the Sea Scouts I would become more interested in 'mains' than 'planes'. No, it didn't work, so being the loving father he was, formed an Air Scout group in which he was the scout leader with a now very happy air scout son. His other daughter Rona didn't share the sailing passion either, and Yvonne had found other activities more exiting for a teenager, so the the Vagabond, along with Frank's sea-faring days, were 'scuttled'.

Peter William Luxford (son), 18 July 2013.

John Macdonald
SS *Empire Elgar*

John 'Jack' Macdonald was born on 21 June 1917, in Arbroath, Angus, Scotland, the son of Alexander and Mary Cochrane Macdonald (née Ramsay), and one of seven children. One of his sisters, Violet, served in the WAAF.

Jack's appetite for the sea was whetted when, as a young man, he moved to Glasgow to work as an engineer in the shipyards, where many of the men talked of their visits to places like New York and San Francisco. Apparently it was the done thing for young engineers to go to sea, sow their wild oats, and then go ashore again. However, in Jack's case he was stuck, as war broke out!

His training as a marine engineer was essentially carried out 'on the job' when he joined the Orient Line. If you wanted to expand your experience, as Jack did, you joined the Pool, which also led to quicker promotion.

Jack married Jean McMorran, who lived in her family's home in Glasgow where Jack had been a lodger. She joined the WAAFs and was stationed in Loth (near Brora), which was handy for Jack on his return to Scapa Flow. Jack takes up the story:

Being a member of the British Merchant Navy Pool, I was allowed three months absence of leave (without pay), to attend college to study for my Second Engineer's Certificate of Competency. I had to sign on at the Bureau, as it was then known, and received about half of what I would have earned whilst at sea.

Following college, I travelled to the headquarters of the BOT (Board of Trade) in Broomielaw, Glasgow, to sit my examinations which lasted the whole week; Monday to Friday. I had to go back the next Monday to get the results; fortunately I had passed because it was all done at my own expense.

The Merchant Navy Pool was right next to the BOT offices, so I rejoined the pool in order to re-enhance my pay. I returned home to my wife's parent's home at 1230 hrs and while we were having lunch, a telegram arrived asking me to report back to the pool by 1500 hrs without fail, which I did.

I was informed that I had been appointed as Second Engineering Officer to a ship based in Murmansk, Russia, and that my train would be leaving Glasgow

John MacDonald in 1948 (*Courtesy of Ronald Stewart*)

Central station at 1830 hrs and to make sure that I was on it. I caught the train to Scapa Flow, where, upon arrival, we were escorted to HMS *Iron Duke*, which had been the Flagship of Admiral Sir John Jellicoe, deployed in the Grand Fleet during the First World War, and was being used as a transit camp providing accommodation for personnel in transit to and from ships of the Home Fleet.

In Murmansk, the Royal Navy had a wireless station, a medical centre, and the 2,847-ton merchant ship SS *Empire Elgar*, which had been specially rigged for heavy lifting. The Navy wanted to relieve all personnel from all three bases, but the Russian Government objected; I suppose it was on the grounds that the fewer foreigners saw the conditions in Murmansk, the better. Anthony Eden had to visit Moscow himself in order to get permission to relieve all personnel, and we stayed on board the *Iron Duke* until the problem was solved.

No convoys had reached Murmansk for around six months because of the German submarine blockade, and so in order to break this, the Navy assembled a fleet of four M-class and four S-class destroyers which set sail for Murmansk. I was on board HMS *Mahratta* (G23). If the destroyers pinpointed any German submarines, off we would go like a greyhound at thirty knots, throwing depth charges left, right and centre to break through the blockade.

On reaching Murmansk, the Merchant Navy crew were escorted to the *Empire Elgar*, where the old crew were relieved to join the destroyers on their return journey to the UK. After about ten days, the first of the convoys came in, and

John Ramsay Macdonald (*Courtesy of Ronald Stewart*)

(under Russian Government orders) we were transported by road to the quay, and sailed out on the *Empire Elgar* to where the convoy ships were anchored, transfered their heavy cargoes, and then sailed back to harbour to discharge the loads.

We had all been issued with winter clothing to protect us against the bitter sub-zero temperatures. The daylight hours were between around 1030 hrs until 1530 hrs, and this gradually became shorter during our time there. The daylight also brought with it the opportunity for German bombers, which were regularly bombing Murmansk.

For recreation at night time, there was a community centre, where we and the convoy seamen (including many Americans from their vessels) used to drink vodka, which tasted like it had been distilled from potatoes.

The forecastle of the *Empire Elgar* was loaded with fourteen-pound tins of corned beef, which we had in various disguises for breakfast, lunch and dinner.

John MacDonald with his granddaughter Kathy. (*Courtesy of Ronald Stewart*)

When out in the roads, discharging any heavy lift off an American ship, we would trade tins of corned beef, and as we were a new part and parcel of the Royal Navy, we were allowed a ration of rum each day, which we would bottle and trade off with the tins for barrels of frozen chicken and other goods—the first taste of chicken was out of this world.

With drink getting the better of them, many fights broke out in the Community Centre between the British and the Americans, and the Russian Police would just stand back and watch it all happen to their great amusement.

J. MacDonald (*Courtesy of Ronald Stewart*)

We had Russian women on board the *Empire Elgar*, who worked twelve hour shifts on the derricks. The OGPU were the 'secret' police then, and when they were in the engine room and we offered them a cup of tea, all we got back was a "Nyet—No". But get them into your cabin with the door shut and they would take anything you offered them as long as nobody was watching them. We got on very well with the Russian officials during our time there, even learning to speak a few basic words of Russian, "Pojalusta—Please" and "Spasseeba—Thank you", although "Zavtra—Tomorrow" seemed to be the most widely used.

There's not a great deal I can say about Murmansk—each day was like the one before it, and being down in the bowels of the ship, we heard no evil, saw no evil, and spoke no evil.

The *Empire Elgar* was on two year articles under BOT regulations, and when our time on her was up, we had to be relieved. When we were leaving, our officers received letters of thanks from the Russians, and a gift of three thousand roubles. It couldn't be spent though; there was nothing to spend it on. This was also the only ship I had been on where we were paid overtime, and I came away with a cheque for £180, which was a lot of money then.

We were embarked once again on destroyers that were escorting a convoy back to Scapa Flow, and again the escort ships moved like greyhounds at full speed when any submarine was detected, with the usual deployment of depth charges. It was rumoured that seven U-boats had been sunk.

SS *Empire Elgar* as *Sea Minstrel*. (*Author's Collection*)

My wife was a radar operator, and was based in Loth, Sutherland, a few miles north of Brora, in the Highlands of Scotland. As I didn't fancy going by the non-stop train from Scapa Flow to Glasgow, and then all the way back to Brora to see my wife, I had a word with the engine drive and the guard and explained my position, and with the help of £1 each, they would stop the train at Brora, and I would be ready to jump off with all my gear. It was unheard of. I enjoyed a few days in the Brora Hotel where my wife visited me when she was free; I owe that engine driver and guard my heartfelt thanks.

Jack left the Merchant Service to have a proper family life in around 1950, and had shore jobs, mainly as a Boiler Inspector. His last job was with the family firm, Ramsay Ladders of Forfar, but this didn't work out. He returned to the sea in 1963, but by that time he was thoroughly deskilled of course; engine room design had changed radically since his days of service. He joined a tanker of the 'World Wide Company' of Hong Kong, and as he had his Chief's Ticket he was appointed as a Second Engineer and a year later was appointed as Chief. Jack left the sea in for good in 1984.

John MacDonald and Ron Stewart (nephew), 10 July 2013.

John Mackay
HMS *Keppel*

John was born in Granton, Edinburgh on 8 February 1920, the son of Ewan and Harriet Mackay. His elder sibling was his sister Jessie who worked in England in munitions when the war broke out. Of his three brothers, Donald served in the army and was captured at St Valerie, just outside Dunkirk, and spent the rest of the war as a prisoner of the Germans. His other brothers, Ewan and Gregor also served in the Royal Navy; Ewan joining when he was just fifteen years of age.

John trained as a painter and decorator at College, though since he was a young boy, he had always wanted to be in the Navy. He joined the Royal Naval Voluntary Reserve at Edinburgh on 17 March 1938, at the age of seventeen. He was called up on 26 August 1939, and was sent for basic Gunner training at Leith docks, being paid 3*d* a day, which doubled to 6*d* a day when he started training on the ASDIC underwater detection device (which the Americans called Sonar).

John's first ship was HMS *Wolfe* (F37), previously named the SS *Montcalm*, which had recently been requisitioned for service with the Royal Navy as an Armed Merchant Cruiser (and later as a submarine Depot ship from 1942). During the time he was with the *Wolfe*, he married Anne Jamieson, who he had met while resting at the Naval Hospital, on 12 November 1941, and lived in Glasgow.

He was then drafted to HMS *Highlander* (H44), an H-class destroyer which had been the Flotilla Leader of Escort Group B-4 of the Mid-Ocean Escort Force in early 1942 and continued to escort convoys in the North Atlantic for the rest of the war.

John joined the Shakespeare Class destroyer HMS *Keppel* (D84) on 25 February 1943 as one of two ASDIC operators, and worked on a four-hours-on, eight-hours-off shift pattern. When working together they would take turns, listening for one hour and then change places.

There were too many men on board to be allocated a cabin, so John shared an open space on the top deck, below the stokers and signalmen, with six others, who were fortunate to have been allocated a hammock; in some other quarters men had to bunk on wooden boards.

John Mackay with his medal. (*Courtesy of Iris Burgess*)

HMS *Keppel* left Loch Ewe on 11 February 1943 on the arduous convoy duties with part of the Third Escort Group sailing to Russia.

'I remember having to chip away at the ice; you could not touch the sides of the boat without gloves on or your hands would have stuck to the sides and your skin would have come off.'

'We were lucky to get a meal if 'action stations' was sounded. I always remember thinking when my next meal would be. The potatoes would be frozen and we would have to try to squeeze the water out of them. The bread would be black with mould which we had to cut away.'

We used to travel in twos, and with the Sloop HMS *Kite* (U-87) beside us we took up our position as Advanced Starboard Attack Party on convoy JW-59 in August 1944.

On 20 August, we picked up a target on our starboard quarter, and along with HMS *Kite* and a Swordfish aircraft from the Nairana-class escort carrier HMS *Vindex* (D15), we attacked a U-boat with depth charges and hedgehogs, and went on to deploy anti-Gnat devices (known as foxers) throughout the night but without success.

The next morning, however, as the *Kite* slowed down to clear her tangled foxers, the German submarine U-344 fired a spread of three FAT torpedoes at the Sloop. The ship was struck by two of the torpedoes on the starboard side and heeled over to that side immediately. The stern broke off, floated for a few seconds, and then sank.

'I was asleep in my hammock when I was woken by an explosion, shortly followed by a second. As 'action stations' sounded, I already had my duffel coat on (the crew was instructed by the Captain to sleep fully clothed in the event that the ship was hit by a U-boat torpedo) and made my way onto the upper deck towards my station.'

'HMS *Kite* was astern of us and was sinking fast, and within a minute of my reaching my post on the bridge, she was fully submerged.
I carried out a sweep of the surrounding area but could not pick up a contact with the U-boat. The Keppel circled the survivors until support arrived.'

'When HMS *Mermaid* and HMS *Peacock* arrived, the *Keppel* drifted among the survivors who were scattered far apart.

I was ordered to go to the foc'sle with a hard line, and from there I could see a large number of men covered in thick oil and clinging to Carley rafts or pieces of wreckage.'

'There were only nine survivors on our boat. It was my job to bury the dead. I did this by putting them in hessian sacking, and sowed them up with a sail-maker's needle; the last stitch was put through their nose to make absolutely sure they were dead. The Union Jack was put over them and then the officer would nod and we would tip them overboard.'

'Our job was to look for the U-boat that had sunk the *Kite*. With the help of aircraft we fired at the U-boat, damaging it. It was leaking oil and we followed it.

John Mackay being presented with the medal. (*Courtesy of Iris Burgess*)

HMS *Keppel* in 1936. *(Authors Collection)*

As it got nearer to the Norwegian coast (which the Germans then occupied) we set off a Hedgehog and it blew the U-boat out of the water, nearly taking us with it.

I remember rescuing a tin of beans out of the water that had come off the submarine, and we had something different to eat that night.'

'I was in touch with a man called Ray Holden, who wanted to know what happened to his brother who was on the *Kite*. I told him we had rescued him but it was so cold where we were that he died from his injuries on board the *Keppel*, and that I had buried him at sea.

He was glad to know what had happened to his brother and know that he had been buried and not just lost at sea.'

'I once met two men; Peter Mackinrow from Glasgow, and another called Mackintosh from Dover. They both said they were going on the Kite and we would meet up in Russia, but they never made it. I am lucky that I survived the arctic convoys to tell my story.'

John Mackay was discharged on 3 January 1946, and returned to his trade as a painter and decorator (which he had trained in at college before the war). He moved his family to Manchester, where he later worked at Withington Hospital as a Planner/Estimator. After he retired, John took up being a decorator again, and worked up until he was 79 years old, when he gave it up to look after his wife.

John and Anne had three children; two boys, John and David, and after the war the family moved to Manchester, where their daughter Iris was born in 1950.

Penwill James Moore
HMS *Malcolm*

I was born in Wellington, New Zealand, on 29 August 1920, the son of Penwill Moore and Nellie Kathleen Moore (née Millar). I had two younger brothers and a sister, and we were raised in Rongotai. After schooling, I studied accountancy at Victoria University from 1938 to 1941, during which time I also worked at the accountancy firm Clarke Menzies Griffin & Co. as an office junior.

I enlisted as a volunteer in the New Zealand Division of the Royal Navy in May 1941, and in December sailed for the United Kingdom in the quadruple screw Motor Vessel *Dominion Monarch*. She was refitted as a troopship in Halifax, Canada, whilst en route to the UK.

After three months at the shore establishment HMS *Ganges* (which was being used as a centre for 'Hostilities Only New Entry Training'), I was immediately drafted to the Admiralty Leader-class destroyer HMS *Malcolm* (D19) as Navigator's Yeoman.

She was re-commissioned after a major refit at Devonport Dockyard, and after working up, she sailed for Liverpool where she became a Special Escort destroyer of Western Approaches based in Gladstone Dock. Our CO (Commanding Officer) was Commander Archibald Boyd Russell, RN, a distinguished senior escort officer, and we were employed on some special convoy duties in the Atlantic including escorting the troop ship SS *Llanstephan Castle*, which had been torpedoed, from the west of Finisterre to the Clyde.

In early July we sailed for Hvalfjord, Iceland, as SO (Senior Officer) close escort for a Russian convoy which was recalled after about two days steaming. We returned to Hvalfjord from where we escorted the Fleet Oiler *Blue Ranger* (X57/A157) to Scapa Flow then back to Liverpool.

On 2 August 1942, we sailed from Gourock, Inverclyde, oiling at Moville, Ireland, prior to rendezvousing with the convoy (WS-21S) of fast large merchant ships on Operation 'Pedestal', bound for Malta, which was effectively under siege, blockaded by Axis air and naval forces. The convoy was subsequently joined by the battleships HMS *Rodney* (29), *Nelson* (28), aircraft carriers, cruisers and more destroyers.

Penwill Moore on 10 June 2008. (*Courtesy of Penwill Moore, Jnr*)

We oiled at Gibraltar and rejoined the convoy. The *Malcolm*'s special task was one of two Destroyers escorting the carrier HMS *Furious* (47) and being close to HMS *Eagle* (94) when she was torpedoed on 11 August. We rescued 198 survivors, and several of the dead were recovered and subsequently buried with proper naval honours.

During the night, in company with HMS *Wolverine* (D78), we attacked the Italian submarine *Dagabur* which the *Wolverine* rammed and sank off Algiers. The next day we hunted another U-boat, which eventually took refuge in Spanish Ibiza. On way to rejoin the convoy we picked up air crew in life raft from RAF aircraft that had been shot down, and then we were redirected to escort HMS *Nigeria* (60), which had been badly damaged by torpedo attack in the Straits of Pantelleria.

We then escorted the *Furious* towards Malta for three trips to deliver Spitfires to within flying range of Malta, and then returned to Liverpool for a boiler clean. Following that we then went to Loch Ewe, where the merchant ships of convoy PQ-18 assembled. HMS *Malcolm* was SO close escort of the convoy, going right through to Archangel, arriving on 21 September. During our stay the docks were under constant air attack.

On 2 October, we were ordered to Vaenga, on the Kola Inlet, to obtain small supply of fuel oil and we then proceeded independently to Seydisfjord, Iceland—a

HMS *Malcolm*. (*Author's Collection*)

very harrowing experience as our shortest course took us close to the occupied North Norwegian coast. We refuelled at Seydisfjord and back to Liverpool, encountering storm force conditions which caused a great deal of damage to the ship.

HMS *Malcolm* was dry docked for repairs and structural alterations which included a substantially reinforced stem. On 20 October, we sailed for Belfast to assemble convoy of a strange mixture of ships which included three LSTs, and as SO, escorted them safely to Gibraltar, through fourteen days of stormy conditions. We refuelled at Gibraltar and learned that we were part of Operation 'Torch'—the invasion of North Africa, and along with HMS *Broke* (D83), the *Malcolm* was to storm Algiers harbour and smash the boom, seize important port installations and prevent the scuttling of French warships.

At around 0300 hrs, we were caught in searchlight beams and were subjected to a withering barrage of fire from the shore batteries. The *Malcolm* sustained several direct hits; the forward boiler was destroyed and the engine room badly holed. The bridge structure, including the chartroom and conning position, were damaged, and the mid-ships area was on fire; and she was forced to withdraw, slowly sinking.

Algiers surrendered later that day, and the following day, the *Malcolm* was assisted to a berth in the old port where temporary repairs were carried out. After a week, we sailed with three corvettes as escort for some merchant ships back to Gibraltar, and then a week later, returned to the Clyde as part of escort for HMS

Duke of York (17) and HMS *Victorious* (R38). We then went on to Sheerness and Chatham dockyard for major repairs.

I then went to the Crown Colony-class light cruiser HMS *Newfoundland* (59), commissioning after building at Swan Hunter's Yard at Wallsend-on-Tyne. Whilst on seven days' leave prior to going to the shore establishment HMS *King Alfred*. I was visiting relations in Salcombe, South Devon, when it was subjected to a Baedeker Raid by a squadron of Focke-Wulf FW-190's and the house received a direct hit. I was rescued after being buried for several hours and was hospitalised for four months before starting my course at *King Alfred*.

Commissioned at the end of October 1943, I then proceeded to the ACO (Admiralty Compass Observatory) for training as a Compass Officer at Ditton Park, Slough. I was appointed Swinging Officer to Force J Group 2 (HMS *Sea Serpent*) for the D-Day landings at Juno Beach, and was the only New Zealand-born 'compass swinger' in the war.

In September 1944, I returned to ACO for further courses, qualifying as full Compass Officer with next appointment as assistant to Swinging Officer at Leith (HMS *Claverhouse*) with short term stint as Relieving Compass Officer to AKHM (Admiralty Kings Harbour Master), Rosyth.

After VE Day, I was granted Foreign Service leave to return to New Zealand with a reappointment at end of the leave to the British Pacific Fleet based at Darwin. VJ Day was declared in August 1945, and at the end of November, I became surplus to requirements and was discharged from active service. I rejoined Clarke Menzies (but remained on the Reserve of Admiralty Compass Officers until late 1950's). In February 1946, I was awarded an ex-serviceman's scholarship from the New Zealand Society of Accountants to travel to the UK, and from May 1946 to September 1948, I worked in a variety of jobs in London. Upon my return to Wellington, I joined J. L. Arcus as an Audit Manager, and on 4 February 1950, I married Esme Mary Grindrod, and we had three children; Susan Elizabeth (now Cook), Jennifer Ruth (now deLisle), and Penwill Christopher. I set up in private practice in 1981 with my daughter Jenny, and continued working until quite recently.

Penwill James Moore, Wellington, New Zealand, 19 July 2013.

J. Gordon Mumford
SS *Soborg*

Too young to enlist in the regular armed forces, Gordon Mumford studied to become a Merchant Marine radio officer, qualifying for a Special Certificate in 1942. However, tragedy hit the Mumford household when Gordon's father died suddenly when he was stung on the lip by a wasp on 25 August, 1942, and Gordon found himself the sole support of his family: his mother, two young brothers aged around nine and ten, and his older sister (her husband was serving in the British army in Burma) and her new-born daughter.

After their father's death, Gordon's mother spoke to Commander Hall who spoke to 'someone' that he knew in Siemens (a radio telecommunications company), and through him, Gordon was offered a position with them. Siemens was one of three companies that supplied the Merchant Navy with radio officers to work with their equipment. The other two were Marconi and MRI (Marine Radio International). This is Gordon's story:

I was born in Chingford, Essex, and lived my early years in a farmhouse in Epping Forest. I had been a member of the Air Defence Cadet Corp since the age of twelve, and at the outbreak of war was sent to RAF North Weald, a fighter and bomber base, where I and my fellow cadets were trained to carry out various jobs such as dismantling machine guns, and checking and cleaning them under the supervision of leading aircraftmen and armourers. There was a small hand-pulled tender that we used to carry belts of machine gun bullets to the Hawker Hurricanes, and I remember sitting on the wings with 'Taffy', the armourer, and loading the belts into the breach blocks of the Browning machine guns.

Towards the spring of 1940, all air cadets were withdrawn from the airfields throughout Britain due to the increasing threat of attack by enemy aircraft, and Epping Forest was no longer peaceful; often suffering badly when enemy bombers dropped their deadly loads prematurely over the outer edge of London's air defences.

I joined the Merchant Navy as a Radio Officer in September 1942, and my first ship was the SS *Soborg*, a small Danish collier taking coal to Iceland to bunker ships for the Murmansk convoys. She was a pre-war relic; a coal-carrying ship with a sturdy riveted hull, and as dirty as hell; the battleship grey paint was peeling in places revealing the red lead undercoat, and there was coal dust everywhere. Her cargo holds were for'ard and aft of the bridge and mid section accommodation, and were covered and sealed with their latch covers and tarpaulin overlays clamped in place.

My accommodation was a narrow shelf (my bunk) with two drawers underneath. A narrow cupboard was bolted to the bulkhead and next to it was a small washstand with a mirror above it. A steam radiator, rumbling and gurgling like a tormented stomach (much like my own), completes the picture.

With the pitch of the ship, rising and falling in heavy seas, and my chair, which was securely fastened to the deck by a chain, moving with the ship, waves of nausea surged through my body and I reached again for the red can that I had been given from the ship's cook. I was lucky; the can had a lid to keep the smell in. There was no cooling breeze flowing from the whirring fan in the radio cabin, just the re-circulation of the cloying smell of vomit intermingled with the rancid odour emanating from the steam radiator.

The incessant chatter of Morse code flowed from the headphones clamped to my head, and drilled into my brain. I resume writing, my hand shakily clutching the pencil as I record the stream of characters coming from the marine radio transmitter at Rugby. Messages were sent in Cypher groups of five, which, until they are decoded, are gibberish, a meaningless jumble of letters and numbers. The four hours of my watch was passing very slowly.

At 1200 hrs, the heavy steel outer door opened with a clang and a blast of cold air, and the Chief Sparks entered, 'This place stinks', he complained, 'Phew, what with that bloody radiator and that can of yours, we're in for a bad trip.'

'If I'd known life at sea was like this, I'd have stayed at home.'

'You'll get used to it', he reassured me, 'It'll take a few days but then you'll be alright. If you think this is bad, just wait until we get out into the Atlantic.'

As I lay on my bunk, the horizontal position calmed my queasy stomach, still aching and sore from retching, and I remember thinking, "I'll be on watch again in four hours". Depression set in. 'My first ship and it had to be one with a two-watch system!' 'Was it only two or three days since I had joined the ship? It seemed longer.'

Amidst incoming reports of enemy E-boat and aircraft activity, the *Soborg* left the Green Hythe buoys in the Thames at first light on 24 September, hugging the eastern seaboard, bound for North Shields.

It was late afternoon when we dropped the pilot and moved into convoy formation, but within half an hour the ship's klaxon woke me. The noise shattered the patterned thud of the engines and echoed along the passageways, bringing the ship to maximum alert.

Grabbing a tin hat, I left the cabin and scrambled up an iron ladder to the armoured machine gun nest above the radio room.

Gordon in tropical uniform in April 1946 when he was Chief Radio Officer on the MV *Luling* in India on his 21st birthday. (*Courtesy of Barbara Mumford*)

This area was known as 'E-boat Alley' because of those high speed motor torpedo boats that operated out of the occupied channel ports. I threw off the waterproof canvas, revealing an ancient Thompson machine gun on a swivel mounting, and double-checked the round ammunition pan that fed the gun. I was used to guns, having been brought up in the country, and did well on the three-week gunnery course prior to joining the ship.

I peer through the gun sights, scanning the surrounding sea and overcast sky, focusing on imaginary targets. In some ways, war was still a game to me. I was at one with the elements: the raw cold wind chilled my face and my seasickness had abated. This is better, more like the action I've waited for.

Tensions were running high among the crew, and for good reason. Two months previously the *Soborg* had been bombed and badly damaged in these waters. Hans, an elderly engineer, told me about what happened in the wardroom.

'Ja, Loister, Jong' (he always called me Jong, which means young person: at seventeen I was the youngest one on the ship), 'Dey bombed us in de Thames Estuary. Do bloody bastards hit us in de stern, right op de twenty fife pounder gon. Many men killed. Ja, alles de gon crew and some of my stokers. Dey ver killed below decks ven de ammunition she blow up. Dey could not get out of de port holes because dey ver too small. De men died screaming. Dit was awful. Dey died half in and half out of de port hols, poor bastards.'

He paused for a moment and then said, 'Vell, Jong, now ve ave got big port holes. Too damn late vir de odders, but maybe ve is ok dis time. Vat is dit dat jo Engless say? Lightning she no strike same place twice.' I hoped that he was right.

It turned out to be a false alarm; the enemy aircraft must have been looking for other targets and had not spotted us in the overcast weather conditions.

Early the next morning, we entered the Tyne and the short voyage to North Shields was over, which became the home port of the *Soborg*.

Within two or three days we were ordered to the nearby port of Blythe, a few miles north of Newcastle, where we took a cargo of coal.

As we loaded at the wharf, the air thick with coal dust, rumours were spreading around the ship about our final destination; the Russian convoys to Murmansk were on everyone's mind. The Germans held Norway, and Narvik is close to the northern route with airfields and enemy naval forces. Nobody liked to think of the Russian run as a destination. Survival in the frigid waters of the Arctic is just a few minutes before hypothermia and death set in.

Fully loaded, the *Soborg* moved out beyond the harbour breakwater into the anchorage, which was protected against enemy attacks by minefields. The captain set off in a naval launch to a convoy conference, and returned in the late afternoon. He was unsmiling as he hurried up the gangway, summoning the Mate to the Captain's stateroom.

During supper that evening, the Mate broke the news (although it had 'somehow' already leaked out beforehand) that we were going to Iceland. The coal we had loaded was for refuelling a convoy bound for Russia, and we were to rendezvous with the convoy in a fjord near the capital, Reykjavik.

Gordon at a book presentation in the Burnaby Museum, Canada, in 2010. (*Courtesy of Barbara Mumford*)

The overcast skies and dirty weather conditions that had dogged us along the coast from the south continued, but it helped to hide us from the enemy. It became embarrassingly apparent only a few hours after leaving Blythe that my training at the radio college was deficient of visual signalling communications, such as semaphore, flags and Aldis lamp signalling, but this would soon change, and the experience would turn me from a raw landlubber into a seafarer.

Rounding the top of Scotland between Inverness and the Orkney Islands, we ran into gale force winds and seas, but we forged slowly ahead bearing north northwest to Iceland. The ship is rolling and pitching violently; waves tower above the vessel, and then, as she slips sideways, they crash down over the cargo deck. I would cling to the aft deck railings in the lee of the mid-ship accommodation and watch the waves smash across the battened-down cargo hatches. The ship would shudder and lurch before returning tons of sea water in cascading masses, over and through openings in the cargo deck bulwarks.

The temperature dropped dramatically as we ploughed ever northward. The ice built up on our superstructure and icicles hung down from the surfaces where partial melting had taken place. Ice also formed on the steel mast stays, doubling or tripling their thickness. An engineer was busy with the deck crew trying to chip off the ice outside water pumps to get them operational. To keep warm, we wore our warmest clothing beneath duffle coats and mittens provided by the ship. The duffle coats, with their protective hoods, were an absolute necessity when working outside in those temperatures.

Nearing the Arctic Circle, the snow-clad shores of Iceland reared up on the horizon, and the convoy ran parallel with the coast as it headed for Reykjavik, until it finally anchored up in the bay. We didn't get any shore leave, our stay was too short.

Two or three days later we were ordered to Hvalfjord, just along the coast. This deep long fjord proved to be our rendezvous point with the Murmansk convoy.

Gordon wearing his war service medals in 2000.
(*Courtesy of Barbara Mumford*)

Ships of many nationalities make up the Murmansk convoy. We tied up alongside a Russian ship for bunkering, and I was surprised to see that there were women in its crew. I had never seen women working as crew members before. The long slow task of unloading the coal into the ship's bunkers began, and continued through the following days and nights. As one ship is bunkered, another takes its place.

Once empty, the crew hosed down the holds of the *Soborg*. New orders were received. We were to load barrels of fish destined for Aberdeen on the return voyage to Newcastle, and later that day, a tug towing the first lighters arrived alongside.

The voyage back was violent; the weather had turned sour and fighting the exceptionally heavy seas and winds, we just about maintained our position. A five-thousand ton cargo ship capable of a top speed of about eight knots, we could cover one mile in 24 hours and we lost the convoy. Eventually the weather and seas abated and as visibility improved, we found ourselves alone in an empty sea.

The Captain altered course for the Orkney Islands, and the safety of Kirkwall, the major port. Fortunately we encountered no enemy forces on that run.

Our stay in Kirkwall was short, because a southbound convoy was sailing the following day to the east coast ports in Scotland and England. We received orders to join it as far as Aberdeen, and the next morning, the *Soborg* left the anchorage and joined the other ships in a slow five-or-six knot coastal convoy.

The voyage was routine, apart from the continuing bad weather. We were sheltered to a certain extent from the incoming weather fronts from the Atlantic by the land mass of Scotland, but the seas still ran high.

The British Merchant ship *Soborg*. (*Courtesy of Barbara Mumford*)

The following morning we turned off from the convoy, and picked up a pilot as we approached the anchorage at Aberdeen, where we spent several days tied alongside the dock. This is where I received my first mail from home. In fact there were several letters from my mother telling me about the nightly bombing raids on London. I was wondering how my mother was adjusting to my father's death which occurred three months previously.

We left Aberdeen on 21 November for Newcastle with ships on both flanks and some ahead of us. The coastal traffic on the HF (High Frequency) bands was heavy as we edged down the coast, indicating enemy action from aircraft and E-boats in the Channel and the coastline of southern England.

We were lucky; our area was quiet, and under the cover of low-lying clouds and squalls intermingled with fog banks, we slipped through the Tyne without incident.

Flags of different colours and patterns were flying from the mast of the Commodore ship as we prepared to leave the convoy. Answering flags were raised from our bridge and the bridges of other vessels also destined for the Tyne. Their import was a mystery to me but fortunately the deck officers understood them. Depleted in numbers, the convoy sailed on south towards the attacking enemy forces. I watched them go with mixed feelings.

Officials from the Ministry of War Transport came on board the following morning (23 November) to sign the crew off the ship's articles, and that afternoon I was on a London-bound train home on leave, and awaiting assignment to another ship.

Gordon worked on a variety of ships: the *Scottish Heather* torpedoed in the North Atlantic, the *Empire Harmony* in the Mediterranean, the *Empire Path* mined and sunk in the Scheldt Estuary, the *Luling* in the invasion of Malaysia, and the *Adolph S Ochs* in Canada and South America. He left the sea on 27 March, 1947.

Gordon and Barbara Mumford, June 2013.

Maurice Newman, OBE, DSC
HMS *Bermuda*

After the leave which followed passing out from HMS *Heron* (also known as RNAS *Yeovilton*) in Somerset, I joined as FDO (Fighter Direction Officer) in early December 1942, on the cruiser HMS *Bermuda* (C52) under Captain Terence Hugh Back, RN, at Scapa Flow. I relieved a Lieutenant Bleasdale, an FDO who had ideas about instituting Headquarters Ships for amphibious landings, and who was off to the Admiralty to pursue these ideas. The *Bermuda* had just returned from the North Africa landings, where she had taken part in the bombardment of Bone.

The ship had been commissioned in John Brown's yard at Clydebank, Scotland, on 12 August 1942. She was a Colony-class cruiser, which was a follow-on design of the pre-war Town-class vessels. She had four turrets, each of three six-inch guns and four twin four-inch high angle guns plus lighter (pom-pom) anti-Aircraft guns. She was also equipped with torpedo tubes, ASDIC, (Anti-Submarine Detection Indicators) and modern warning and fire control radars. She also had two aircraft hangers and launching and recovery facilities for the Supermarine Walrus float-planes.

My duties were to be FDO, ARO (Aircraft Recognition Officer) and ALO (Air Liaison Officer) as well as Quarter-deck Divisional officer, which entailed being available for personal assistance to anyone in the quarter-deck division who needed it. I also stood watch-keeping duties at sea and in harbour, along with the other junior executive branch officers. In harbour, when it was my turn to be officer of the watch, I was assisted by a petty officer quartermaster, a corporal of marines and two side boys. This was particularly useful to me because I had a very bad auditory memory, and when the commander, in particular, would come along and reel off a list of things that had to be done in our watch, I had no hope of remembering them. So the moment he was gone, we would form a group and write down everything he had said. In night watches, and sometimes also in day watches, I would do rounds of the ship.

As fighter direction officer, I had my air plot in the bridge structure immediately under the bridge, sharing an office with the surface plot run by the ship's schoolmaster immediately over my cabin.

The air plot crew consisted at first of myself and three other ratings. We were later joined by Captain Clemenson (Royal Artillery), who had been left on the ship. He had been appointed as FOO (Forward Observation Officer) to liaise with the army in bombardments in the North African campaign—but the army had forgotten him! He was seconded to the air plot for watch-keeping purposes and the rating complement expanded to, I think, five, only two of whom would be on duty at any one time.

My job was then to direct aircraft from the ship, assess the air situation and keep the captain informed. It was on the air plot that a record was kept of all the aircraft in the area. The aircraft positions were plotted on a concentric-ringed grid, covered with Perspex and positioned at a forty-five degree angle. For communications we had phones to the bridge and radar room, also loudspeaker communication between us and the air-warning radar operator. The air-warning radar was Type 281, later replaced by Type 281B.

As speed and accuracy in plotting would be vital in an action, I concentrated from the start on training, with competitions that involved plotting blindfolded from all sides of the plot, so that the crew achieved a very high degree of competence, and when the Fighter Direction School was established at Hatston, the main town in the Orkney Islands, we were invited to give demonstrations there.

Ascertaining height of aircraft was in those days difficult and I kept plans of the radar lobes in the plot and checked the first appearance of an echo with the lobe, which proved adequate in practice, though we had to adjust the theoretical lobe with actual calibration runs with aircraft.

HMS *Bermuda*. (*Courtesy of Juhani Sierla*)

We made one or two trips to Iceland, on one of which we tracked aircraft which were obviously German, flying up towards Iceland and back again. I reported this to my captain, who authorised me to go ashore to meet with the admiral in charge, and arrange for land-based US aircraft to be directed from HMS *Bermuda* (by me) onto these aircraft and shoot them down.

I duly went ashore to ACHQ (Area Control Headquarters) and, with much difficulty, was finally introduced to the admiral. When I suggested this operation, his response was 'You can't come in here with all this war talk, my boy. Take a seat. The truth is, those aircraft are very useful to us. They transmit the meteorological information of the area back to Germany and we are able to use it. By doing so, we are also able to break their codes. Thank your captain for his suggestion.'

Life on board Ship

The European class system was quite clear aboard Royal Navy ships. Generally, officers didn't in any way socialise with the men from the lower deck, partly for discipline reasons, partly because of social class. For New Zealanders who weren't used to much of a class system at all, this was very different, although people never knew quite where to place us colonials, or 'Black troops', as some called us.

While I was in training, I considered that the people in charge of the seamen (Petty Officers and Chief Petty Officers) were, without exception, absolutely first class and dedicated: it was their life. They were the backbone of the British Navy. After being commissioned, however, I found that the officers in charge were more of a mixed bag. In my case they were mostly Royal Navy, and so they were part of this class system. They were all pretty efficient, mostly very English, though sometimes cliquey.

We were RNVR (Royal Naval Volunteer Reserve), a slightly inferior race— not that we felt it, but there was a difference there all the time. I was lucky in that generally I got on very well with the RN officers, particularly with those on my own level. One junior RN officer, Lieutenant W. J. Woolley, and two RNVR officers, Lieutenant Reg 'Tiger' Gilchrist, RNVR, and Lieutenant D. A. 'Prof' Kidd, RNVR, became life-long friends until they died.

The navy divided the day into watches and everything was done in these watches. There was the forenoon (0800 hrs until 1200 hrs) the afternoon (1200 hrs until 1600 hrs) the first dog-watch (1600 hrs until 1800 hrs) the second dog-watch (1800 hrs until 2000 hrs) the first watch (2000 hrs until 0000hrs) the middle watch (0000 hrs until 0400 hrs) and the morning watch (0400 hrs until 0800hrs).

There was a good spirit in our wardroom. Every Saturday night in harbour, we had a formal dinner, black ties and all, where we entertained visitors, followed by a social evening of singing and impromptu acts by one or two talented officers.

A new dish to me was kedgeree, which was often served in the wardroom. It consisted of lots of rice and not much fish. Once in Northern Iceland, a small boat was sent away to do an exercise in dropping small depth charges (designed for dealing with midget submarines). After the depth charges had exploded the boat was filled with the masses of the cod found floating in the water. This cod fed the ship of about 800 men extremely well for a day or so.

My cabin in the *Bermuda* was quite small, about six feet by ten feet. There was a ventilator trunk beside my bunk, and sometimes in the northern latitudes, I used to wake in the mornings to find a sheet of ice across my top blanket, stretching across from the ventilator. My first job of the day was to clean the ice off the blankets! At one end of the cabin was a cabinet containing a little wash basin, mirror and toilet basin, while opposite my bunk was a narrow writing desk with bookcase above and somehow a chair fitted in below it. This was my home for about twenty months.

From time to time, groups of six CW (Commission worthy) ratings were sent to *Bermuda* for training, as we had been sent to Lookout. One of these groups consisted of New Zealanders, and on one occasion, the Master of Arms, a fearsome looking gentleman, approached me and asked me to speak to one of the New Zealanders who was breaking the censorship rules in his letters home; talking about his duties and where he was, both of which were forbidden. I was impressed that the Master of Arms did not want an offence to appear on the rating's record. I duly saw the rating concerned and there was no further difficulty. He was later to become well-known as the playwright Bruce Mason. These were the only times we had New Zealanders in our ship's company apart from me.

I remember in particular, the noise of the guns firing, as my cabin was just above and astern of the two forward gun turrets, each with three six-inch guns. When they were fired everything in my cabin leapt up. The noise was indescribable; books fell out of the little book-case and glasses broke (That was the worst noise). The memory of it ranges alongside the noise of being dive-bombed on my first night at the training ship HMS *Ganges*. A diving Junkers Ju-87 'Stuka' makes a very nasty screaming noise. I heard it only once and that was enough for a lifetime.

Communication between ships at sea was mostly done with flag hoists and signal lamps. Radio silence was normally kept because the Germans did have direction finding, which meant they would be able to locate ships. Various flags had different meanings. There were two or possibly three flags that meant 'Request permission to proceed in execution of previous orders,' and the reply would come back either 'affirmative' or 'negative' on a single flag.

One time when on exercises 'in line abreast' on the way back from Russia, I could not keep the ship exactly a 'cable' (200 yards) from the next ship without creeping ahead or slipping back. The admiral signalled, 'Bermuda keep station. Hoist the name of the officer of the watch,' and up went the flags 'N-E-W-M-A-N' for all the fleet to see. I had to shout for the mess that night.

Actually, we had to alter speed in changes of two revolutions of the propeller shafts and our speeds did not quite synchronise with the other ships. On this occasion the PCO (Principal Control Officer, who was in charge in the event of sudden action until the captain arrived) was on the bridge with me, had been showing me how to reduce our speed slightly by making tiny alterations of course, and then correcting them, which worked perfectly so long as you didn't look at our wake, which wagged like a dog's tail. You can't always win.

Arctic Convoys

Until the fall of Stalingrad, supplying munitions to the Soviet Union by the northern route was essential for their success in fighting the Germans. HMS *Bermuda* acted as 'distant cover,' some sixty miles or more from the convoys, wherever large enemy ships were thought to be lurking.

Our first convoy was Convoy JW-51B, which had sailed from Loch Ewe on 22 December 1942. The convoy became scattered in a storm off the Faroe Islands and was ordered by the Admiralty to Akureyri, in Northern Iceland, to reassemble together with its covering fleet. I believe it was on this trip to Iceland that we located a high mountain on the north-east corner of that country with an echo from our air warning set and were able to pinpoint our position—six miles from the Admiral's. Signals passed: from HMS *Bermuda*: 'Suggest your noon position six miles 0-9-0 from true position.' From the Admiral: 'My noon position correct.' But when we sighted land, *Bermuda*'s position, fixed by radar, proved to have been the correct one. I wonder if the Admiral shouted for our captain.

The convoys had three enemies; U-boats, aircraft bombers and heavy surface ships, including battle cruisers and cruisers. In the case of Convoy JW-51B, we were part of a battle-fleet under Vice-Admiral Tovey in HMS *King George V* (41), with HMS *Howe* (32), both 45,000-ton battleships, two cruisers, HMS *Kent* (54) and HMS *Berwick* (65), and six destroyers patrolling the area near Jan Mayen Island to meet and deal with any heavy German units attacking the convoy from that direction. I well recall keeping station on *King George V*, which seemed enormous, towering above our 7,000-ton *Bermuda*.

For this convoy, the 'distant cover' consisted of a force under Rear Admiral Burnett, called 'Force R', consisting of the cruisers HMS *Sheffield* (C24) and HMS *Jamaica* (44) and two destroyers. Although our force under Admiral Tovey saw no action, 'Force R' was heavily engaged against the German heavy cruisers *Lützow* and *Admiral Hipper*. Burnett had raced off to the north-east to gain the advantage of light at dawn, a ruse which succeeded, *Hipper* being completely surprised and hit before she had any idea of Force R's presence. *Hipper* was so badly damaged in the battle around the convoy—which became known as the 'Battle of the Barents Sea'—that it was withdrawn from service and took no useful part in the rest of the war.

There was virtually no air-liaising work for me to do on these northern patrols, so I served my share of bridge watches as officer of the watch, when it was my duty to 'con' the ship along its zig-zagging course with a more senior officer (the CPO) alongside to take charge of any aggressive or defensive action until relieved by the Captain.

Duty on the open bridge in the Arctic was a very cold affair. Even the fleece-lined boots and coats (supplied by the naval outfitters) and gloves only slightly relieved the cold. Fortunately we were moving so fast that snow and even rain blew over our heads, landing rather on those at the back of the bridge. In fog, which was frequent, we usually followed another ship, the senior officer always in the lead. Although only 200 yards away, we frequently could not see the ship ahead, and spent our watches straining our eyes looking for its wake. Sometimes it was discernible by only a few bubbles, but somehow we never lost contact.

Our second convoy was JW-52, which left Loch Ewe on 17 January, 1943, and sailed west of the Faroe Islands along with the cruisers HMS *Kent* and HMS *Glasgow,* providing distant cover under Rear-Admiral Hamilton. Although attacked by Heinkel torpedo bombers and shadowed by U-boats, the convoy suffered no losses, and half the attacking aircraft were brought down by gunfire. Our group, over the horizon, were blissfully unaware of the action in which the convoy itself was involved. It was while covering this convoy that Oberleutnant Benker in U-625 attacked both us and HMS *Kent* with torpedoes—unsuccessfully, fortunately for us. We were not to know of this for fifty years, when the books were opened. The convoy sailed safely into Kola Inlet, North Russia on 27 January 1943.

We then provided distant cover for the return convoy, RA-52, which had only one ship, the American freighter SS *Greylock*, torpedoed and sunk 600 miles north east of Iceland on 3 February by U-255 under the experienced Kapitänleutnant Reinhart Reche.

On one of our first Russian convoy patrols (in which we were usually in company with one or two other cruisers and/or battleships), we arrived at Kola Inlet in North Russia in fog and, using the gunnery radar sets and the proximity of the air and surface plots, found our way into our anchorage, while the other ships waited outside until the fog cleared. While not fighter direction, this was, as far as we know, the first instance in which the fighter direction techniques and the link with the surface plot were used in navigation.

When we were able to see the land about us in Kola Inlet it proved to be low-lying rolling country covered in snow, out of which stuck a few crooked sticks which were probably stunted trees.

We spent the summer of 1943 south of Britain, but November we were back on northern patrol, covering convoy JW-54A, which had sailed from the Minches, north-west Scotland, on 15 November. Our group, under Rear Admiral Palliser on HMS *Kent* and with HMS *Jamaica* (44) also in company, provided the distant cover.

Much of the trip was in mist and cloud, so we went through undetected and were in the Kola Inlet by 24 November. I believe it was on this trip that we shipped a load of Russian gold received in part payment for munitions. The security for this operation was prodigious, which did not stop one rating from being 'up before the captain' for trying to steal a block of gold as it was being passed from hand to hand along the ship, from the lighter alongside to the safe custody in a *Bermuda* hold. On the return trip we provided distant cover for the returning convoy RA-54B. Gales, thick weather and arctic winter once more provided the overcast scud, low visibility and darkness that effectively hid us and the convoy from the airborne eyes of the enemy, and it passed through unscathed, as did we.

Part way to Britain, we turned and escorted convoy JW-54B through the Barents Sea to Russia through the same bad weather. This convoy had sailed nearer the Norwegian coast than usual, with the objective of enticing out the German battle cruiser *Scharnhorst* so that our heavy units could deal with it and remove its menace once and for all. The *Tirpitz* had already been incapacitated by our midget submarines, and the *Lützow*, together with the *Admiral Hipper* had been withdrawn from the area after being damaged in the Battle of the Barents Sea—only the *Scharnhorst* remained a threat.

As we on HMS *Bermuda* lay at anchor in Scapa Flow making ready for the next convoy, Fraser's ruse of using a convoy (ours) as decoy paid off and in the ensuing 'Battle of the North Cape', *Scharnhorst*, out to attack the convoy, was sunk. Sir Robert Burnett, known in the fleet as 'Bullshit Bob', was the Admiral commanding the 10th Cruiser Squadron, of which we were part. With three cruisers; his flagship HMS *Belfast, Norfolk* and *Jamaica*, he played a major part in the battle.

On his return to Scapa he came aboard the *Bermuda* and gave an account of the battle to our ship's company. When he ended he said, 'I'm only sorry you chaps weren't with us.' I heard a rating near me mutter, 'Thank God we weren't'—a remark whose significance I never forgot. Many of the ratings were not volunteers but had been conscripted into the navy and felt it was a necessary evil from which they could not escape. Many of them saw no glory in risking life and limb in a war from which they could see no personal benefit. Rhetoric about the Nazi menace did not affect some of them much.

The next convoy, JW-56A, which sailed on 12 January 1944, was my last. The weather deteriorated so much that the ships' cargoes were damaged and the convoy had to reassemble in Akureyri, a fjord in Northern Iceland. We discovered an American air force base ashore and arranged to direct some of their anti-submarine aircraft from the *Bermuda* and HMS *Cumberland* (F57), a County-class cruiser in our group. The *Cumberland*'s FDO was Lieutenant Michael Sandeman, RNVR, (of the Sandeman Wine family) and although we 'met' over the R/T (Radio Telephone) during this operation, we did not meet in person until he settled in Christchurch after the war and we became firm friends.

One afternoon, when it was Sandeman's turn to direct the aircraft, Lieutenant Jim Woolley, RN, and I went ashore to climb a mountainside. We were halfway up when we saw a blizzard approaching across the fjord. We raced down to our caps and jackets, which we had left on a rock, by which time we had small icicles hanging down from our hair. Some US officers warmed us with rum and coke in their officers' mess, to the extent that I obliged with the Canterbury College Haka performed on the bar. Jim Woolley and I kept up our friendship and used to meet every time I went to the UK. Sadly, he died in 2003.

There was a wolf-pack of ten U-boats lying in wait for this convoy, but the close cover ships were so efficient in dealing with U-boats, even when in packs, that only three ships out of twenty and one small escort vessel were lost. The U-boats were firing acoustic homing T5 torpedoes, known by the British as 'Gnats', but these all exploded in the wakes of the fast moving escort ships and did little damage. The resulting explosions were heard in the U-boats who reported to German radio a great victory. One of the U-boats was sunk by depth charges. It had been in service only six weeks.

On one northern convoy trip, a British Conservative member of parliament joined us to experience what happened on such trips. We became friends and at the end of the voyage he offered, if I was interested, to nominate me after the war for the Conservative College, to train to become a Conservative MP. That would have been different again!

One incident while working out of Scapa Flow taught me something of naval discipline. Two ratings from one of our battleships had been court-martialled for a misdemeanour involving sheep, the case taking place the very day I was detailed to be officer in charge of a drifter returning men from Flotta, a small island in Orkney, where there was a 'wet canteen', to their ships; the men in various stages of inebriation. When the drifter approached the battleship the men started making sheep noises 'Baa, baa', which, try as I might, even with the help of petty officers on board, I was unable to stop. On arrival at the battleship I saw the Admiral and the Captain pacing the quarterdeck, high above where the men disembarked from the drifter.

Back on my ship I was working in my cabin when there was a knock on the door. 'Lieutenant Newman, sir, the commander would like to see you, sir.' The Commander showed me a signal: 'To all ships in the Fleet Anchorage, repeated *Bermuda*: 'Personnel in ships' boats approaching HM ships in the Fleet Anchorage will not make unseemly noises'.' 'What is the meaning of this, Newman?' I told him, and was told in no uncertain terms that I should have stopped the noise. Having accepted the reprimand with the proper 'Ay-ay, sir', I went on to say I was a relatively inexperienced officer and asked how I should have prevented it. 'Candidly, Newman, I haven't the foggiest idea.' 'Ay-ay, sir.' End of interview; discipline and honour satisfied all round.

Spitzbergen

In May 1943, in company with HMS *Cumberland* and some destroyers, we took aboard a contingent of Norwegian soldiers and reinforced the garrison at

Spitzbergen, 600 miles from the North Pole. They were as fine looking a lot of young men as I had ever seen. They slept in hammocks in our passage-ways, and I never knew how they were otherwise looked after. The run up was fast and direct and when we entered a fjord near Barentsburg, Svalbard, there were lines of smoke along the hillside where the Germans had landed, annihilated the garrison and set the coal mines on fire.

We were there for about four hours, disembarking men and stores, while our destroyers dashed back and forth across the entrance on U-boat patrols. Fortunately none appeared. One of our radar officers, Sub-Lieutenant Appleby, was in private life a geologist and was allowed ashore with his chip hammer and bag for rock samples—and delayed the little fleet's departure by being late back. It was a most unpopular action and we never heard what the captain, Terrence H. Back, had said to him, but it would have been devastating. We later heard that the Germans had returned and attacked the garrison again, and that only one Norwegian had survived.

On the return trip from Spitzbergen, when the ship was about eighty miles away from a very high Iceland mountain, the ship's air warning radar started to pick up echoes which I promptly reported to the bridge. The captain immediately brought the ship to 'Repel Aircraft Stations'. I kept monitoring the echoes and realised they were not moving at all, which was very unusual, so I reported this information to the captain. Eventually the radar officer suggested that it was probably a column of polarised air, of which he had read that it could show on radar. I told the captain over the intercom and, in a rage, he ordered me to the bridge where he asked me exactly what I thought was responsible for the echoes. I replied that the radar officer believed it to be a column of polarised air. At this the captain's anger subsided and he said, 'I thought you said polar bears.' He then proceeded to inform the crew, 'Relax Repel Aircraft Stations. Revert to second degree of readiness. The FDO tells me it's only a flying polar bear.'

Aurora Borealis

One of the enduring memories of these voyages is that of the 'Northern Lights', the Aurora Borealis, which we saw on numerous occasions in the high latitudes if the weather was clear. Imagine yourself on the bridge peering ahead into a dark void and gradually the high sky lightens a fraction, followed by the appearance of dim yellow-green shapes like big cigars which start moving and changing colour to include mauves and reds forming into waving shapes like giant curtains across the sky, and you are seeing the Aurora. It is hard to realise that it is about 600 miles above the earth, but it has a fascinating beauty as, after a period it dims gradually back into the darkness of the night sky.

Maurice Newman, OBE, DSC, passed away in Christchurch, New Zealand, on Monday, 6 April, 2009.

Frank Roe
SS *Elona*

I was twenty-one years old when the Second World War broke out and served throughout as an officer in the Merchant Navy and the Royal Fleet Auxiliary.

My earliest experience of danger was in December 1939. At the time I was on board MV *Cardium*, a Shell International tanker of 8,236 tons, and we were part of the unescorted convoy OG-16, formed from Convoys OA-80 and OB-80 and consisting of thirteen ships bound for Basra out of Southampton. The ship next to us, the British Steam Merchant *SS Armanistan,* was carrying 8,300 tons of general cargo including sugar and iron rails when she was torpedoed by U-25 (Korvettenkapitän Viktor Schütze, Knights Cross) on 3 February 1940, west of the River Tagus, Portugal. The *Armanistan* started to settle by the stern and disappeared bow up in no time. Fortunately all the crew were saved by the Spanish Merchantman *Monte Abril* and were landed at Tenerife. The Commodore broke radio silence to call Gibraltar and we awoke next morning to see a couple of Royal Navy destroyers escorting us. Luckily the U-boat left us alone after his success and no further ships were lost.

After this, I spent the whole of 1940 sailing around the Indian Ocean where German AMCs (Armed Merchant Cruisers) operated. On one arrival at Aden the authorities were surprised to see us; apparently an AMC had been following us. All our ships carried thousands of tons of petroleum products, a frightful source of danger, because when bombed or torpedoed, not only was the ship a blazing inferno but the sea around was on fire too. There was no chance of escape.

The Russian convoys were a different kettle of fish. I took part in Convoy PQ-6, the seventh of the arctic convoys, which departed Hvalfjord, Iceland, on 8 December 1941 consisting of eight ships; one Russian, five British and two Panamanian, and the escort included the cruiser HMS *Edinburgh* (16) and the E-class destroyers HMS *Echo* (H23) and HMS *Escapade* (H17), two minesweepers and two armed trawlers. At that time I was on board the SS *Elona*, a tanker of 9,192 tons. We arrived in Molotovsk, Russia, just before Christmas, having been stuck in the ice and were rescued by a Russian icebreaker.

As we were leaving in March, with a Russian minesweeper ahead of us in the narrow channel, there was a mighty explosion as he set off a mine. He probably saved us from being mined ourselves.

From there we went to Murmansk to form a convoy. A small Russian vessel, with a blue light, was supposed to guide us. It did, but we lost him in a blizzard. Unfortunately, we hit an obstruction, and water poured into the wing tanks. We could cope with that with our cargo pumps, as the centre tanks were always filled with ballast. The Russians came and filled all the gaps with a bitumastic cement (a solvent-based bitumen rubber mastic joint sealant) which would last until we reached England. I heard later that around eighty bottom plates had been removed—a lot of damage.

While in Murmansk, we were in the saloon one evening when there was a loud explosion. We rushed out on deck but had suffered no apparent damage, but when morning came, we found a piece of land-mine around a metre across on the deck. It was sent ashore to be identified. A German plane had been over that day reconnoitring ships in the anchorage. The next day they came over again, this time three bombers each with a stick of four bombs. The first plane straddled us, two bombs each side. The second plane straddled us amidships and the third did the same up near the bow. That was the closest attack I had during the war.

We departed Murmansk on 1 March 1942 as part of QP-8, a convoy of fifteen ships, and reached Reykjavik on 11 March. One ship, the Russian cargo ship *Ijora* carrying timber, had been straggling behind the convoy when she was sunk by the German destroyer *Friedrich Ihn* on 7 March.

Editor's note: U-25 was later lost around 1 August 1940 in the North Sea after hitting a British mine. There were no survivors. By this time the Captain had left the ship and survived the war, dying in 1950. During his career he sank thirty five ships totalling 180,073 gross registered tons.

Frank Roe passed away on 9 September 2012.

SS *Elona*
(*Courtesy of
Derek Whitwam*)
John Seares

John Charles Seares
HMS *Belfast*

I was born in Forest Gate on 30 August, 1923, the son of John and Elizabeth Louisa Seares (née Tomlinson), who were originally from Bethnal Green. I had a sister, and two older brothers who served in the RAF; Arthur, who was a Leading Aircraftman, and Frank, who was a Warrant Officer Radio Operator/Air Gunner. Following in their footsteps, my younger brother, Raymond did his National Service in the RAF as Ground Staff.

I was a cycle messenger for the ARP Warden in Stratford from October 1939 to January 1941. I was sixteen years old at the time, and I volunteered for the Royal Navy in 1942 as an Ordinary Seaman, and did three months training from 21 July to 13 October at the shore establishment (stone frigate) HMS *Collingwood* at Fareham, Hampshire.

On 3 November 1942, I was drafted to my first ship; the light cruiser HMS *Belfast* (C35), which was at Devonport Dockyard, Plymouth, and was commanded by Captain Frederick Parham and Rear Admiral Robert Burnett. My action stations were as Gun Loader on P1 turret; Secondary Armament four-inch guns.

I served two commissions on HMS *Belfast* between 1942 and 1946. She was the flagship of the 10th Cruiser Squadron Home Fleet, and was still the largest and most powerful cruiser in the Royal Navy, and most importantly she was equipped with the most advanced radar systems. We left Plymouth in December 1942 en route to Scapa Flow.

This was the beginning of fourteen months for me on the arctic convoys. We were all very young and were going into the unknown. We encountered mountainous seas as high as a tower block of flats; lifting the ship out of the water, and us praying that 'the old girl' would come through it—and she did. Sub-zero temperatures; you could not let your nose run or it would freeze on your face, and you could not touch anything without gloves or you would just stick to it, and god forbid anybody went overboard because you would die in seconds from the cold.

John Seares on board HMS *Belfast* after the Russian Medal presentation in May 2010.
(*Courtesy of Mavis Seares*)

John Seares on HMS *Belfast* in February 1943. (*Courtesy of Mavis Seares*)

HMS *Belfast* on patrol in very rough seas in 1943. (*Courtesy of Mavis Seares*)

The ice and snow settling on the super structure increased the weight of the ship by at least 300 tons, and it was down to the foc'le men who had the job of chipping away the ice.

On 15 February 1943, we left Loch Ewe, sailing into a gale as escort to twenty-eight Merchant ships in what is often referred to as the 'forgotten convoy': JW-53 (our first arctic convoy). The escort was made up of three cruisers, one anti-aircraft cruiser, one escort carrier, sixteen destroyers, two minesweepers, three corvettes and two trawlers.

As we sailed north the gale developed into a hurricane and ships began to sustain damage, and six of the merchant ships; the *Empire Baffin, Explorer, James Bowie, John Laurance, Joseph E Johnston* and the *Komiles,* were forced to return to Hvalfjord, Iceland. At one stage the convoy was so scattered because of the weather conditions, it took the Navy to round us all up and get us into convoy order again.

The cruiser HMS *Sheffield* (C24) and the escort carrier HMS *Dasher* (D32) had to return with severe weather damage, the former with one third of the roof of 'A' turret gone, the latter with damaged flight deck.

The loss of the escort carrier meant that we had no air cover and, as expected, a few days later, a German spotter plane arrived which flew round the convoy all the daylight hours to keep an eye on us. The next day, ten Junkers Ju-88 bombers, which had taken off from Banak, Norway, dived through the inferno of our combined anti-aircraft fire, and claimed a near miss, and a follow-up attack twenty four hours later again yielded no results.

We kept moving relentlessly towards North Russia, and at this point were relatively safe from attack by U-boats; the weather conditions and the pancake ice floes went a long way to protecting the convoy. The blizzards, when they came, were always welcome as they hid us from the enemy.

We arrived at the Kola Inlet in two groups on 27 February. The inlet is a long fjord with hills on either side, and the town of Murmansk is situated near the top end. We were all exhausted by the time we reached the anchorage, because over the last few days we had either been on duty or at action stations for most of the time.

We left the Kola Inlet on 2 March as cover for Convoy RA-53. During this convoy of thirty ships, three were lost to U-boats. The pressure of such events in the North Atlantic meant that it would be another nine months (until November 1943) before the route would be used again.

On 26 December 1943, we encountered the *Scharnhorst*; she was picked up on our radar. We fired star shells to illuminate the target as we were too far away, so enabling the main armament to engage her.

HMS *Belfast* remained protecting the arctic convoys until 1944 when she spent five weeks supporting the Normandy landings and reportedly fired one of the first shots on D-Day itself.

HMS *Belfast* in Jun 1943. (*Courtesy of Mavis Seares*)

John Seares with the P1 Gun crew on board HMS *Belfast*, February 1943. (*Courtesy of Mavis Seares*)

HMS *Belfast* on eight-day patrol off the Norwegian coast in January 1943. (*Courtesy of Mavis Seares*)

Clearing the deck of HMS
Belfast of ice in February 1943.
(*Courtesy of Mavis Seares*)

She was always a happy ship, and I am lucky that I still go aboard her at her moorings at Tower Bridge, which is only about an hour from where I live. Sadly, most of my shipmates have already crossed the bar.

John Seares, 18 June 2013.

Doug Shelley
HMS *Milne*

I was born in West Road, Shoeburyness, Essex, in 1925, the son of Walter and Elizabeth Shelley. I had a sister, Nora, and a brother, Edgar, who died of leukaemia, and a half-brother, who was with the Airborne when they went to Arnhem, and the Germans blew them out of the trees. The whole brigade died. I have a step-brother, Arthur, who wanted to go as well, but because he was an officer's batman, they wouldn't let him. He was choked about it. He had a big photo of all the lads, and they were all killed, and he was the sole survivor, and had to live with that.

I knew that when I was eighteen years old, that I would be called up, and that could include going down the mines with the Bevin Boys, so when I was seventeen, I went along to the drill hall in Romford, Essex, with the intention of volunteering for the Marines. 'You'll be lucky', the chap said, 'they are full up'. I asked him what else they had, and he gave me the choice of the Royal Air Force or the Royal Navy. I chose the Navy, and went to HMS *Glendower* in Caernarfonshire, Wales, for my basic training.

I remember my first morning there. I was in a chalet, and at six o'clock in the morning, the Chief was banging on the door, shouting 'Wakey-wakey', or words to that effect. The sunshine was burning my eyes out and I opened the door and there was about four foot of bleeding snow on the ground. I thought, 'Bloody hell, what have I done here!' After all the square bashing and early morning six-mile runs, I was sent to Chatham for a Gunnery course.

I was drafted at 0230 hrs one morning to the M-class destroyer HMS *Milne* (G14) at Scapa Flow. She was one of the first class of British destroyers to have their four point seven-inch guns in fully enclosed mountings. The ships were tied two to a buoy; they were all waiting for the ships carrying the raw materials to escort to Russia.

We went down to Loch Ewe and picked up the convoy and off we went. We called in at Reykjavik, Iceland, to refuel, and while we were there, we were dive-bombed. Fortunately our 'Chicago Piano'—the pom-poms—blew the thing out of the sky.

Doug, his sister Nora, and half brother Arthur, who was killed at Arnhem. (*Courtesy of Doug Shelley*)

My 'action station' was in 'B' turret. I spent a lot of time in there; even slept in there. We had our duffle coats on, and all the cold weather gear on, and we had a harness we had to wear that came over and clipped together, and it had two red lights, one on each shoulder. This was because if we got walloped, and fell overboard into the Barents Sea, you could be seen by the flashing red lights. If you were fortunate you would be hooked out, but after five minutes in the water and you would be a block of ice. The shock of the freezing cold alone could kill you.

The speed of the convoys varied between seven knots and fourteen knots, depending on the ships you had. PQ-17 was the worst one of all. Out of thirty five ships only seventeen arrived in Russia. The convoy was ordered to scatter by Admiral Sir Dudley Pound, who panicked when he heard that the German battleship *Tirpitz* was in the area, and the escorting destroyers were ordered to join the cruiser force in a hunt for German surface ships, and the merchantmen to proceed independently. They had no defence against air attacks and the U-boats. The Admiral was held responsible for the fiasco and died shortly after he resigned from office after suffering two strokes.

The worst part of the convoys was when we approached the Kola Inlet because of the U-boats, because they knew you were covering for ships that carried raw materials for the Russians, and they were out to stop it getting to them. It was a bastard of a place; the seamen who went in there had a rough old time of it. They would go in and unload and then wait for the return journey, but while they were

Doug Shelley met Prince Andrew in 2012. (*Courtesy of Doug Shelley*)

there the Russians never even acknowledged them. It was all Stalin. He screamed his head off for the raw materials and treated us all with contempt. That was the last convoy for a few months, and what worried Winston Churchill more than anything, more than the campaigns in North Africa and Burma, was that if we lost the battle of the Atlantic, we were finished.

I raise my hat to the men of the trawlers. The skippers were RNVR, who came out of places like Fleetwood and Grimsby, and were fantastic blokes.

There were seven M-class destroyers; the *Milne*, *Marne*, *Matchless*, *Meteor*, *Musketeer*, *Mahratta*, and the *Martin*. Three of them got walloped; the *Marne*, *Mahratta*, and the *Martin*, because the U-boats were firing torpedoes that would home in on the moving parts—the screws of the ship, and when they hit, they'd blow the back of the stern right off.

One of the U-boats sank itself when they fired an acoustic torpedo, and it went in a circle and came back onto them. They were too shallow in the water when they fired it, and it homed in on the submarine's own screws. How bad was their luck.

I spent seven months on the convoys, and then came home on 5 June, the day before D-Day. After my leave, I went to Chatham where I didn't wait long before I got a draft ship to the Golden Hind, which was a dispersal camp in Australia. I wasn't there very long either, and was then drafted to the Battle-class destroyer HMS *Armada* at Sydney, and I was on her for about twelve months. The *Armada* was actually adopted by the town of Brentwood, Essex, in 1945.

HMS *Milne*. (*Author's Collection*)

I finished up in Hong Kong, by which time the war was over, and I had to wait for my relief to arrive. I returned to the UK (to Plymouth) on HMS *Anson*, which had just taken the surrender of the Japanese under the flag of Rear Admiral Cecil Harcourt. Once I was back at Chatham, I waited for my number to come up, and was demobbed in 1947. I hadn't a clue what I could do as a civilian, so I took a job as a driver for the ministry, but after two years it was boring me to tears, so I went and signed on with the Merchant Navy, and that more or less saw me through.

Doug Shelley, 19 June 2013.

Syd Simpson
SS *Charlbury*

My first trip to sea was in December 1939, when I was fourteen years old, aboard the 5,221-ton cargo ship SS *Peterton* and we were bound for Montevideo in Uruguay. Passing the scuttled German heavy cruiser *Admiral Graf Spee*, with her mast and funnels showing above the waterline, we youngsters took great pleasure in giving her the 'fingers' salute. We were probably one of the first British ships to see her after the great 'Battle of the River Plate.'

I did three trips to Canada and America before a spell on the British coast aboard the 1,780-ton SS *Collingdoc*, which, before she was purchased by Ministry of War Transport, had seen several years' service as a Great Lakes steamer under her original name SS *DB Hanna*.

Whilst en route from the River Thames to the Tyne on 13 July 1941, we struck a mine four cables (about 960 yards) off Southend Pier resulting in the loss of Chief Engineer William Martin Wilson and Second Engineer William Edward Stutchbury. The rest of the crew were landed on the pier.

The ship was later salvaged and towed to Rosyth, and then to Scapa Flow where she was scuttled as a block ship in March 1942. My next ship was the SS *Atlantic*. By this time (August 1941) I was sixteen years old and was a deck boy, and on my way to Archangel as part of convoy PQ-1, which consisted of eleven Merchant ships (which carried among its cargoes of raw material, twenty tanks and 193 crated Hawker Hurricane fighter planes), and was the second of the Russian convoys, the first being codenamed 'Dervish'.

The following year I was signed on as an Able Seaman aboard the 4,836-ton SS *Charlbury*. En route from Cardiff to Buenos Aires with a cargo of coal, we detached from the South Africa-bound convoy ON-93 and sailed independently without escort. On 28 May 1942, we were intercepted by the Italian Marcello-class submarine RM *Barbarigo* off the coast of Brazil. The Italians wasted no time in firstly raking the ship with machine guns, and then firing a torpedo which missed as the skipper turned hard to starboard.

Then they started shelling from their deck gun which lasted for some time. Two men were killed and several injured. Eventually, he torpedoed us just aft of the engine room. The explosion blew the propeller off, resulting in the prop shaft turning, with no resistance, at an alarming speed. Then the order came to abandon ship. The lifeboats were all ready to be lowered (a wartime measure) and the wounded placed aboard before lowering.

By this time I realised I had shrapnel wounds to my kneecap and my nose, but my main worry was the terrible pains in my lower abdomen which I'd had for some six weeks. Four boats were lowered and were pulled away from the doomed ship. Within ten minutes she had broken her back, and the two halves, bow and stern, lifted up and went to the bottom. Of the four lifeboats, one was so severely damaged as to be useless due to the machine gunning having damaged the buoyancy tanks. The crew were shared amongst the other three lifeboats.

Keeping together was difficult and the three boats gradually drifted apart. It became a constant battle bailing-out due to the machine gun damage and the bad weather. We had a ration of water, hard tack biscuits and pemmican (which tasted like Marmite), and rain water was collected on a tarpaulin and scooped up eagerly for drinking.

Days went by and we began to have hallucinations of seeing land that wasn't there, and it was getting close to the tenth day. We were unaware that the Chief Mate's boat had been rescued and had informed them about the other boats—it

SS *Charlbury*. (*Courtesy of David Whitwam*)

was lucky not to have been fired on. The rescuing ship, the American light cruiser USS *Omaha* (CL4), spotted what they thought was a German sub on the horizon and were all ready to blaze away at it with everything when a lookout shouted, "IT'S A LIFEBOAT!"

After a day or so they located us and we were landed at Recife-Pernambuco, Brazil. We had been in the lifeboat for ten days.

My abdominal pains were diagnosed as appendicitis. After the operation and recuperation, I found all the crew had gone to America by air. I followed them after a week or so, eventually joining a ship, the *Ocean Messenger,* in Portland, Maine, which arrived in Cardiff in November 1942. I then joined the Deep Sea Rescue Tugs, where we wore Royal Navy uniform and were under naval discipline, but drawing Merchant Navy pay. We were in Yugoslavia when the war ended.

Syd Simpson passed away on 27 March 2011.

Alf Steadman
HMS *Wren*

I was born in 1924 in Benfleet, Essex, one of three sons and four daughters of George and Alice Steadman. Although our family home was in Plaistow, we were in temporary residence in a cottage in End Way (now called Essex Way) where my father was working as a bricklayer.

I joined the Royal Navy at the age of seventeen in January 1943, and after training at HMS *Collingwood*, in Fareham, Hampshire, I was drafted to the British Sloop HMS *Wren* (U28), on which I served the whole of my naval career.

I picked her up in Londonderry and we sailed to join up with other Bird-class Sloops; the *Starling*, *Woodpecker*, *Woodcock*, and *Wild Goose*. We were to be known as the Second Escort Group, under the command of Captain Frederic 'Johnnie' Walker (who became known as Britain's No. 1 U-boat killer). The Second Escort Group was deployed as a Support Group and deployed for support of convoys under threat of attacks and to supplement escort of other Atlantic convoys.

After a few months, I was given the job of Navigator's Yeoman as the captain (Lieutenant Commander R. M. Aubrey) told me, 'Your credentials from Civvy Street shows you've had the education to do it', which meant I worked with the Navigator (Lieutenant Robson, RNR) from 0800 hrs to 1700 hrs in and around the Charthouse, keeping charts up to date with sunken ships, the position of convoys, and U-boats.

At 'action stations', my job was to work on the plot in the Wheelhouse. The plot was a lit-up glass-topped cabinet with a sheet of plain chart paper on top of it, and I had to record the position of our group of ships and U-boats as given to me by the ASDIC operator so I keep the bridge informed of changes in their direction. The job of Navigator's Yeoman had its advantages; I was answerable only to the Navigator and the Captain.

On 16 March, HMS *Wren* was deployed with HMS *Woodpecker* (U68) for escort of joint military convoy KMF-11 to Gibraltar and WS-28 to Freetown and joined HM Destroyers *Badsworth*, *Douglas*, *Eggesford*, *Goathland*, *Whaddon*

HMS *Wren* in the stormy seas of the Arctic. (*Courtesy of Alf Steadman*)

and the Polish destroyer *Orp Krakowiak* on the Clyde. Convoy KMF-11 was detached from the joint convoy on 21 March to go to Gibraltar after which, on 24 March, we resumed Atlantic support and convoy defence duties with the Group, and were based at Liverpool.

We then went to sea working with the Corvettes that were doing escort work with the convoys.

On 1 May, 1943, we had just picked up a convoy in the Liverpool Bay area when we were directed to pick up survivors of the British Motor Merchant *Port Victor,* which had been torpedoed (by U-107) a few hundred miles off the coast of south west Ireland.

We picked up the master, seventy-four crew members, ten gunners and sixty passengers (including twenty-three women and children) from the lifeboats from the *Port Victor* and took them to Liverpool where we were then further directed to join convoys ONS-8 and HX-240 off of Iceland which were bound for Newfoundland. This meant that we would not be joining the Second Escort Group until we returned.

In June we were sent to the Bay of Biscay (which was known as the 'Valley of Death' among U-boat men from 1943 onwards). The Germans had control of the French coast and had turned the port of St Lorient into their main U-boat base, and our job was to try and stop U-boats getting out into the Atlantic or getting in to the port. We were often under attack from German aircraft while we were there, and it was there that HMS *Woodcock* left us and HMS *Kite* (U87) took its place.

In October 1943, we sailed to Avonmouth docks at Bristol for a refit, after which we rejoined the Group and were ordered back into the Atlantic to break up

HMS *Collingwood*, 2 November 1943. (*Courtesy of Alf Steadman*)

the Wolf packs which were forming; these were a constant danger to the convoys. In November, we got a new captain, Lieutenant Commander S. R. Woods.

On 20 February 1944, HMS *Woodpecker* got hit by an acoustic torpedo from U-256 (These were a new development; the torpedo was attracted by the noise of the propellers and would home in on them). We were some 1,200 miles from home but the *Woodpecker* did not sink, so we started taking her in tow. After a couple of days an ocean-going tug arrived from a convoy that was on its way to the Mediterranean. The commander of the escorts was our old skipper, Captain Aubrey, who since leaving us had been made up to a full Commander, and on hearing of the plight of the *Woodpecker*, immediately dispatched the tug to us. It took the stricken vessel in tow to Plymouth. She had only a skeleton crew on board as most of them had been distributed across the Group.

Sadly, on 27 February, the *Woodpecker* foundered and sank in an Atlantic storm. The skeleton crew was rescued before the ship went under.

One special job we were given was to escort a couple of convoys going to the Mediterranean through the Bay of Biscay because the Germans were now using what were called the 'Chase-me-Charlies', the forerunner of the flying bomb. These were mounted on small gliders that were carried under an aircraft and when released, could be controlled by radio towards the target. The aircraft were thus able to remain out of the range of our guns. We had a lot of scientists on board who were hoping we would be attacked by it. The only defence they had discovered (according to a report by Lieutenant Green) by pure luck, was that the frequency from an electric razor messed up their radio control. So we all brought up our electric razors—the idea was to divert them away from any ship in the convoy so that they would drop into the sea. As it turned out, we did recover one of these new bombs which had been diverted by messing with its frequency, and we pulled it out of the sea to take back to England.

After a month at sea in the Atlantic, we arrived back in Liverpool, only to be directed to Scapa Flow for duty with the Home Fleet. Along with HMS *Magpie* and HMS *Whimbrel,* we joined convoy JW-58, which left Liverpool on 27 March, destined for the Kola Inlet; our main task being to give special protection to the American ship USS *Milwaukee*, which the Americans were giving to the Russian Northern Fleet. This was always such a dangerous journey because the Germans could follow convoys all the time as they had aircraft and U-boat bases on Bear Island, to the north of the convoys as well as bases on the coast of Norway, south of the convoys.

The weather made a lot of difference to our routine; in rough weather we would get a respite from the U-boats and aircraft but it meant we had to put up with being thrown around with the heavy seas. In calmer weather we were busy seeking out any contacts of U-boats. There were many but their attacks were not successful and one U-boat was sunk by the Group during the voyage of the convoy without any loss of ships. We landed safely at the Kola Inlet on 4 April.

I do not remember where we anchored but we were let ashore. I found it a very eerie because it didn't matter where you went there was somebody with a rifle watching you. The one surprise I had was standing on a jetty in deep snow waiting for a boat to take us back to our ship, and I got a tap on the shoulder. Turning around it was an old mate I used to play football with at a youth club before joining up; Ron Crocker, who happened to be on HMS *Diadem.*

Shipmates Maurice Jones, Wally Ruddock, Alf Steadman and Bobby Gotobed on 2 November 1943. (*Courtesy of Alf Steadman*)
William Thorne

The *Milwaukee* had a skeleton crew on board, who were spilt up among our ships for the journey home. We took fifteen on board the *Wren*. The first thing they asked was where the gum and coke machines were, and they couldn't believe we didn't have them, but they did love their tot of rum every day.

At 0200 hrs in the morning of 6 May, we were west south-west of Ireland when HMS *Starling*, HMS *Wren* and HMS *Wild Goose* successfully sank U-473 by depth charges.

During a one-month spell in the Bay of Biscay, we had a successful encounter with the U-boats. On 10 August, we were near La Rochelle when U-608 was sighted. A British Liberator of 53 Squadron dropped depth charges and we fired our own, the combined barrage sinking the submarine. The following day, the victory over the U-385 in the Bay of Biscay was shared by HMS *Starling* and Australian manned Short Sunderland of 461 (RAAF) Squadron. During the command of Second Support Group by 'Johnnie' Walker, twenty submarines were sunk by sloops of the group.

When we arrived at Gladstone Dock, we were greeted with the dockyard full of naval personnel cheering us in.

At the end of October 1944, the *Wren* was directed to Hull to have a refit for duties in the Far East, but it never came about. We were docked in Hull Fish Dock, which was at the eastern end of Hull.

It was while we were on leave in Hull that I met my future wife, Peggy, at a dance in Madeley Street Baths, and while writing to one another from then on, we decided on a date for the wedding; 27 July 1946.

After around two months we were sent to Leith, and in September 1945, we were paid off HMS *Wren*. After a week or so in Portsmouth barracks, I was drafted to HMS *Lochinvar*, the shore base at Port Edgar, Scotland, until I was demobbed on 23 April 1946.

Alf Steadman, 19 June 2013.

William John Thorne
Northern Wave

I was born on 1 September 1921 in Clerkenwell, London, the son of William and Annie Thorne. I had an older sister, Eileen, and two younger brothers; Leslie, who joined the Royal Navy in 1942 as a Radio/Telegraphist on HMS *Orion* in the Mediterranean, and John, who joined the Royal Navy after the war, on 1 October 1945, enrolled as a Ship's Writer.

Following my enlistment in the Navy, I travelled to Ipswich, Suffolk, on 24 March 1941 to commence my training as a signals rating at HMS *Ganges*, a shore establishment which was situated at the confluence of the rivers Orwell and Stour.

After being kitted out, we went into training, which comprised initially, rifle drill, marching and walking around the parade ground holding small flags aloft ostensibly simulating fleet manoeuvres. Good fun, but it made your bloody feet ache.

Having completed our preliminary training, drilling etc., the Signalmen and Telegraphists (in embryo of course) were transferred to a camp which had been set up in the grounds of a country estate, Highnam Court, just outside Gloucester on the road to Newport, South Wales. We arrived there in April 1941 and commenced our training by putting into practice the Morse Code which we were supposed to have learned by this time. Lectures were given in small marquees and also 'buzzer' exercises. All visual signalling was carried out in the open air and whilst the weather was fine, it was enjoyable; when it rained it was lousy, in fact, a pig's orphan.

Our Chief Yeoman of Signals was E. Peacock, a native of Portsmouth, who stood about five feet two inches and was dwarfed by all the class. He was a naval reservist, recalled for the duration of the emergency, as were most of the instructors and possibly because he was a family man and at least thirty years older than his trainees, he treated us most kindly and tolerantly. All in all, he was one of the nicest individuals that it was my good fortune to meet during my sojourn in the service.

The object of the whole exercise was to produce as many communication ratings within the allocated period, approximately six months and ratings were

William Thorne. (*Courtesy of Sally Pilkinton*)

expected to pay attention at all times. Then came a warm and sunny afternoon in May and Chief Yeoman Peacock was holding forth on Fleet dispositions.

Most of our training was carried out in the open air and trying to read Morse from a tiny light bulb in full sunlight could be sheer purgatory. The set-up was a twelve foot pole with a small cone-shaped object on top, with a battery operated lamp of low power inside the cone. As I have already said, it would be diabolical trying to peer at the light when the sun was in one's eyes. It was at Highnam that the matter of my colour blindness once again came to the fore. I had already failed the colour test at HMS *Ganges* but in response to my pleading that I must be a Signalman like my dear old Dad, they permitted me to continue training. However, the Signal Bo'sun (Boatswain) at Highnam was not so sure and insisted that I undergo further tests, this time with coloured lights and not the Japanese test, which was the accepted method.

I made a couple of errors, but further pleading brought me success and I was now on my way to becoming a Signalman. Under combat conditions I found that very few flag signals were used and that most of the signalling was carried out with a signal lamp. On a few occasions when in company with other vessels and a flag signal was hoisted, if in doubt of a flag's colour, I would simply say 'What is the colour of the second flag please Skip?' and history can vouch for the fact that no ship was ever lost because of my lack of colour vision!

Having qualified as an Ordinary Signalman and the training period completed, our class was split up and travelled to their designated Depots. My Depot was to be 'Chatty' Chatham, and on the morning of 15 August 1941, I reported my arrival to the Regulating Office, which was situated in the Drill Shed.

I was a month short of my twentieth birthday and was most unworldly wise, having never before been away from home or from dear old Mum. I was not

William Thorne. (*Courtesy of Sally Pilkinton*)

prepared for what happened next. With my kit-bag on my right shoulder, my hammock balanced on my left shoulder, with my small attaché case somehow rammed under an armpit, I began the journey to the Mess, which was to be my home whilst awaiting draft to my first ship.

As I made my way across a tarmac area in the vicinity of the Drill Shed, a nasty man dressed in the uniform of a Gunner's Mate, yelled into my shell-like ear, 'You don't walk across the f****** quarter deck, you f****** well run'. I thought to myself 'that's not very nice, you nasty man'. I often wonder what my reaction would have been today. In any case, I don't suppose my running across the Quarter Deck shortened the war and it must have looked comical when I broke into a shuffle, due to the bloody great load I was carrying.

My stay at Chatham consisted of daily signalling exercises, eating and sleeping. Due to the Depot's vulnerability from enemy bombing attacks, those ratings who were not involved in fire protection, were compelled to sleep in what was known as the 'Tunnel' and which appeared to have been excavated from the hillside. I knew very little about this place, other than to sling my hammock, have as sound a sleep as possible and get out early in the morning. The call to arise came something like this; 'Wakey wakey rise and shine, the morning's fine and the sun's burning your bleeding eyes out. Show a leg there!'

The atmosphere in the 'Tunnel', which appeared to have no ventilation, was, to put not too fine a point on it, ghastly. There were at least a couple of hundred matelots kipping down there in very close proximity. One could almost taste the aromas borne on what passed for air and would liken it to a gorilla's armpit, 'orrible!!

Sketch of *Northern Wave* by William Thorne. (*Courtesy of Sally Pilkinton*)

I departed Chatham on 16 September 1941 after getting my first draft, and, with a certain amount of trepidation I arrived in Londonderry the following day and reported aboard His Majesty's Trawler *Northern Wave*, a ship of 650 tons gross. She approximated in size to a corvette and a few feet shorter than a destroyer. Built in Bremerhaven, Germany, during the 1930s, she was one of a class of fishing trawlers which operated from Grimsby and I think I am correct in saying, Hull also, and the owners were the Unilever Group.

The fishing grounds were in the White Sea and Bear Island areas and Icelandic waters were also fished. As a class, the ships were readily identified by their curved stem which continued downwards to the bottom of the stern-post, thus giving a shallow draught forward and becoming increasingly deeper as it reached the stern. This shape assisted greatly when at a later stage we found ourselves in pack ice. The method of advancing was for the engine to thrust us forward as hard as possible, the ship would hit the ice, slide upon the ice until the screw could push her no further, stop, the weight of the ship would then break the ice and the performance would be repeated ad nauseam.

Northern Wave had been involved in the withdrawal from Norway and was, when I arrived, engaged in convoy and anti-submarine escort duties. As a class, the *Northern* boats acquitted themselves very well.

A word here concerning our armament: Forward on the forecastle was mounted a four-inch gun of First World War vintage. It could only fire at low angle and therefore was useless as an anti-aircraft weapon. To hit an aeroplane, it would have had to be flying at about one hundred feet and be thirty miles away! On the lower bridge, outside the wheel house, were twin Lewis guns, one pair on each side of the bridge and also of the First World War. Abaft the funnel was a water-cooled Vickers .5-inch machine gun which would almost always jam when it was most needed, and finally the Holman Projector, which I shall mention again later.

My first trip to sea was from Londonderry to Loch Ewe, which is a sea loch on the north-west coast of Scotland. Having entered the loch from the sea, one was struck by the sheer lonely magnificence of the place; rugged, bleak, inhospitable, and lonely, yet savagely majestic. There was, and no doubt, still is, a village called Aultbea, which housed a naval shore establishment, a necessity in view of the number of convoys which were assembled and departed from there.

When we arrived at Loch Ewe, an aircraft carrier was already at anchor. I think it was the HMS *Formidable*, but I am not certain.

We departed from Loch Ewe in early November 1941, our destination being Reykjavik, Iceland. I clearly recall asking Sub-Lieutenant Ranger, our navigating officer, if the sea could become rougher than that which we were at that moment experiencing. Not a daft question really, because I was new to the game. My previous sea service was a rowing boat on the Serpentine. The wavelets were not more than three feet high. Mr Ranger replied that it could be worse. He wasn't kidding. Within twenty-four hours my question was answered in full. Dear old Mother Nature sent us a force eight north-easterly gale which in due course climbed even higher up the Beaufort scale, possibly as high as force ten or force eleven and producing waves thirty-five and forty-five feet. We were in no little trouble because just before the gale hit us we had dropped a pattern of depth charges on a suspected U-boat presence and possibly because an error was made when setting the depth for the charges to explode, one charge detonated prematurely, which damaged the ship's plates and sea water began to enter the ship. The detonation was of sufficient force to put the pumps out of commission and as a consequence, the crew, including

William Thorne visited Eddie in Vaenga hospital on 13 January 1943 and gave an impromptu concert. (Courtesy of Sally Pilkinton)

yours truly, were compelled to man a chain of buckets and bail the old ship out. All this time the wind was rising and we knew that we were in for trouble.

As the wind rose to gale force, so the seas rose with it and soon nothing could be heard but the howling of the wind through the rigging and the sound of the sea as it crashed down upon the poor old ship which, let us not forget, was in a sinking condition. The noise was mind shattering.

In view of our predicament, one of the escorting destroyers, HMS *Shikari* (D85), was detailed to stand by us in the event of our being overwhelmed by the seas which were belting hell out of us. We were just able to keep the ship's head to the sea by virtue of a slight increase of power which the Chief Engineman managed to coax out of the engine. Had the worst happened, it would have been impossible for the *Shikari* to rescue anyone, such were the awful conditions which obtained. The wind was producing waves of terrifyingly mountainous proportions, but due to my having to cling to the rail, I was unable to use a tape measure to verify the height of the seas. By nightfall, the engineers had managed to re-commission the pumps and bailing out was discontinued, I am pleased to say.

That first night out from Loch Ewe was horrendous. I was working watch and watch, there being only two signalmen aboard and my relief was so poorly that I had to remain on watch from midnight to 0800 hrs. I found myself a corner at the rear end of the bridge and clung to a rail which fitted under my armpit, because it was impossible to stand upright due to the tremendous roll of the ship. Being young, bloody terrified and wishing that I had never left my dear old Mum, I watched in terror as the crests of the gigantic waves approached the ship as though to engulf it and then at the last moment the ship would lift and be borne rapidly upwards on a rising sea.

The bridge on which I stood was about twenty-eight feet from sea level and the waves were at least ten feet above the bridge. It was all the more frightening inasmuch that it was dark and I was alone; the officers being occupied with navigation and keeping the ship afloat.

During the hours of darkness it was impossible to see the accompanying destroyer, due to the height of the seas. We were able, however, to communicate with each other by using an Aldis lamp and flashing Morse signals on the very low cloud ceiling, clinging all the time with one arm hooked over the rail and holding the signalling lamp in the other hand. This was a little tricky at times but worth the effort to pass messages to someone who was in the same parlous state as us. During this awful night, the *Shikari* informed us that she had sustained damage to her superstructure. When at last daylight arrived, we were able to observe her when both she and we reached the crest of a wave simultaneously.

Whoever initiated the damage report was not joking. Her forward four-inch gun turret was crushed as though it was cardboard and part of her bridge was torn away. It is incidents like these that demonstrate the awe-inspiring power of the sea.

We limped into Reykjavik harbour six days after departing from Loch Ewe, the normal time for the trip being three days. Although I have seen pretty rough conditions since then, I think it was the most frightening because it was my first trip and the waves threatened to sink us. I saw larger seas at a later stage, but which did not have the ferocity of those on this particular voyage.

I will never forget the frightfulness of this trip. The noise of the wind and waves, water and yet more water everywhere; Water which managed to find its way into the ventilators and brought down into the mess-deck all the coal dust which had permeated the vents during coaling of the ship. This was delightful; coal dust and sea water swilling about the mess-deck whilst trying to have a meal and the smell of the bilges wafting up from below . . . oh joy! I considered myself fortunate that I always had a good appetite, despite being assailed by the aromas and nothing could prevent me from eating, not even when it was impossible to sit at the mess-deck table, due to severe rolling of the ship.

A very humorous situation would arise when the ship was rolling badly and one was endeavouring to eat soup. The mess floor was covered with Government Issue heavy brown linoleum and with the sea water and coal dust mixture sloshing about the deck was very slippery indeed. There was a clear space across the mess-deck, the full internal beam of the ship and when the old ship was rolling heavily, it was impossible to sit down to a meal. The only alternative was to stand and when trying to eat soup in a situation like this, it was commonplace to slide with one plate of soup from one side of the mess-deck to the other, usually in the company of another rating. Not a drop was spilled!

One evening whilst this particular storm was doing its utmost to put us on the sea bed, I came off watch at midnight, shattered and frightened bloody stiff and stumbled below into the mess-deck which was comparatively quiet after the thunderous commotion on deck, when I saw a mature man of about forty years of age, on his knees, praying for a safe relief to all our trials and tribulations. This terrified me even more, because this chap from Fort William, Inverness-shire, wore the usual identity tag which in his case, bore the legend 'agnostic'. I could, under the circumstances, appreciated the need for a bit of assistance from the Deity, but it proved to me that we were in a parlous state for an agnostic to make the call on behalf of us all.

The next couple of days were a case of 'the mixture as before', mountainous seas, thunder, lightning and everything that the elements could throw at us. Being on the bridge, cold, wet and bloody miserable for twelve hours out of twenty-four, was not exactly a sinecure and to obtain extra warmth I would, when there were no signals being passed, wrap myself in the largest flag in the flag locker; it happened to be a red one, flown during gunnery exercises.

With HMS *Shikari* still in company, we eventually arrived safely in Iceland and were ordered to sail to Hvalfjord which is a short distance from Reykjavik and where the Depot Ship HMS *Blenheim* would assist us in repairing the 'poor old tub'. It was in Hvalfjord, that during yet another gale, I saw an army Nissen hut lifted from its base and slowly, despite the many soldiers hanging onto it, gradually bumped its way down the ravine in which it was situated and finally went over the edge and into the fiord. The winds up in that region can be diabolical.

Repairs having been completed, we escorted two merchant ships back to the UK. The weather was an anti-climax after the outward voyage; ridiculously calm. The sea was like a sheet of glass and I freely confess to being sea-sick, as were many others. It proved to me that fear on the outward trip overcame the tendency to mal-de-mer.

It was on the return journey that I saw for the first time, dolphins accompanying the ship. When darkness fell they could be seen heading at full speed towards the ship, leaving a bright phosphorescent wake, which until one became accustomed to it, seemed for all the world like a torpedo track. Many times I stood back instinctively, waiting for the explosion which never came, thank Gawd.

Having arrived in the Minches (the stretch of water between the Inner and Outer Hebrides), one could usually relax and the captain decided to make a detour on our way south, through the Sound of Mull. I came off watch at midnight, made myself a cup of 'kye' (cocoa) and made my way forward to the mess-deck. I was so affected by the sheer tranquillity of the night that I burst into song. It was the Serenade from 'The Student Prince'; Sigmund Romberg and all that. In those days I rather fancied myself as a light baritone and so I bawled out 'Overhead the moon is beaming', etc. A voice, which I recognised as that of the old man himself, called down, 'Is that you Thorne?' Thinking I was about to be congratulated on my singing, I replied 'Yes, Sir, Captain'. 'Shut that bloody row!' Hurtful, to say the least. Win some, lose some, I suppose.

It was during the return to our base at Londonderry that the captain, Lieutenant George Pardoe-Matthews, decided that an exercise be carried out with the Holman projector, this being a weapon to deal with low-flying aircraft. This was Heath-Robinson at his most sublime. Imagine a steel tube, approximately six feet in length, fitted to a swivelling base abaft the funnel. A metal rail encircled the tube which was hinged near to deck level and which prevented the tube from being lowered too far, presumably to avoid blowing off the heads of anyone who happened to be passing at the moment of truth. A steam pipe from the engine room was connected to the bottom end of the tube and a pressure relief pedal to release the steam into the tube. There were handles brazed to the tube to enable it to be pointed in the required direction. I saw it all on this particular day.

I was on the bridge when the skipper ordered the exercise to begin. Our coxswain, Paddy Cullen from Donegal, grasped the Holman Projector with his left hand, pulled the safety pin from the grenade (the bomb), which appeared to be a home-made affair, something like a tin of fruit, dropped the bomb into the tube and depressed the foot pedal to discharge it at an imaginary aircraft. Nothing happened. Consternation all round.

It should be explained that once the bomb was in the tube, there was no way of retrieving it other than by blowing it out with steam pressure and on this day, there was no pressure for the simple reasons that no-one in command had thought to instruct the engine room staff to turn on the steam.

Panic calls to the engine room bore fruit and wisps of steam suddenly appeared from the tube. The situation was desperate for the fuse time was running out. Give Paddy his due, he stayed at his post well knowing that at any moment a one-pound tin of high explosive was about to make mincemeat of him. More commotion, 'Stormy' Bob, our Chief Engineman, arrived on deck to see for himself what was happening, when suddenly sufficient pressure built up within the projector and the bomb was discharged from the tube, but only with sufficient force for it to trickle out of the tube and fall onto the 'Fiddley top' (the deck on which the funnel stood) and thence to fall onto the main deck, right at the feet of a seaman, Freddie Ford, who wasted no time running forward as fast as he could. That was the situation when 'Stormy' appeared on the scene.

He picked up the missile, threw it overboard and before it could hit the sea, the bloody thing exploded. I stepped back behind my armour plating on the bridge, feeling that I was too young to die and waited for the noise to abate, wondering how many had been killed. Although it takes time in the telling, the whole incident occurred in possibly no more than half a minute. The cook came rushing out from the galley, covered with soot and swearing like a fish-wife. The bomb had blown off the top of the galley stove-pipe hence the soot-covered cook. It could have been much worse.

When things had settled down, it was decided, nay, Pardoe-Matthews ordained, that we should carry out yet another exercise, this time with one of the PAC (Parachute and Cable) rockets. This was also designed to put enemy aircraft in jeopardy, but in fact was far more hazardous to the person firing the damned thing. The rocket was fired by an explosive charge from a launching pillar which was fixed to the bridge decking. Attached to the bottom of the rocket was a Bowden type steel cable housed in a metal container which stood on the deck and was fitted in a figure of eight conformation, the idea being that when the rocket was fired ahead of the attacking aircraft, it would carry the wire with it and when it reached its maximum height, a parachute would open and the cable would be suspended in mid-air for a short time, thus endangering the enemy plane. The danger arose from the possibility of the wire fouling as it unwound and carrying parts of the bridge skywards. To be honest, I preferred not to fire the PACs; they were so unpredictable.

After all this nonsense and against all the odds, we arrived safely in the entrance of the River Foyle on our way to Londonderry. We anchored off Moville, a small town belonging to the Irish Republic and in no time at all, small boats were alongside selling their wares; butter, eggs, and Guinness. The next morning we were berthed alongside the town quay in Londonderry, and I must say I for one was delighted to be there safe and sound. That was the completion of my first real sea trip and I can't in all honesty say that I found it enjoyable.

When we had been in Londonderry for a few days, we were ordered to Belfast for a refit. This was good news because it almost certainly meant that home leave would be granted. We were not disappointed and we were home for Christmas. The ship's company returned from leave a couple of days after the festival and we left Belfast on Friday, 2 January 1942, reaching Londonderry the next day.

On Sunday, our dynamo gave up the ghost, and the immediate reaction was that leave would be imminent. No such luck. It snowed heavily on the Monday and it was extremely cold. I wrote some letters home, to my fiancée and my mother, and then went aboard HMS *Malcolm* for signalling exercises. There was little doing for the next couple of days except for normal duties and playing cards. On 9 January, we were coaling ship with a view to justifying our existence, and the next day I badly burned the palms of my hands due to a cracked Aldis lamp battery.

Two days later, we sailed from Londonderry to participate in an exercise between our ship and a Royal Air Force Wellington bomber which was testing a new piece of equipment, probably something concerning radar. We returned to port at 1930 hours, my having been on the bridge non-stop for eleven hours (and not even paid union rates). On 15 January, our sailing orders arrived which specified a noon departure. At 1100 hrs the orders were cancelled due to engine failure, though this didn't surprise any of the crew. Work commenced immediately and was satisfactorily completed within twenty four hours, and we departed on 16 January at 0830 hrs.

Iceland or bust was the order of the day and the weather as usual, did not disappoint; it was blowing a bloody gale and the sea was very rough. We were to join a convoy which was assembling in Loch Ewe and the destination was Reykjavik. On Saturday 17 January, with a dreadful gale blowing, we received an SOS from a ship in distress which had been driven ashore off Barra Head, the southernmost tip of Barra Island, the most southerly point of the Outer Hebrides. We stood by waiting to render assistance to the stricken vessel, but fortunately the lifeboat service beat us to it and performed the necessary life-saving relief.

Having been delayed by this incident, it meant that we had missed the convoy out of Loch Ewe and would have to chase like hell to overtake it. We sighted the Butt of Lewis in the Outer Hebrides, and then the convoy at 2315 hrs, and joined up with it shortly after that.

This was the evening, I think, that I first saw the Aurora Borealis (the Northern Lights) in all its splendour. The lights flashing across the northern sky were breath-taking. As one of the crew (a fisherman from Hull and had seen it all before) remarked to me, 'It would cost you a fortune to see this in peace time, Bill'. An accurate statement, which was to be repeated some months later when steaming through ice fields, by which time I was convinced that I would never pay good money to travel up in those latitudes, bloody hell, no!

By evening the gale renewed itself and we had a very trying night. Once again, due to the poor engine, we were unable to maintain pace with the convoy and were gradually left behind. Having altered course two or three times during the night looking for the convoy, we surrendered and came about at 0400 hrs. We were approximately two hundred miles out.

Tuesday 20 January saw us in the vicinity of Skerryvore, a tiny island with a light, about one hundred and fifty miles south-west of the island of Tiree, in the Inner Hebrides, in response to another SOS. Due to the diabolical weather, we were unable to find the ship which was supposedly in trouble, or even Skerryvore, come to that. We gave up the chase and continued on our return journey to Londonderry. The weather moderated and by the time that we managed to sight the island of Inishtrahull at 2100 hrs, a couple of small islands about five miles off the North Donegal coast and about twenty miles from the entrance to the River Foyle, we were in thick fog. We steamed backwards and forwards all night and by a stroke of good fortune found the entrance to the river at 1000 hrs; arriving in Londonderry at 1216 hrs.

Back in 'Derry', life returned to the humdrum, but an incident occurred which was sheer tragic-comedy and a waste of effort and a pointer to service thinking. On 23 January 1942, I was cleaning some of the brass-work on the bridge when I became quite ill with severe stomach pains and a general feeling of nausea. I endured this situation until 1145 hrs when a 'cooks to the galley' was sounded. Thinking that the working period was almost over, I made my way below and turned into my bunk with the hope that my indisposition would pass before we turned to at 1400 hrs and that I would be able to carry on as normal.

It did not require the brain of an Einstein for me to realise that the cause of my trouble was the tinned salmon sandwich which I had eaten on my return to the ship the previous evening. The can had been opened at tea time (four hours earlier) but the remaining food had been left in the can. Enquiries must have been made as to my whereabouts and within minutes of my 'turning in', an officer arrived. He asked me to describe the symptoms and, apparently satisfied, departed, presumably to request the attendance of a doctor. The time was 1210 hrs.

I was in great discomfort all afternoon and no sign of the medico. Towards early evening one of the lads suggested that I might try a sip of weak tea and feeling better than I had been all day, I sat up on the edge of my bunk and lo and behold, a doctor appeared, in company with an officer. The time was exactly 1830 hrs. Because the symptoms had almost disappeared, the verdict was that Willie John had possibly suffered food poisoning but that there was no excuse for taking to my bunk without permission.

The next morning found me standing to attention before the august presence of that Old English Gentleman, George Pardoe-Matthews, Lieutenant, RNR.
The charge was read to the effect that 'you turned in without permission, blah blah'. The fact that I thought I was going to depart this bloody life had no place here. Being heinously guilty, I was sentenced to fourteen days number Eleven's, which is on the scale of naval punishments. This particular number indicated that one rises

before the rest of the crew, shorter meal periods and continuing work a couple of hours after the remainder of the crew had ceased work for the day. I often thought to myself during daylight hours that had it been possible for the buggers to put one in the family way, they would have done so with much pleasure.

Being young and daft, I protested at the severity of the punishment by simply saying 'that is hardly fair, sir'. Pardoe-Matthews being a man of few words replied equally simply 'Commander's report'. Things were now getting out of hand because the matter was now being taken ashore to Commander of the trawler base, a man who was friendly with our skipper. So, charming, bloody charming, two days later I was standing before Commander 'T' and his acolytes; the charge was now insubordination, for if you recall I had said 'that's hardly fair, sir'. This old man of about forty-five years of age asked for the charge to be read and giving me little or no chance to speak in my own defence, looked at me with a kindly fatherly eye and said 'Captain's report'. Hells bells, this was almost tantamount to being brought before God himself.

The captain of the base was Captain Rucke-Keene, Royal Navy. Some days later I stood before this officer in the off-cap position and also present were Commander 'T', two aides, Lieutenant Pardoe-Matthews, our First Lieutenant and two Sub-Lieutenants. Finally the charge was delivered by the Master at Arms, thus making an impressive array lined up against me.

Captain 'D': 'Tell me Thorne, did you volunteer for the Navy?'

Me 'Yes, sir'.

Captain 'D': 'What was your job in civilian life?'

Me 'Postal sorter, GPO, sir'.

Captain 'D' 'Describe in your own words what actually occurred'.

I did exactly that and Captain 'D' asked me to wait outside. After a few minutes I was recalled to the office and Captain 'D' told me that he had decided to give me a complete discharge. I thanked him and he said that if I thought a change of ship would be helpful, then I only had to say. I declined his offer with thanks and told him that I was perfectly adjusted to the crew and would prefer to remain where I was.

A most perceptive man who read the signs of petty tyranny very clearly. I was treated somewhat differently thereafter and I felt that he had read the riot act to our officers.

February and March consisted of routine matters; cleaning the bridge, brass-work, signal exercises, watching the trains depart for Larne and the cross-channel ferry; going to the cinema, having a 'cuppa' in the United Services Club and listening to the squealing of the pigs on their enforced journey to the abattoir. Most of these activities were in the company of my very good ship-mate, William Faithful Banks. Bill was a Telegraphist who lived in the vicinity of Marylebone Railway Station. Like me, he was tee-total, chiefly because he was engaged to be married and needed to save for the event. I hope that he survived the war and has lived happily ever after.

We said goodbye to Londonderry on Wednesday 25 March, and after a most uneventful journey, arrived at Reykjavik, Iceland, at 0130 hrs, Sunday 29 March, and anchored for the night. I should mention, however, that for two of the four days, a north-easterly gale attacked us but things were not too uncomfortable. We left Reykjavik harbour at 0900 hrs and proceeded to Hvalfjord and took on coal. As usual, coal dust managed to permeate throughout the mess-deck and all other parts of the ship and the smell was with us for days after. Whilst we were in the fjord, HMS *Richmond* (ex-USS *Fairfax*), a four-funnelled ex-Yankee destroyer (affectionately known, due to its unattractive appearance, as a four-funnelled fish shop) came alongside us and it took no great intelligence to realise that she had almost been cut in half. She had apparently been rammed by a 10,000 ton oil tanker. I was greatly surprised and delighted to see a Post Office colleague from London, Tony Currie, who was a Telegraphist aboard the *Richmond*. He was a native of Belfast and a superb soccer player.

On 3 April, we were coaling ship once more; a matter of topping up, and then we returned to Reykjavik with the intention of swinging compasses (to adjust them). Having arrived at Reykjavik, we attempted to carry out the intended operation, but once again, due to the gale force winds, we were unable to do so. Instead, we tied up alongside the jetty to take on water and make more repairs. Another pleasant surprise when I saw an old school chum from Barking, Essex, Tom Piper, who was likewise serving in the Navy.

We anchored out in the harbour on Sunday 5 April. The gale was still blowing like a bastard and as the waves broke aboard, the water almost turned to ice, it was so cold. The next day (Easter Monday), we managed to swing compasses at long last and which when satisfactorily completed, we made our way back to Hvalfjord and secured alongside HMS *Blenheim*, the Depot ship. The next day we took aboard twenty-five tons of coal and eighteen tons of fresh water, whilst the gale kept up its banshee wailing through the rigging.

Letters home were written and mailed, and at 0700 hrs on Wednesday, 8 April, we left Hvalfjord in convoy with thirty-two Merchant vessels and six escort ships, comprising four trawlers (anti-submarine and rescue), and two Fleet Minesweepers; HMS *Speedy* and HMS *Hebe*. When we turned 'right' at the exit from the fjord, I knew for certain that the rumours ('buzzes') were accurate and that it was a case of 'Murmansk, Russia, here we come', sung to the tune of Crimond. The convoy was designated PQ-14.

On Thursday, 9 April, a gale was howling down upon us, bringing heavy snow with it and adding to the bloody misery of it all. As we steamed up the western coast of Iceland towards the North Cape, we were joined by the cruiser HMS *Berwick,* and I thought that she was to become part of the escort, which would have been most welcome, but she was simply out on patrol and after accompanying us for a couple of hours, she departed, having first wished us 'the best of British'.

Friday arrived with the blizzard howling at full blast, with the visibility down to fifty yards. The ship was by now heavily encrusted with ice and as the snow landed aboard the ship, it turned into ice. Although there were only two signalmen aboard and meant that we were working watch and watch (four hours on and four off), as we came off watch, we had to join other members of the crew and assist in chipping the ice from the rigging and upper works of the ship, in order to prevent her from becoming top-heavy and thus reduce the chances of capsizing.

The blizzard had blown itself out by the next day, and we found ourselves in pack ice. This meant, of course, that at least enemy submarines could not attack, but on the other hand, enemy aircraft would have found us sitting ducks, unable to manoeuvre and just awaiting their pleasures.

The Arctic sun decided to show itself by 1000 hrs; the sky was a beautiful blue and the ice which surrounded us took on the same blueness. All in all, it was a glorious sight and apart from the circumstances which had taken us there, was well worth seeing.

Our method of progression through the ice was a painfully slow procedure; engine at full revolutions, slide up on the ice and full stop. The weight of the ship broke the ice, opening a narrow channel which enabled us to go ahead at full revolutions, slide up and so on. During this period, we managed to smash the ASDIC dome which was bolted in position beneath the keel. The dome contained the impedimenta for ascertaining the position of enemy submarines and needless to say, it was a heavy loss to an anti-submarine trawler and was irreplaceable at the time. The dome was usually hoisted aboard when entering harbour, particularly in shallow waters.

At 0300 hrs, we emerged from the pack-ice only to find ourselves enveloped in fog. I would never have credited that the weather conditions could alter so rapidly. A heavy swell was running (not a stout member of the peerage in a marathon) and although out of the pack-ice, we were now entering floe-ice.

We were now making better progress but the ice, although of smaller dimensions than the previous type, began to hit the ship with some force, due to our increased speed and below decks in particular, the noise of the thumping was rather frightening and one began to wonder whether the ship's side could withstand the battering it was receiving. It could, and it did, thank the Lord. I must state, however, that one could see the inner bulkhead give inwards as each chunk of ice hammered at the hull. Not a situation to encourage one to sleep below, despite being dog-tired.

Having lost most the convoy due to the fog and ice, we settled down to escorting what was left. At 0800 hrs we managed to find two oil tankers, and shortly after this we were joined by the cruiser HMS *Edinburgh*, which was to be part of the escort. Later that morning we were joined by four destroyers and four corvettes, but of the thirty-two merchant ships which had left from Iceland, we could now only muster seven.

HMS *Bulldog* was to be leader of the escort whilst the *Edinburgh* took up a wandering commission around the convoy periphery. It was interesting to watch her zig-zagging at speed away from the convoy, thus making it more difficult for U-boats to attack.

At midday on 13 April, the engines of an aircraft were heard, but thanks to the fog which had closed in, there was no chance of the enemy spotting us and reporting our position to their base. The following day, the weather was beautiful, with the wind blowing from astern (from the west). HMS *Edinburgh* was still with us, and we had been joined by another destroyer, all grist to the mill.

An enemy long-range reconnaissance aircraft was sighted at 0800 hrs on 16 April, circling the convoy (or what was left of it), and this was joined by another at 1100 hrs, no doubt divulging our position back to their base. This made us a little 'windy'.

The following day, the destroyers were sent to investigate sighting reports of three U-boats. It was not a pleasant thought that there were people out there, whose sole object in life was to send us to the bottom of the sea.

I had just been relieved to go to lunch, and had just settled down at the table feeling more than ready for my grub, when there was a heavy explosion, magnified by our being below water level. We didn't need to be told that a ship had been torpedoed, and we rushed up on deck, food forgotten, and wondering which ship had been unlucky. It took no more then five seconds to reach the deck, and I was just in time to see the last moments of the stricken vessel. She was the British Steam Merchant *Empire Howard*, which was carrying the commodore of the convoy along with all sorts of equipment for the Russian forces.

Our skipper rang down to stop engines to enable us to rescue survivors. All very well, but stopping the engines made us vulnerable to enemy action. There was a pall of smoke overhanging the scene, plus the smell of oil and high explosive, and a heavy swell running, which made picking up survivors very difficult. Now to the crux of the matter; The *Northern Wave*'s engine was not renowned for its obedience to commands, and this occasion was no exception. She refused to respond to 'all stop' and continued on her easterly course. Meanwhile, our seamen had managed to launch a small boat and went about the business of picking up survivors from the *Empire Howard*. The *Northern Wave* carried on regardless, and looking from my vantage point on the bridge, I spotted a man in the sea directly ahead of us.

We had prepared for such an emergency by throwing grappling nets over the ship's side which would allow men to grasp a hold and climb to safety. However, as I watched, we hit this poor fellow with our stem, and whilst I watched he swept along our starboard side and attempted to grab the net, but he was unable to hang on and was last seen disappearing under the stern of our ship with the screw still turning. I was convinced that he was a goner. The air temperature was twenty degrees Fahrenheit, and he had been in the water for eight to ten minutes, and now I had seen the poor sod go under our stern.

Our engineer managed to correct the fault, and the ship was hove to. We picked up the small boat which had performed sterling service, and had rescued fourteen merchant seamen. We picked up eighteen survivors, but tragically, one died and was buried at sea. A postscript of this incident is that members of the crew willingly gave their bunks to the survivors, who were, needless to say, were in a dreadful plight.

My bunk was occupied by a rather ebullient Yorkshire lad, who, despite his experience, was full of beans on no time at all. An irrepressible character, he said to me, 'I thought that I had had it'. I asked him what he meant. He was able to describe to me all that happened to him from the time we hit him with our stem, being drawn down under our propeller, and being picked up. That is what I call being a survivor. He could not have known that I had watched helplessly from the bridge throughout the whole episode.

A hero of a different sort was our steward who, with the ship almost stopped, observed a life-raft on the port side with about eight merchant seamen aboard. Because of the cold were unable to help themselves any further, grabbed a small calibre rope (a heaving line) and jumped into the freezing cold sea and swam to the raft. He made fast the rope and members of our crew were able to pull them all to safety. It was one of the bravest acts that I have ever seen, and he was subsequently awarded with the DSM.

Immediately the *Empire Howard* was torpedoed, the escorting destroyers went into action against the submarine, or submarines, which were responsible for the sinking, and whose presence was no longer in doubt. Despite the tragedy that had just occurred, I could not help but admire the sight of destroyers at full speed searching out the enemy, and dropping depth charges as fast as they could. Accuracy did not appear to have too great a place here. The general idea seemed to be to drop as many charges on the bastards as possible and frighten them off.

One of our three big-ends in the engine decided to overheat at this point; the white metal had melted, and there we were, with the survivors on board, proceeding to Murmansk; dom-dom-BANG, dom-dom-BANG!

Naturally we were concerned about this situation for it meant that enemy submarines would be able to home in on the noise we were making, and disclose the position of the convoy. U-boat hydrophones could detect underwater sounds such as we were making, from many miles away.

Eventually, the thudding of the big-end was so great, and dangerous to all the ships in company, that we stopped the engine and hove-to, while the chief engineman uncoupled the connecting rod from the crankshaft. This was an uncomfortable time, being stopped, alone, all other ships having carried on towards Russia, and with the knowledge that U-boats were in the vicinity waiting to have a go at anything that floated.

Having completed the disconnection, it was a great relief to hear the skipper say, 'Full ahead', and off we went, trying to overtake the convoy which had about an hour's start. It was marvellous to steam along without that bloody noise.

All the time I spent at sea, with the enemy lurking somewhere above or below, it appeared to me that I was their prime target; me, Willie John. No doubt this was because for much of the time there was little signalling to be carried out and I was alone with my thoughts.

At 0400 hrs, almost broad daylight in that part of the world, the convoy was attacked by a succession of enemy bombers, mainly Junkers Ju-88s. Their targets were, of course, the oil tankers and merchantmen. It was an odd sensation to watch the bombs leaving the aircraft, and with the best will in the world, could do sod-all about it. There was, of course, plenty of anti-aircraft fire, but too inaccurate to inflict any losses on the enemy.

After each bombing run the aircraft would push off to return to base for yet more bombs. The attacks were still going strong at 0900 hrs, but apart from near misses, we suffered no actual losses.

Two Russian destroyers, having chanced their arm and put to sea, joined us, and very welcome they were. A feature of their behaviour was that they would only venture out no more than a couple of days, if as much as that. They would also suddenly rush to the perimeter of the convoy and blast away with their anti-aircraft guns at the shadowing aircraft, with not a snowball in hell's chance of bringing anything down. We had become so accustomed to being trailed by German reconnaissance planes that we didn't waste ammunition on them, yet here were our allies pumping shells into the sky as fast as they could.

By 1300 hrs, all aircraft had departed from the scene, and shortly after this we ran into fog and frost, but by 1600 hrs these conditions had eased. With this easement, another enemy plane arrived and began to circle the convoy. He received a bit of a shock, contrary to our normal procedure of conserving ammunition; everyone blasted away at him and he was pleased to shove off.

Saturday, 18 April was quiet until action stations were sounded at 2200 hrs. We received a radio report that three enemy surface ships had been observed leaving Altenfjord, Northern Norway, and were on a course which would seem to indicate that we were the target. I remember being alone on my section of the bridge, and in the dark would imagine that I saw torpedo tracks heading towards our ship. The truth was that I saw shafts of moonlight shimmering across the surface of the sea, creating the illusion of tracks.

The weather conditions remained atrocious; the German ships abandoned the idea of trying to intercept the convoy, assuming that was their intention, and we were stood down from action stations. The snow and freezing fog which deposited ice on the superstructure of the *Northern Wave* added to our worries. We had also developed boiler trouble and once more we were compelled to heave-to while emergency repairs were carried out. Thirty minutes later, we were on our way again. At this stage of the game I felt bloody tired, having had no more than three hours sleep in the last two days, and keeping visual watch didn't help. My eyes felt as though they were embedded in ashes; not at all nice.

Land Ho!, and although we were delighted to have arrived (almost) at our destination, not one of us was prepared for the inhospitableness of the terrain which appeared at daylight; Snow and ice everywhere, few trees, and all that pervading, diabolically freezing cold.

We entered the Kola Inlet at 0700 hrs on Sunday, 19 April, and took a pilot aboard. Proceeding up-river, we arrived at Vaenga Bay, a large expanse of water with an entrance and an exit, and we secured alongside HMS *Edinburgh* which had preceded us to the anchorage in the centre of the bay.

The survivors from the *Empire Howard* were transferred to HMS *Edinburgh* to be examined by the ship's medical staff, and we were now free to get some kip. It was twenty below zero, and lay fully clothed on my nautical couch (bunk) and went to sleep immediately. Within seconds of going to sleep, I was awakened by two bloody great explosions which it appeared were the result of a bombing attack. I was out of my bunk in a flash, tiredness forgotten, up on deck, and then climbed aboard the *Edinburgh* (she being better armed than my ship) and I sheltered there until the raider cleared off. It had been a solitary Messerschmitt Me-110 from a base in Finland, the border being only a few miles away. There was no time for the ships to open fire on the bomber, having 'crept' in as it was, and then all was quiet once more.

I emerged from my place of safety—I am joking. I was in such a hurry to climb aboard the *Edinburgh* that I hadn't spotted the refuge I had selected was actually underneath loaded torpedo tubes. I returned to the *Northern Wave* to get a couple of hours sleep.

Orders were received to proceed to Rosta, a coaling wharf on the way to Murmansk, and we arrived there on Monday, 20 April. The coaling was done by men and women carrying the coal in baskets. Some of the crew were given shore leave, a 'make and mend' (repair their kit and uniform) being granted to all the ship's company.

We were snowbound all the next day, and apart from an air raid on Murmansk which we could hear clearly, we just stayed where we were, trying to keep warm, in a mess deck which relied on a coal-burning stove for heating. The fog lifted sufficiently for us to return to Vaenga, and berth back alongside HMS *Edinburgh*.

While there, we were visited by Vice-Admiral Bonham-Carter, who congratulated us on our successful arrival at Murmansk, etc., etc. Bloody hell, did he not know that once the ship was at sea, there was nowt for it but to keep going? I never once felt that I was a hero, just a twit for placing myself in such an invidious position.

We were treated to another bombing attack on 23 April, which resulted in the loss of one merchant ship. The following day brought more air raids but fortunately we suffered no losses. Over the next two days, the engine room staff was still hard at work trying to repair the damaged boiler tubes and pumps, etc,. to enable us to make the journey home safely.

On the evening of 27 April, we received orders to report to the base at Polyarny, and with the engines having been put right, almost certainly a temporary thing, we went down river towards the sea. The base was situated in an almost land-locked harbour and access to it was gained by winding one's way through what seemed like umpteen fjords, and challenged from shore gun emplacements no end of times. Signalmen had to be quick to respond to the challenges, or else! Polyarny was very quiet and peaceful when we arrived. There were four submarines at anchor, and one destroyer, sunk.

A homeward bound convoy left the Kola Inlet on 25 April, and we should have been in company, but yet again our engine was not up to scratch, and she failed her trials.

We departed Polyarny for Murmansk on 29 April, and arrived there at 1300 hrs. We were still having mechanical trouble and we were moved to the floating dock where engine and boiler repairs continued to be carried out. Because of our enforced stay, food shortages began to rear their ugly heads; we were reduced at one stage, to a slice of Russian rye bread and a tin of plums between two men for the main meal of the day. The desperate food situation applied to quite a few British ships, and I think it's fair to say that the trawlers were the hardest hit.

There was a great deal of aerial activity, while we were there, with Russian and German aircraft engaging in dog-fights, and all the time the Russian anti-aircraft batteries would fire away, seemingly oblivious to the fact that their own planes were having to avoid the shells. The drama was unbearable.

Two British destroyers, HMS *Foresight*, and HMS *Forester*, came into harbour bearing dreadful battle scars, and had sustained casualties. The *Forester* had a hole in her hull, just below the bridge, and one could see through to the other side.

We carried out engine trials on 8 May, which proved satisfactory, and we anchored off Mishukov Point, between Vaenga and Murmansk. My Lord, it was cold. The next day we were in Murmansk and yet another bombing raid took place, and then we sailed back to Polyarny at 1900 hrs, this time acting as NAAFI ship, transferring stores from Vaenga to the British Naval contingent at Polyarny. HMS *Forester* buried her dead at sea some time between 0930 hrs and 1030 hrs on 10 May.

After another air raid by five enemy aircraft on 12 May, the next week was uneventful, and at 1800 hrs on 21 May, we joined up with the homeward bound convoy QP-12.

Although it was good to be leaving such a dreadful place, there was, never-the-less, a great deal of trepidation regarding the trip, having seen the results of the enemy's actions while we were waiting for our sailing orders from Murmansk.

We took up our position on the port quarter of the convoy, which comprised fifteen merchant ships and seventeen escorts. The weather was reasonable, although the next day the wind was strong and the *Northern Wave* was rolling like a pregnant pig, and our escort of two Russian destroyers turned back during the second day.

We altered course south of Bear Island on Sunday, 24 May, with things going reasonably smoothly, then to emphasise that life can be a bit of a bastard, the ship had developed boiler problems again, and in consequence, our speed dropped considerably. Luckily for us, 'Stormy' Bob (again) managed to rectify the trouble and we caught up with the convoy during the early hours of the next morning.

At around 0800 hrs, we had visitors in the shape of three Focke-Wulf long-range Condor aircraft; their sole purpose was to circle the convoy for hours on end and making sure they kept out of the range of our guns.

The sea was very calm for a change, and the cloud ceiling was high. The Commodore of the convoy aboard the CAM ship SS *Empire Morn*, ordered the Hurricane aircraft she carried, to intercept the enemy planes and shoot them out of the sky, if possible. It should be appreciated that once the plane has been catapulted from its carrier, there was no possibility of return, and it was compulsory for the pilot to ditch into the sea.

The *Northern Wave* was ordered to take up position on the starboard quarter of the convoy, with a view to pick up the pilot when he ditched his aircraft into the sea. The take-off was timed to coincide with the two Condors at their furthest point west of the convoy, and the single plane at his furthest point east. The Hurricane was catapulted off at 0900 hrs, and the pilot, Flying Officer John Bedford Kendal, flew his plane in a southerly direction and then climbed very rapidly eastwards and into the clouds.

From my vantage point on the bridge, and using binoculars, I next saw the Hurricane emerge from the clouds and dive upon the German plane which was on its south to north leg. We heard the rattle of machine guns and the next thing we saw was the enemy aircraft losing height and on fire with a trail of smoke. It reached sea level and disappeared from view; it was almost certain that is crashed into the sea.

The Hurricane now came on an east to west course, and as he approached the pick-up ships at what seemed to me like an almost stalling speed, we heard the pilot speaking on his radio that he intended to ditch. He was told to jettison fuel and to choose his spot for pick up. I watched with interest as he approached HMS *Badsworth*, a Hunt-class destroyer, and our co-pick-up vessel. When the aircraft was about a cable's length (200 yards) on our starboard side and seemingly gliding towards the *Badsworth*, when suddenly, and for no apparent reason, the Hurricane nose-dived into the sea, and vanished.

HMS *Badsworth* was equipped with a fast motor boat which had already been prepared for the pick-up, and I have never seen such a superb effort by the boat's crew. They were away and at the scene of the immersion in less time than it takes to tell. The water was still swirling when they arrived and seemed to be having some difficulty in reaching the pilot. When the motor boat began its return to the *Badsworth*, we took the view that the pilot had gone to the bottom with his plane, but shortly afterwards the *Badsworth* signalled all ships that the pilot had been picked up and was uninjured. At 1300 hrs, another signal was received from the *Badsworth* stating that all ships should dip their ensigns as a token of respect for a very courageous young pilot who had just died. This was a sad moment for us all.

Later that day, we broke down again, and we were taken in tow from the fleet minesweeper HMS *Harrier*. This, for us, was a unique and pleasurable experience, for, steaming under our own power, and pulling out all the stops, and with some pushing, could manage possibly ten knots. The *Harrier* pulled us at twelve knots— almost unbelievable. Meanwhile, 'Stormy' Bob and his artificers persevered to get the engine started and the tow was cast off at 1130 hrs on 26 May. (As an addendum to this journal, I would add a remarkable coincidence when some time ago I met an elderly gentleman, Fred Sharpe, like myself, now in his eighties, also an ex Royal Navy Rating. I asked him the name of his ship, to which he replied 'HMS *Harrier*'. I responded 'a fleet sweeper' (minesweeper). He said 'did you know her Bill?' I replied, 'I certainly do Fred. We (my trawler *Northern Wave*) were in the Barents Sea on our return to the UK when we broke down. *Harrier* took us in tow'. Fred then astounded me by saying, 'and the tow rope broke!' Which it did! In other words, Fred Sharpe was aboard at that time in February 1942 and we met for the first time in our lives in Cookham, sixty years later!

At 0015 hrs the next morning, SS *Empire Morn*, HMS *Ulster Queen*, *Cape Race* and *Southgate*, escorted by HMS *Badsworth* and HMS *Venomous*, departed from the convoy; their destination being Loch Ewe, Scotland. The North Cape of Iceland was sighted at 0245 hrs on 28 May, and despite the cold and bleakness of the terrain, we were bloody pleased to know that were had overcome the worst part of the trip.

We arrived at Reykjavik, and anchored in the outer harbour, at 0100 hrs the next morning. There was mail in plenty, and decent food available at last. The next day we moved to the inner harbour, and took advantage of the shore leave that was granted.

We hovered around Reykjavik for some days, and on Monday, 15 June, the *Northern Wave* made the four hour trip to Hvalfjord and went alongside SS *Delaware*, a collier, and took on board 113 tons of coal. There was a show of strength the following day when one American battleship, three cruisers and five destroyers arrived, followed by the British cruiser, HMS *Cumberland*. It is remarkable how safe one feels when surrounded by big ships.

With the topping up of stores and fresh water, etc., completed, we departed for home at 2230 hrs (in broad daylight), accompanied by *Jaunty*, a sea-going tug, and a tanker. The weather was superb, and the sea as flat as could be, and we sighted the Butt of Lewis at 1600 hrs on 24 June. The trip through the Minches was uneventful and we arrived at Moville, at the entrance to the River Foyle at

1800 hrs the following afternoon, where we anchored for the night and proceeded to Londonderry the next morning.

Home leave was granted, and then between July and mid-October, the *Northern Wave* underwent a refit and other necessary activities. We were then sent to the Mount Stuart dry dock, Cardiff, to have steel girders welded into the ship's bows, which meant one thing only; a return to North Russia. Oh joy.

Following an incident in the early hours of 17 November in the Mersey Reaches, when the *Northern Wave* was rammed (ever so gently) by the Cunard liner RMS *Samaria* during thick fog, bending our starboard gunwale inboard like a banana, the next few weeks saw us escorting coastwise shipping to various small ports around the coast of Ulster and returning to Belfast each time. We also visited Tobermory on the Isle of Mull as our 'working up ship' period; the purpose of this being to improve the efficiency of the ship and its crew.

We left Belfast at 0600 hrs on Saturday, 12 December 1942 with four LCTs (Landing Craft, Tanks) in company, and headed for Stornoway, on the Island of Lewis, and after topping up our coal from an old hulk which was floating in the harbour there, arrived at Loch Ewe three hours later.

It was decided by the powers that be that we should not have too much time to dwell on our future, and hey presto! In the afternoon of 15 December, we were once again on our way, destination North Russia on convoy JW-51A. I listened most attentively for the hoorahs of the crew when they learned where they were going again, but no cheers were to be heard. This trip was direct to Murmansk, avoiding Iceland altogether, and the weather was, as always, diabolical, and darkness was with us for all but for a faint glimmer of daylight for half an hour at noon, then darkness once more. Due to the amount of ice (small bergs and plenty of floe ice) visibility was never really bad, and I am in no doubt that the ice and the darkness together, saved us from the attentions of the enemy.

It is difficult to describe the conditions to people who have no experience of those areas. The nearest I can get is to ask a reader to visualise the sea, without a ripple on its surface, yet with a swell so high and rolling, that were the sea to be covered with grass, one could liken the result to the hills and valleys of Devon and Somerset. I have never seen anything larger at sea. The ships, small and large, simply climbed up the hills, looking like mini-toys, and then down the other side but completely stable all the time.

These conditions remained for two days, and all the time the floe ice was doing its utmost to smash its way into the hull of the ship; it was noisy and rather frightening.

We arrived at the Kola Inlet at 0800 hrs on Christmas Day 1942, and proceeded up to Vaenga Bay, where we secured alongside the cruiser HMS *Jamaica*. Boxing Day was celebrated with a visit from German bombers; three raids, in fact, which did no damage but resulted in the loss of two enemy aircraft which were brought down by the concentrated fire of our ships.

On 27 December, we called at Rosta for coal, and whilst there, we could hear bombs exploding on Murmansk. We left for Polyarny, and after the usual cautious approach along the various fjords, we secured alongside the jetty.

Returning to Vaenga on 31 December, we could hear the uproar of a bombing raid on Murmansk. It was minus twenty degrees, and the weather was so atrocious that we were forced to anchor at Mishukov Point, about half way to Murmansk. We were in what is known as 'black ice'; a thick fog which froze on one's face as it stuck. The fog was so all-enveloping the cold and the silence was unbearable. The engine room of a trawler was always hot, and it was necessary for me to enter it from time to time to place my Aldis lamp batteries on charge, or take them off charge. It was on one of these visits that I noticed that the internal steel bulkhead at the top of the engine room was thick with ice, due to the freezing cold external surface.

It was essential that one avoided touching metal parts of the ship unless wearing gloves. I made this error on one occasion only, and lost some skin from the tips of my fingers.

The two 'heads' that were normally available for the use of the crew were frozen solid for most of the time, adding to the misery. To relieve oneself of water at night, it was a question of wrapping up, climb the ladder, and then urinate immediately outside the companionway entrance, making sure not to touch the brass handle with bare hands. The following morning brought a horrible sight: Amber-coloured ice.

We saw the New Year in at Mishukov Point; not exactly a riotous time, and so ended 1942, which for me had included a broken engagement, and on Sunday, 3 January 1943, the weather having improved, we received orders to proceed to Murmansk to coal ship, but once again, due to the obscene weather, the operation had to be abandoned until the following day. To keep the Signalmen busy and away from mischief (I ask you!), we were told to soogee the bridge paintwork. Soogee is a mixture of soft soap and soda in very hot water, and we applied this using cotton waste material to swab the paint work. In spite of the heat of the water, it froze immediately it hit the iron and wood work. We protested at the ridiculousness of the situation, but our protests fell on 'cloth' ears.

In a similar vein, I had requested that I be permitted to grow a 'set', i.e., a beard and moustache. It grew very well; luxuriantly is the word, but I found, like many of my shipmates, that being on an open part of the deck, the fog froze on the beard and was far from comfortable. In no time at all, I requested permission of the commanding officer, to shave. Permission was not given immediately, and I had to wait two days before I could remove the offending growth.

My duties as Signalman meant that all my watches were on the open bridge, and on this trip we had been issued with leather, as opposed to rubber sea boots. They were fine in the warmth (a comparative term) of the mess deck, pliable and comfortable, but fifteen minutes on the bridge were sufficient to make them rigid, and one would stagger around like Frankenstein's monster.

Coaling recommenced on Monday 4 January, and my function was simply to record the number of buckets of coal received into our bunkers. The work continued until the next day, in filthy weather; frost, snow and ice. It was in the half-darkness that Eddie, a Telegraphist, fell down through an open bunker lid, into the bowels of the ship, and hit the bottom with a thump. He was sufficiently shaken to be permitted to take to his bunk, but on the following day he complained of a severe pain in his shoulder.

A signal was sent ashore, and a Russian Army medico (female) came aboard and examined Eddie, and pronounced him bruised, but fit. We completed coaling, and returned to Vaenga on Thursday. Throughout this time, Eddie was complaining of terrible pain in his shoulder, and a British doctor was called to see him. The lad was transferred to the naval hospital at Vaenga (courtesy of our Russian allies) when it was discovered that he had a shattered scapula.

On our way down to Vaenga, we saw HMS *Onslow*, which, unbeknownst to us, had been involved with enemy surface ships that had attacked the convoy, of which she was an escort. The convoy was the one after ours, and therefore we considered ourselves very lucky not to have been chosen for attention.

Our ship always seemed to be chosen to do all sorts of jobs, and one such task was to convey the bodies of two British sailors out to sea, and beyond Russian territorial waters, there to commit them to their permanent resting place. I have a vivid recollection of standing on the bridge, peering over the top and looking down on the two flag-draped bodies which were lying on the foredeck. It was horrible to think that these lads were dead, and it could have been so many of us, and although it made me feel sick to think of the sadness for all concerned, try as I might, I could not prevent myself from looking at those two figures. There was another fear to worry this brave matelot, and that was the fact that we were out at sea, unaccompanied, with a strong likelihood of a U-boat being in the vicinity. I was pleased when the funeral service was over and we reached the Kola Inlet without trouble.

Food stocks were becoming depleted, and what we did have was devilish. However, we were invited alongside the American merchant ship *John H. LaTrobe*, which was anchored at Vaenga. The freezing fog conditions were still with us; the temperature being below zero. The reason for the visit was simple; the United States' ships were 'dry', and ours were not, and so, by the expedient passing of a few bottles of whisky, rum and gin, the Americans supplied us with sides of beef, squabs, steaks, and cigarettes. It was a most satisfactory arrangement for all concerned.

We received instructions to go alongside the pier on Sunday to take on water. Due to the wind direction, we approached the pier head-on. The ship was travelling at around two knots, and when we were only a short distance from the pier, the CO rang for 'full astern'—another mishap! The valve control jammed, and the ship continued straight ahead, with no room for manoeuvre, and hit the brand new jetty stem-first causing the pier master to jump for his life. The *Northern Wave* juddered to a stop at least five feet into the timbers of the pier. I have no idea how that one was squared up.

During the same morning, there was a heavy bombing raid on Murmansk and a couple of miles downstream at Mishukov, resulting in the loss of three merchant seamen, and two wounded, their ship being hit but not sunk. Later the same day, we also heard that the captain of the *Onslow* had been awarded the Victoria Cross for his part in the battle with enemy surface ships, on the inward-bound convoy.

On Tuesday 12 January, we secured alongside HMS *Seagull*, a Fleet minesweeper, which was anchored in Vaenga Bay. This was a welcome break for us; *Seagull* was the senior ship, as it were, and so we were not required to keep signal watch on the shore station. That evening, our crew were invited to a concert party on board her and I was asked to take my guitar with me and together with an officer of *Seagull* playing clarinet, we were able to contribute to the fun and festivities.

The next day we were back to keeping watches after leaving the *Seagull*, and were secured to another trawler, *Lady Madeleine*, which was berthed at the pier, not far from the section that had been almost demolished. I made a visit to the hospital to see Eddie; what a cold, miserable mile-and-a-half walk that was. Our ship's crew, including myself, gave a concert to the lads in that hospital, and although it was amateurish, it was done with sincerity, and was appreciated by all.

Back again to Rosta for more coal where the work was completed on 16 January, and returned to Vaenga, and secured alongside HMS *Hyderabad*, a corvette, who took over the responsibility for all signals. We went back to Murmansk for more coal, to be taken from the SS *Daldorch*, and I noted that Murmansk was now surrounded by barrage balloons as we steamed down river to Vaenga.

Monday 25 January saw us returning to Mishukov Point, and after a twenty-four hour turn around, were steaming back to Vaenga. The following day we moved down to Polyarny and anchored for the night. There appeared to be no rhyme or reason to our peripatetic existence; we departed Polyarny at 0800 hrs on 29 January, and arrived at Vaenga at noon, happy in the knowledge that we were soon to be leaving for home.

At 2200 hrs, we had collected eleven ships and were on our homeward voyage with convoy RA-52. As we steamed northward towards the ocean, still in the Kola Inlet, in the darkness, except for the light reflected by the snow, two Handley Page Hampden bombers, which had been supplied by us to the Russians, were returning from an operational sortie against the Germans. They were not quick enough to reply to the challenge of the Russian shore batteries when they opened up on them. They were flying low, and their course took them over the convoy. As a consequence of the Russians opening fire, so did every ship in the convoy.

The planes flew over us at mast height, and the noise was terrific. The darkness helped, and they managed to get clear; it was a sticky couple of minutes for them. To give the Russians their due, every man appeared to be on the ball.

The next two days were uneventful, apart from the freezing cold and frequent snow storms. On Monday 1 February, we altered course to avoid three U-boats which were known to be in the vicinity, and at 2110 hrs, we dropped three patterns of depth charges on a suspected U-boat presence, but could not claim a successful outcome.

In the forenoon half-light, we spotted floating mines, which I found unnerving, because one realised that mine-laying submarines had been at work during the night, and we must have passed through them.

On Wednesday, 3 February, I was on afternoon watch with Lieutenant Perry, RNVR, a barrister in 'Civvy Street', and as I gazed around the convoy, all was serene. Suddenly there was an explosion and I looked at the ships nearest to us, the American merchant ship SS *Greylock*, and saw a column of water on its port side. The first torpedo was immediately followed by a second. We picked up seventeen survivors and there was no loss of life. The ship took thirty-seven minutes to sink. A melancholy sight; we stood by to sink her if necessary, rather than allow the enemy tow her in as a prize. The torpedoes, however, had done their work, and the last I saw of her was her stem which, just before she slid to the bottom, rose about ten feet out of the water, almost as a farewell gesture, and then she was gone.

We were soon in the midst of a blizzard, but of course, we couldn't be seen by the enemy, although we knew we were being shadowed by at least one U-boat. Sighting reports were received fairly frequently, which put us on guard.

There were no further incidents, and we sighted the North Cape of Iceland at 1130 hrs on Friday, 5 February. We called in to Reykjavik for coal, and after taking on stores, we were on our final leg to Belfast, all alone. Despite the gale which blew from astern, we made good time, and that was the last I saw of the northern latitudes, thank the Lord.

Shortly thereafter, the ship was paid off, and the crew dispersed in all directions. This was a very sad moment, and we all felt miserable, having been through some trying times together. Glad to see the back of Pardoe-Matthews, may his tribe be opposite to that of Abou ben Adhem.

Stanley Welch
HMS *Apollo*

I was born in the District of Southwark, London, on 18 March 1925; my mother (of Irish descent) was disappointed as she wanted me to be born on 17 March (St Patricks Day). I was one of three boys, and had one sister.

I was six months old when the family moved to Dagenham, and when I was about the age of seven, we moved to Welling, Kent.

My eldest brother Joe was in the army. He was a regular and served in the Royal Signals from early 1939 to 1946. During that time he served in the Western Desert, Greece, Crete, Syria and finally the 14th Army in Burma. He was lucky to escape from Crete as one the ships he was being evacuated on was sunk. He was declared missing for a few months but eventually turned up in Egypt. It may not be generally known but he fought against the French in Syria. His name is in a book called *Nemesis* by Max Hastings. My other brother and sister served in the Air Force after the war.

Prior to entering the services, I belonged to the Air Training Corps and was keen to join the Air Force at 17¼ years old. I volunteered for Air Crew but for some reason wasn't selected. Just after my 18th birthday, I was called up for service in the Royal Navy.

On 27 May 1943, I stepped off the train at Skegness; there was a reception committee waiting for me and, of course, others. They were not wearing red coats as Holiday camp employees did even though we were going to a holiday camp. They were, instead, wearing blue serge. As we drove through the entrance to Butlin's Holiday camp (HMS *Royal Arthur*) I noticed a notice a sign that had been left from a more peaceful time 'Our true intent is for your enjoyment' never a truer word has been spoken in jest.

After spending a month being taught how to march in step, and rifle drill, etc., I was sent to Dundee. Here, we were billeted in a nice hotel and attended a Radio College, which had previously been used to train Radio Officers in the Merchant Navy. I thought 'this isn't too bad, first a holiday camp then a hotel'. In November, once I attained twenty words per minute in Morse code, I was sent to another holiday camp in Ayr (HMS *Scotia*) this time it wasn't quite as pleasant—unheated chalets. It was so cold if you scrubbed your hammock and hung it out to dry you could pick it up later and stand it in the corner.

We had more instruction in Morse code, other codes and ciphers, and then in January it was back down South to a place called Borstal, which was an annex of Chatham barracks. It was alongside the original prison for youths just outside Rochester.

On 11 January 1944, I joined the Abdiel-class fast cruiser Minelayer HMS *Apollo* (M01) at Hebburn in Newcastle. I arrived at around 2100 hrs, and just half an hour later we sailed. I was sat down in front of a receiver and checked out by a three badge Leading Telegraphist and, after satisfying him that I could do the job, went on solo watch.

We had a mixed lot on our mess deck, Signalmen (bunting tossers), Telegraphists (sparkers) and Coders. Within those were two journalists, a stockbroker who was an Advertising Manager for Persil (he had also been a fighter pilot in the First World War) and a professional soccer player for Perth. The rest were sprogs like me (laboratory assistant) and a coal heaver.

Our first destination was Scapa Flow for commissioning trials; anti-aircraft gunnery firing at drogues. I was on the bridge talking to the (Australian) pilot of the towing plane, although he didn't think much of our accuracy. He said to me, 'Tell your skipper I am pulling this bastard not pushing it'.

When the first guns were fired, one of the crew was sitting in the heads, and the toilet pan disintegrated under him. Fortunately he was unhurt apart from his dignity. I know the ship was laid down to do forty-seven knots, and we did manage to achieve forty-two knots in a calm sea. Quite impressive—she was like an overgrown MTB (Motor Torpedo Boat).

After Scapa we proceeded to Milford Haven in Pembrokeshire, South West Wales, where we spent the next fifteen months picking up mines, though, on a couple of occasions, we loaded up mines at the naval base at Loch Alsh, Scotland. On our first operation we called into Plymouth en route. Naturally, I think we were all apprehensive because in the newspapers at that time there were descriptions of massive defences installed by the Germans along the French coasts. Before leaving for France that evening, a church service was held on the quarter deck in which 'Drakes Prayer', which was written before he attacked the Spanish Armada in 1588, was read.

I was eighteen at the time like many others on board, and wondered what the hell were getting into. After a few trips the mine lays became routine. We worked in conjunction with Coastal Command Short Sunderland aircraft. They carried out flights over the English Channel and sent position reports of any enemy shipping which we intercepted and decoded.

On one occasion we arrived off Brest, reduced speed to ten knots and started to lay the mines. About a quarter of mines had been laid when echoes appeared on the radar. It was assumed they were hostile. An enemy report was sent and mining was stopped and we vacated the area as fast as possible. The cruiser HMS *Black Prince* (81) and three Tribal-class destroyers; HMCS *Haida* (G63), HMCS *Huron* (G24) and HMS *Tartar* (F43) and at times HMCS *Athabaskan* (G07)—which was sunk by the enemy one night when we were absent, were our escort on the seaward side.

The *Black Prince*, which had received the enemy report, had observed a radar target heading towards them and gave the order to fire. The target they observed was our ship—the *Apollo*. Our radar IFF (Identification Friend or Foe) identification system had broken down, and despite visual signals and radio, our escort started to bombard us for twenty minutes with ninety eight shells—and we still had 120 mines on board. What saved us was that the *Black Prince* thought we were much closer than we were and under-ranged. I think we had a few shrapnel holes in one of the funnels. Whether it was because of this incident or the sinking of the Canadian destroyer *Athabaskan*, Admiralty decided not to use a cruiser for our escort as they did not want to risk a cruiser being sunk by the Germans. After this we laid many more mines without incident.

After the completion of mine-laying, we proceeded to Portsmouth where we had some work done involving installation of extra communication equipment. Later on, around 5 June, we joined the invasion fleet anchored between the Isle of Wight and the Needles, where ships were anchored in their hundreds. During the day captured German aircraft with the invasion markings on their wings (white stripes) flew over the Fleet to acquaint crews with aircraft recognition. That night the fleet started to move out—but we did not.

On 7 June, we had guests come on board. General Eisenhower, Admiral Ramsay and all their staff, and our W/T office were taken over by their own Wireless Telegraphists. We then set sail for the Normandy beaches. On arrival you could see wreckage of landing craft. The ship started cruising along the line

HMS *Apollo*. *(Authors Collection)*

of ships carrying out bombardment, ships like HMS *Warspite* (03) and the *Lord Roberts*, a monitor ship which had one sixteen inch gun on board, and every time it fired, the recoil from its massive gun caused it to heel over then slowly to move back onto an even keel.

Among the ships were American ships and, as we were carrying the four star flag of an American general on our main mast, they dipped their flags in salute. As our W/T office had been taken over by the Admiral's staff, I was at a loose end and just stayed on the upper deck watching the bombardment. Now and again various Generals (including General Montgomery) came on board to liaise with General Eisenhower. I decided to go down below to get a cup of tea from the W/T Office. I stood outside the office drinking my tea when there was a crunch, and the ship started to heel over. The wireless staff came running out the office and up the ladder nearly knocking the tea out of my hand. I went and looked in the office, it was empty. As the ship appeared to have stabilised I went up to our mess and took my personal papers out of my locker.

On the upper deck there were aerials laying on the deck and various other bits and pieces. It appeared that General Eisenhower had asked our captain to go closer in to shore to observe the action. Unfortunately the ship had gone round the wrong side of a buoy and finished up on a sand bank. Endeavouring to free the ship we lost one screw and one blade of the other three-bladed screw. General Eisenhower disembarked onto a destroyer.

Later that night we limped back to Portsmouth at five knots in a convoy. As the remaining screw was unbalanced the ship appeared to be bending amidships as we progressed. En route the ships in the convoy were firing at strange aircraft with flames coming out of the tails. These were the first of the doodlebugs—the V1s.

As a result of the incident the captain faced court martial. One contributing factor was the bridge was so crowded with the VIP's staff that the navigator was asked to leave the bridge.

The captain lost one year's seniority. As a footnote to this, in 1787 a Royal Navy ship ran aground on a sand bar while pursuing a Dutch ship, and the pilot was court-martialled. The name of the ship—HMS *Apollo*!

On 13 June, the *Apollo* was towed by a Dutch sea-going tug up to Newcastle for repairs which would take two days. On arrival, we tied up alongside the HMS *Manxman* (M70) (the same class as the *Apollo*). She had been torpedoed and had a massive hole in the hull. I noted it was where the W/T office had been. Repairs to the *Apollo* were not completed until 30 September; during which time each watch was given six weeks leave each.

My leave started out with a bang. I left our local station and walked home. As I was walking up the back garden path I heard a doodlebug approaching. Suddenly, its engine cut out and appeared to be diving toward me, but fortunately it passed overhead and landed in a wood adjacent to the housing. I heard later

Stanley Welch. (*Courtesy of Stan Welch*)

on that one had hit the local railway station. I thought to myself 'Bugger this, I'm going back to sea—it's safer'.

After completing working up trials in Scapa Flow, the *Apollo* was transferred to Western Approaches Command. Due to the use of the snorkel, U-boats were posing a threat as they did not have to surface to recharge their batteries and could operate closer to the shores of UK. Fourteen deep minefields were laid in the Northern and Southern approaches.

We left Scapa Flow on 12 January 1945 to carry out Operation 'Spellbinder', which was to carry out attacks on a north-bound enemy convoy and lay a minefield in the path of the convoy adjacent to Utstra Island on the Norwegian coast. The operation was to be carried by three forces of the Home Fleet ships.

Force one; the cruisers HMS *Norfolk* (78) and HMS *Bellona* (63), and destroyers HMS *Onslow* (G17), HMS *Onslaught* (G04), and HMS *Orwell* (G98) would attack the convoy. Force two, which comprised HMS *Apollo* and two destroyers, would provide a smoke screen for the mine-laying. Force three consisted of two aircraft carriers. Aircraft from the carriers shot down a Junkers Ju-88 and drove off approaching torpedo bombers.

This was a night time operation; the sea was like a mill pond and with a cloudless sky and full moon. Visibility was unlimited.

After we finished our mine-lay we headed back to Scapa Flow at high speed. At a pre-briefing we were advised that there were fifty aircraft based at the local airfield and that radar ashore was not very efficient as the soldiers were busy fraternising with the local girls. During the mine-lay a shore based electronic navigation aid was utilised to provide accuracy. Apparently those on the upper deck could see the headlights of the German army on a coast road.

On 15 January, we returned to Western Approaches Command, laying another ten mine fields; the last being laid at the end of March. Most of the time we had an escort, and there was the odd occasion when they carried out depth charge attacks. Returning in fog to Milford Haven in February, we collided with the corvette HMS *Clarkia*. Luckily damage was not severe but provided us with a holiday in Pembroke dock. It was a break from the Irish Sea.

Our final operation was to take part in Operation 'Trammel'. For some time the UK had tried to get permission to lay mines in the Kola Inlet (North Russia). There had been a problem trying to detect U-boats in the Kola Inlet owing to 'Thermal layering', where differing temperatures at different depths affected ASDIC results.

With an escort of three 'O'-class destroyers (also carrying mines) and after a delay in refuelling, the mine-lay was carried out with a further shield of seven frigates on our seaward side. I believe one of the frigates was sunk. We had Russian observers onboard who were a bit apprehensive about the safety of shipping due to the mines. So we steamed over the minefield just to prove it was quite safe, except of course for enemy submarines.

Little did we know the European war would be over in a matter of weeks and it was a pity that the mines had not been laid earlier.

Our final operation was on 'VE' Day when we took Prince Olaf and his Cabinet back to Oslo. It was a beautiful day, and we met a German minesweeper whose Captain came on board to guide us through the minefields.

Sailing up the fjord leading a number of ships was an impressive scene as the Norwegians came alongside in their boats singing their National anthem. In Oslo the German soldiers were still driving around in their trucks, whilst fighting was taking place between the Quislings (collaborators) and the free Norwegian Army who had been secretly training in Sweden. I saw some females who were having their hair shaved off for fraternising with the Germans. Whilst I was ashore a German soldier came up to me and said, 'We did not lose the war it was the people in Germany that had'. I said, 'I couldn't care less it's over and done with'. Obviously he was not aware of the destruction that had taken place in Germany. I believe the phrase he used was made by some Germans after the First World War.

The number of mines we laid, according to official figures, was 8,571. How effective that had been is unknown. One U-boat was confirmed as having been sunk in the Kola Inlet and, in recent years, the wrecks of two U-boats have been found off Newport, where mines were laid by *Apollo* and HMS *Plover* (M26).

Unfortunately, I was drafted off the ship at this time. I was sorry to leave it and many shipmates. HMS *Apollo* was to join the Pacific Fleet, and after a couple of months, I finished up at the naval base HMS *Golden Hind* in Sydney. In January, I was sent to Shanghai as base wireless staff, swapping from ship to ship as they arrived. I must have spent a few weeks on about seven cruisers and one destroyer. Our main task was to take two hourly position reports from merchant shipping transiting between Hong Kong, Shanghai and Tsingtao. The reason was that piracy was taking place along the Chinese coast.

Finally I was demobbed in August 1946, and returned to my old job as a laboratory assistant in a chemical laboratory in Bankside Power Station on the south bank of the River Thames. Unable to settle down there, I spent a year at Radio College to obtain a Merchant Navy Radio Officers certificate. Whilst impatiently waiting for a ship I saw an advert for vacancies in the New Zealand Navy—they had purchased six Loch-class frigates from UK and wanted ex-RN members to crew them. It was for a three year engagement—but that's another story!

Stanley Welch, Paraparaumu, New Zealand, 17 June 2013.

Sydney Wells
HMS *Magpie*

I was born in Bootle, Liverpool, the son of Sydney William and Muriel Vesta Wells, on 10 September 1925, and had three brothers and three sisters. My father was a school teacher and we moved with his various positions. The family moved to Isleworth when I was about two years old, and later to Totteridge, Potter's Bar. After a bombing, my mother and my siblings went to Selsey Bill, and I stayed with my father, who was teaching at Southgate, to finish my education. When war was declared on 3 September 1939, one of my brothers (who was two years younger than me) and I volunteered to help, and we were tasked with filling sand bags which would be used to make air raid shelters.

After my schooling had finished, I was working in an estate agent's office when, on one of my outings with the estate agent in May 1943, at the age of eighteen, I was walking along Edgware Road when I spotted and saw a recruiting office, walked in, and volunteered for the Royal Navy (my brother had joined the Merchant Navy and, with no training needed, and in early 1944, aged just sixteen, was on his first passage to South America). The medical was carried out and then I just waited for my call up, which duly arrived: Seamanship Training at HMS *Collingwood*, Fareham.

After that I was sent on a Gunnery course at Whale Island, where I wanted to do training to be an AA (Anti-aircraft) gunner, but because of my education, they made me do the control rating course (rangefinders) and said that if I failed on purpose in order to do AA course, to think again; I would be made a quarters rating, which meant I'd be in the bowels of the ship with the magazines, and at action stations all hatchways were secured tight—not good if you were torpedoed. So my action station was on the bridge.

It was there that I waited for a posting, checking the notice board daily, but it wasn't long before HMS *Magpie* (U82) appeared on the list. She was a modified Swan class Sloop which was engaged for duty with the outer escort group, and so with my kit bag, hammock and travel warrant, I journeyed up the West Country via Bristol to join her in Oban, where she and the group were carrying out initial trials before going on convoy duties in the Atlantic. She was one of five escort sloops under the command of Captain 'Johnnie' Walker, RN, on HMS *Starling* (U66), and had just returned from a successful trip in the Atlantic. I think on that particular trip they sank five U-boats.

When we sailed, and got into the Irish Sea, it was rough, but I wasn't seasick, and after a few days out, I thought to myself that this wasn't bad, but obviously I hadn't experienced the real rough seas at that stage. When I did, I was on the quarterdeck, leaning over the guard rail, with the waves washing against my legs, and I was feeling that bad that I didn't care if the sea took me over or not. All I could cope with food wise was beef cubes and ship's biscuits. That's all that kept me going, and it took a few trips for me to get over my seasickness. There was one chap on board who, in private life, was a jeweller, and he was so seasick, he didn't get out of his hammock. I don't know if or how he was punished, but he couldn't get out.

Being on a smaller ship, we didn't have a galley chef like there was on the cruisers where set meals were dished out. We had an allowance, and had to go to our canteen and buy what we wanted, whether it be tins of red lead (tomatoes) or yellow peril (smoked fish), but I must say that our meat ration was superb compared with what the civilians were getting. A lot of it was American meat, but it was good.

My 'action station' was on the bridge, and my job was to convey instructions from the First Lieutenant to the depth charge quarters and guns. In practice this would mean I would call down the voice pipe. If it seemed likely that a U-boat was in the vicinity, because of the acoustic torpedoes they were using, we would drop our speed to ninety revs, and send over depth charges in patterns.

Sydney Wells. (*Courtesy of Sydney Wells*)

We used to take convoys from Belfast or Londonderry over as far as Newfoundland, and there wait for another convoy to escort to bring to England, and then wait for another convoy that was going to America. As a result of that we'd be at sea for some weeks, with no opportunity for getting time ashore, and by that time we were eating a lot of dehydrated food stuffs because the potatoes had become too soft. The only time we could have gone ashore was in Reykjavik, Iceland, because we had broken down, but on that occasion, the ship was not allowed into the harbour, and had to anchor outside it. The sea was so rough we had trouble tying the ship to a buoy because we only had rope hawsers; they wouldn't allow us to use steel hawsers because they were dangerous. One of our leading seamen in Liverpool was caught by one of the steel hawsers when it snapped, and it got his legs and flipped him right up in the air. The wires can sing, and when you hear the hawsers sing, you get right out of the way.

I also did my turns in the crow's nest as lookout, and going up one rung at a time in the rough weather, the yard arm would almost be in the sea, and I used to wonder how the hell the ship was going to come upright again, but it always did.

We went from Rosyth to Scapa Flow in late March or early April, 1944, and we were in the naval canteen at Scapa having a drink, and we met some other sailors who had just come back from the previous convoy. We got talking and they told us they pitied us having to go up there again because the U-boats were even surfacing to take pot shots at the ships. With that in mind, we left Scapa to pick up convoy JW-58 which was moving through from Iceland. We were escorting the USS *Milwaukee* (CL5) which was being delivered to the Soviet Northern

HMS *Magpie*. (*Courtesy of Derek Whitwam*)

Fleet on the lend-lease agreement (and was subsequently commissioned at *Murmansk*).

It was so very cold; we were warned not to touch handrails without wearing gloves or we might not get our hands back. We were kitted out with sea boots, a thick white woollen jersey, duffle coat and a beanie. There was a warning given out to men on the minelayers. It brings to mind the story of a lad on a minelayer. They were all warned not to wear their duffle coats because they have a toggle, and they can get in the way. This chap chose to ignore the warning, and as a result, when one of the mines was loosed, the toggle of his duffle coat got caught up in the chain and he went over the side and down with the mine.

The U-boats were the greater menace to the convoys than the Luftwaffe, but at this late stage of the war, the Enigma code, which the Germans were using in this sphere of the war, had been broken, and their submarines were suffering great losses because their communications could be decoded and understood. From the advantage it gave us, we were usually able to plot where the U-boats were and instruct the convoys accordingly.

When we reached Polyarny, which wasn't as far up the Kola Inlet as Murmansk, we were ordered to tie up alongside a Norwegian tanker, so we didn't get ashore again; for some reason, we weren't allowed, yet some of our shipmates on HMS *Bluebell* did. We waited there for two or three days until the next convoy going back.

When we reached Scotland on that last journey, we then sailed right round the north and down to Milford Haven. As we waited to go in, another vessel was on its way out, and as we were due to anchor, this other ship was hit by a torpedo from a U-boat, so we went to try and hunt down the submarine.

HMS *Magpie*. (*Courtesy of Sydney Wells*)

We ended up going right round towards Portsmouth, and we called in at either Torbay or Torquay, Devon, which was under heavy air attack by German aircraft, but we had instructions not to open fire. Although we were fitted with anti-aircraft guns, we were not to give our position away by engaging the enemy.

We finished up at Portsmouth, where we joined the ships there waiting for the D-Day Landings at Normandy. The invasion had been set back by twenty four hours due to bad weather, and because we weren't allowed to use signals, the *Magpie* was selected to go round to each of the various ships there, and relay the news by megaphone.

It was here too, that we were all told to write out our last will and testament— before D-Day, because they expected seventy five per cent casualties. Not that as a young man I had anything to leave to anyone. We all had our letters from Eisenhower about what was going to happen on D-Day, and all the best, so to speak.

We escorted Landing Craft in to Gold Beach on 6 June 1944, and were then involved in escorting materials for the formation of the Mulberry Harbours as well as the slow process of escorting the ships laying the pipe line under the ocean on Operation 'Pluto'.

On VE (Victory in Europe) Day, we were in Weymouth, and expected some shore leave to celebrate, but were ordered out to sea again to seek out surrendered U-boats, and then following VJ (Victory in Japan) Day I was on a troop ship to the Mediterranean, where I joined the destroyer HMS *Brissenden* (L79), which was engaged for a time on duty blockading the coast of Palestine. I spent a further year on HMS *Orion* (85) before returning to England for demob.

The one thing I had made my mind up about when I joined the ship was that I was not going to be scared, and I don't know if it was the comradeship, but I didn't at any time feel scared. I consider that we were a lucky escort group. There was only one occasion, which was the last time that we were part of the Russian convoys, that one of our escorts was hit, and on being towed back to port it sank before it got back into harbour.

I went to Wellington, New Zealand, in 1952, on what I thought would be a two year stint working for the English company John Dickinson Stationery. I had left my golf clubs in England, and decided to buy a set at the sports club nearby. I was served by a young lady called Doreen Rachel (although she was known as Pat), and we got chatting, and arranged a game of golf, and two years later we were married. Sadly, I lost my wife in July 1992.

I joined the Johnnie Walker Club, and went to Liverpool on the fiftieth anniversary of the end of the war, and met a lot of shipmates there. We went to the Cathedral for a ticket-only service, and then we went to the Royal British Legion branch and later paraded along the seafront in Southport. I was surprised that many young people turned out to watch us.

I hadn't really bothered about my medals; I had three of them, and they got shoved in a box somewhere and my grandchildren used to play with them, and they eventually got lost.

We later found one, the Atlantic Star, in the garden, and it was only since I have been in the Russian Convoy Club that I got interested in acquiring the medals, and one of the chaps managed to replace the ones I had lost. I also received the Palestine Medal, which is the only one I have with my name and navy number on the rim.

> We sailed from Scapa Flow:
> Seamen, seamen, do not weep,
> It was not you who shagged the sheep
> It was the Gunner's Mate

Sydney Wells, 15 July 2013.

Derek T. Whitwam
HMS *Berwick*

I was born in Huddersfield, West Riding, Yorkshire, on 21 November 1925, the son of Norris and Nellie Whitwam, and had three sisters.

After buying myself out of Huddersfield College at the age of fourteen, I worked for a small cloth manufacturing company until we shifted to Workington where my father had obtained a position as weaving manager for a branch of John Crowther Limited. I spent two years there as an apprentice electrician with a night job working the limes at the local variety theatre from 1800 hrs—2200 hrs, six days a week, which bought in eight shillings and an extra eight shillings bonus per month. After leaving the company, I worked as a timekeeper for High Duty Alloys, who made parts for aircraft.

On 25 May 1943, at the age of seventeen, I had just arrived from Workington at the recruiting centre in Carlisle along with three other lads—two from Kendal and one from Carlisle, and we were all wondering what we'd let ourselves in for. My father's last words as he saw me off still rang in my ears, 'beware of loose women'. We were given a travel warrant—Carlisle to Fareham—leaving on the 2035 hrs train and arriving at Euston at 0533 hrs. We then crossed over to Waterloo by underground to catch the 0727 hrs train in order to arrive at Fareham at 0959 hrs to report to Naval Patrol for transport to the training ship HMS *Collingwood*.

After being given an official number, and being photographed, etc., for our pay book, we were assigned a hut '5X Maintop Division'. Others arrived during the day, all from the London area, about twenty-eight in total. The next few days were taken up with uniform issue and kit, marking the same and learning how to sling a hammock. Unfortunately our travelling companion from Carlisle was sent home as he had lied about his age.

Two or three weeks into our training, on 18 June, a lone German bomber, probably lightening his load before heading home, dropped one bomb which landed on a hut in the row next but one to ours, killing thirty-four recruits and injuring over sixty more. A Leading Seaman was also killed.

Derek Whitwam, 2nd from left, front row of Class Maintop 5X in May 1943. (*Courtesy of Derek Whitwam*)

Eight weeks of seamanship training and square bashing was followed by two weeks of gunnery training. When asked what we wanted to do I opted for motor mechanic training, but after transfer to a camp in Belmont Park, I was told that there were too many doing the course, so it was back to barracks for me. I was then drafted to a camp at Stockheath where I, along with several others, were put into 'Fighter Patrol'; given khaki battledress and did little else all day except Physical Training, unarmed combat with a former all-in wrestler, football, and practising the use of Sten guns.

Following a Tannoy request for volunteers for 'something secret', we were sent to HMS *Heron*, the Naval Air Station at Yeovilton in Somerset, where we passed out after four weeks as Plot Control Ratings 3rd class. After the initial training at HMS *Collingwood* in Fareham, and the four week course in Plot Control at HMS *Heron*, I and three other would-be matelots caught the overnight train to Rosyth and joined our ship, the County-class heavy cruiser HMS *Berwick* (65), which was in dry dock at the time having had a refit. The three others were Vic Cooper from Orsett, Essex, 'Ginger' Thomson from London, and 'Tommo' Thomas from Surrey.

No-one seemed to know what to do with us on arrival, not having had Plot Control ratings before, so they put us in a General Mess. It was quite a secretive affair at the time; we didn't have a badge and were told to wear a W/T (Wireless/Telegraphist) badge. We were given Action Stations firstly on the twin four-inch

Mark H/A AA guns but I wasn't tall enough to lift the shells out of the locker so was transferred onto loading magazines on the twin Oerlikon 20 mm cannons. Some semblance of lateral thinking came when they realised it was rather stupid having us on guns when, in an air raid, we should have been in the Fighter Direction Office doing what we'd been trained to do, supervised by the Fighter Direction Officer, Lieutenant (later Lieutenant-Commander) Allday.

We left Rosyth around the end of November 1943 to Scapa Flow for her working up trials, and that was my first time on the water since having a row on Derwent Water.

We went up to Akureyri, North Iceland. It was a memorable sight with the city lights reflecting in the snow, especially after three years of blackouts in the UK. We left there after twenty-four hours as distant cover for convoy JW-56A. The weather was terrible with howling winds and sixty foot waves and the ship shuddering as it ploughed through the rollers. Luckily I was never seasick. I don't recall it ever being so bad again.

Distant cover was always done by the battleships and heavy cruisers, which were not any good in the convoy against the U-boats, and along with light cruisers, would be in the distance in case the *Tirpitz* came out, which was always a big concern. That big German battleship tied up an awful lot of our ships just on the threat of being around. It didn't have to actually do anything; such was the fear of its might.

The weather was rough up towards the Barents Sea; to give an idea of how high the waves were, the *Berwick* had three sixty-foot tall funnels, and the water was running down inside them. The waves hit the ship with such force that it seemed to just stop, and then move on again. Being on the lower deck, we rarely

Derek Whitwam in 1944. (*Courtesy of Derek Whitwam*)

knew where we actually were. All the officers knew of course, but no-one told us anything, and it was only if one of the officers came and told us, we could have been anywhere.

On Operation 'Goodwood', we were part of the group that went on a raid against the *Tirpitz* with a large fleet which included escort carriers and one or two fleet carriers, and this was when the escort carrier HMS *Nabob* was torpedoed. The weather had closed in and they couldn't fly the aircraft off, so the fleet was divided to go and disappear for a while and refuel, and it was at this point that the submarine fired two torpedoes; one hit the stern of the *Nabob* and one hit and sank the frigate HMS *Bickerton*. The *Nabob* managed to get back to Scapa Flow, but it was never any use after that and was scrapped.

On 5 September, we escorted RMS *Queen Mary* to Canada. She was full of wounded American soldiers from the Landings at Normandy. Winston Churchill was also on board; he was going to attend a conference in Quebec. We went in to Halifax, Nova Scotia, and stayed there for about a week, during which we stocked up on tinned food. The *Queen Mary* went on to New York to drop off all the wounded, and then we escorted her back to Greenock. It was a good trip both ways; we went at around thirty-two knots and the sea was like glass in complete contrast to what we had been used to.

We were in Rosyth at the end of October 1944, and picked up a contingent of Norwegian mountain troops, and took them in convoy JW-61A (as part of the Third Escort Group), to Murmansk, and at the same time we escorted two fast liners, RMS *Empress of Australia* and SS *Scythia*, which held over ten thousand Russians who were being repatriated after being captured in France working for, or in forced labour for, the Germans. There were also around a thousand British troops on board in case of any problems. The Norwegian soldiers, a lot of who escaped from Norway during the earlier part of the war, were largely sea sick on the journey, didn't take their rum rations and so shared it out amongst the rest of the lads in the mess (which was very thankfully received).

The convoy reached the Kola Inlet unscathed by 6 November, and after we reached Murmansk, we had some time ashore around the area. There was nothing much there; duckboards and muddy streets, but then it wasn't that far from the front line, so conditions couldn't have been good for the people there. The Norwegian soldiers disembarked to work with the Russians, going in through the north of Finland and down into Norway to ensure their own sovereignty. We had a visit to the ship by a Russian concert party, consisting of a choir and band. We left with a return convoy (RA-61A) on 11 November.

As soon as the war finished in Europe, we went to Trondheim. The port was being liberated from the Germans. Trondheim Fjord is about thirty miles long, and we were waiting at the inlet for a German ship to come out and take us through the minefield, but nothing turned up. Our skipper decided to go in anyway; the Royal Canadian Navy destroyers HMCS *Haida* and HMCS *Huron* went ahead and we followed on, and we got so far when this large fishing trawler came along. We had eight eight-inch guns and four four-inch guns trained on it. The German admiral of the port got into a little boat and came across to us to surrender the port. It was quite an emotional time and I remember the first church service in Trondheim Cathedral after liberation.

After leaving HMS *Berwick*, I went back to HMS *Collingwood* on 24 July 1945, and then went to the radar school at HMS *Valkyrie* in Douglas, on the Isle of Man, for a ten-week RP2 (Radar Plot Second Class) course. Our billets were a row of boarding houses on the Esplanade. Twice a day we had to march up to the radar school on Douglas Head. This part of the course was eight weeks and included VJ Day. From the Isle of Man to HMS *Heron* , the Fleet Air Arm station in Somerset, for four weeks doing Plotting, Navigation, and the use of anti-submarine plotting tables, and then one week at HMS *Dryad* at Southwick (near Portsmouth) was next, where there were mock-ups of ships' anti-aircraft plots. This was also where Eisenhower had his headquarters for D-Day.

Finally, I went back to HMS *Collingwood,* where on 21 October 1945, I got a draft to Malta sailing from Tilbury on a troop carrying aircraft carrier en route to the Far East, and was then drafted to a minesweeper. I was demobilised in England on 3 June 1946, and I was finally released in Class 'A' on 18 September 1946.

I then went on a three-year adult apprenticeship scheme in the textile industry, and decided in 1948 to move to New Zealand, which took quite a while to sort out, and left the UK in November 1949.

It was a seven-week journey, which was staggered because it was the Christmas and New Year period, and the New Zealand Government didn't want us to arrive until work started on 11 January. It was not an uneventful journey; one chap died when he dived into the swimming pool and broke his neck, two people were taken off the ship before we got here one in Malta and one in Port Said, and we had about twenty or thirty people jailed in Perth, off Freemantle, and we had to bail them out, and after we finally arrived we were more or less straight to work.

I started up and ran sixteen automatic power looms at the Wellington Woollen Manufacturing Company, prior to returning to the UK for five months with my family, and then went back as weaving manager until the mill closed down seven years later.

I then worked for the New Zealand Wool Board, firstly as Woolmark Officer and then as Woolmark Manager until I retired in 1986.

Apart from the odd ferry trip, that was the end of my sea faring days.

Derek Whitwam, Lower Hutt, New Zealand, 7 July 2013.

Alexander Wilson
HMS *Zephyr*

Alexander Gibson Wilson was born on 14 May, 1926, in the small fishing village of Port Seton, to parents John and Margaret. He had one brother, Jack.

I remember visiting the newly completed British light cruiser HMS *Orion* as a child in the early to mid-1930s. A boat took visitors from Port Seton to join the ship for a tour. Being brought up by the sea, when war came, I thought only of joining the Navy.

I was seventeen years old, and joined up in the Edinburgh Music Hall in George Street. My mother didn't know anything about it until afterwards.

I began my basic training at HMS *Ganges* at Shotley, East Suffolk, where, during the whole of the eight week course, we never went outside the gates. Whilst there, I learned basic Seamanship and Gunnery and climbed the famous mast. We also had to go through 'collision training', which consisted of being placed in a steel drum which was then filled with smoke and then filled with water. The idea was to find our way out.

After the training was completed at HMS *Ganges*, I was sent for further training in Chatham where, after being classified as having excellent sight, I was given intensive training on various guns, including the four-and-a-half-inch naval guns and the Bofors anti-aircraft guns. I was also trained in the use of the Rangefinder.

In September 1944, my training complete, I travelled up to Newcastle where my ship, the Zambesi-class destroyer HMS *Zephyr* (R19), had been constructed at the Walker Shipyards. I was part of the first crew on board, and after joining the ship, we sailed up towards an area known as the 'Measured Mile' off St Abb's Head, Berwickshire, for speed trials. Whilst sailing up past the Longstone Lighthouse by the Farne Island, the ship came across an MBG (Motorised Gun Boat) which signalled to the *Zephyr* by an Aldis Lamp: They had a mine attached and didn't know what to do with it. They were told to sink it and report it.

After the initial speed trials, the *Zephyr* sailed to the western side of Scapa Flow to the Lyness Naval (Destroyer) Base, where further trials involved live practice firing during which a tug would be towing a target. My role was to learn how to successfully and safely put shells into the breach of the guns. At this point, HMS *Zephyr* became the Flotilla Leader (first in, Last out) under the command of Captain John Hamilton Allison, DSO, RN.

After extensive trials, the first real action was at the end of October 1944, when the *Zephyr* travelled over to the Norwegian coast as part of a Strike Force to engage German convoys as part of Force Two on Operation 'Hardy'. The Strike Force consisted of the heavy cruiser HMS *Devonshire* (39), the aircraft carriers HMS *Trumpeter* (D09) and HMS *Campania* (D48) and the destroyers HMS *Saumarez* (G12), HMS *Serapis* (G94), and two other Home Fleet destroyers, and was engaged in air mine-laying and shipping strikes. The aircraft from the carriers would take off and attack German coastal installations.

The crew were told by the captain that the RAF were going to try and sink the *Tirpitz* and that their task was to pick up any downed pilots. I can't remember picking up any pilots, but I remember hearing that the *Tirpitz* had been sunk.

My job on board was keeping lookout up on the bridge, which of course, was completely open, and I would sit in the swivel chair using the Rangefinder, often in the company of the captain. It was cold and pretty unpleasant up on the bridge; the funnel would belch out noxious sulphur fumes.

The main part of the *Zephyr*'s role was to escort the merchant ships up to Murmansk and Archangel. We would sail to Iceland where we would be joined

Alexander on board HMS *Zephyr*. (*Courtesy of Alistair Wilson*)

by more ships; a mixture of French, Canadian, Polish destroyers. The *Zephyr*, being Flotilla leader, would be in the outer screen with an inner screen and up to thirty or forty merchant ships being protected. The convoy would travel to Iceland, through the Denmark Strait, Jan Mayen Island, and Bear Island, before sailing on to Murmansk, the White Sea and then Archangel.

During one of these convoys, on New Year's Eve, 1944, I was on 'lookout' on the bridge when he heard and felt a big 'thump'. The alarm bells and 'action stations' were sounded and life belts were put on. The Petty Officer then told us to prepare to abandon ship. Being a good sailor, I couldn't swim, and told the PO. He replied, 'there was never a better time to learn'. A homing torpedo from the German submarine U-1020 had hit the Boiler Room, causing extensive damage.

We were loaded into a twelve foot lifeboat. It was cold and we were all wet, but probably too young to be scared. We couldn't be picked up straight away due to the perceived U-boat threat, and so remained in the water for some time. When we were finally picked up, we were put back on the *Zephyr* which was listing badly, but they managed to tow her back to Scapa Flow, where a patch was welded on and the water pumped out. Petty Officer Wilson had been killed, and the hole in the hull was big enough to put a bus through it. The ship was then towed down to Dundee for repairs where it was met by cheering crowds. It took three months to repair the damage.

Alexander Wilson and his wife Rita, who passed away in December 2011. (*Courtesy of Alistair Wilson*)

On 18 April, following the repairs, the *Zephyr* went on one more convoy (JW-66) to the Kola Inlet, and arrived safely and without incident. Unfortunately, during the return convoy (RA-66) on 29 April 1945, a fourteen strong U-boat pack laid in wait off the Kola Inlet. The Captain-class frigate HMS *Goodall* (K479) of the 19th Escort Group was struck by a torpedo from U-968. I remember first hearing the explosion then seeing the ball of fire as the sky was lit up. The ammunition magazine detonated, and the explosion had blown away the forward part of the ship. There was a heavy loss of men, and the *Zephyr* was unable to assist in the rescue of survivors as only the low-sided vessels were of any use. It was the trawlers and tugs that were able to pick up the men.

HMS *Zephyr* left Rosyth along with the destroyers HMS *Zest* (R02), *Zodiac* (R54) and *Zambesi* (R66), and picked up inshore mine-sweepers in Granton. These were the screen vessels for the cruisers HMS *Birmingham* (C19) and HMS *Dido* (37), which they picked up on 8 May on the passage to Copenhagen to accept the surrender of the German cruisers *Prinz Eugen* and *Nürnberg* following the German armistice. German aircraft circled this convoy and action stations were called. The crew weren't allowed down below for twenty four hours because of torpedo threat. Then, two ships were reported dead ahead which turned out to be Swedish destroyers, and these were quickly followed by hundreds of fishing boats crammed with people waving their hands, flags, and handkerchiefs. It was the end of the war and the flotilla was there to liberate Denmark.

Despite the celebrations, tensions were still running high. As the *Zephyr* sailed passed a German cruiser which failed to salute the Senior Ship (*Zephyr*), the captain gave the order to train every gun and torpedo on the German ship until it eventually saluted by dipping its flag. The ships docked in Copenhagen at the Langelinie Pier. A band played on the pier and the celebrations were joyous. The docks were full of German soldiers being marched down onto the prison ships. News of the Flotilla's arrival spread and hundreds of people began to arrive at the docks. The captain tried and failed to keep them off the boat. I would love to experience it all again.

We spent some time in Copenhagen, touring the city and being escorted by local dignitaries. The city was largely intact although they were shown the remains of a school which had been bombed by British de Havilland Mosquitos by mistake. The intended target, the Gestapo headquarters, lay nearby. I remember the poignant sight of the resistance fighter's bodies lying in the streets covered and buried in flowers.

We then sailed down to North Germany itself where the ship docked in Kiel, the naval base and shipyard site where Germany's deadly 'Wolf Pack' of submarines was born; the city was a major U-boat base and production centre.

It was a tense time, and all the sailors were armed and carried machine guns when on shore. It was in Kiel where a German in a rowing boat attempted to reach the *Zephyr*. I shouted to him to keep back and fired a machine gun to warn

Alexander *en route* to the anniversary of liberation celebrations in Copenhagen in 2006. (*Courtesy of Alistair Wilson*)

him. The German was then shot and taken on board where he was patched up by the doctor. It was 'just a flesh wound', and he was given a bunch of cigarettes and put ashore again.

The City of Kiel was in an appalling state. There had been close to 100 heavy raids by Allied bombers between 1940 and 1944 as it was a high priority target, and eighty per cent of the town's buildings had been destroyed. I felt sympathetic to the German civilian's plight, but fraternising was strictly prohibited although I did shout to a German woman who was pushing a broken pram through the rubble with three children in tow. She was terrified, but I reassured her and gave her cigarettes, coffee, and chocolate for the children.

My memories of the *Zephyr* are happy ones. I had joined her as a Boy Seaman and while I was on board her was promoted to Ordinary Seaman, and then Able Seaman.

She was a happy ship and I had a good bunch of shipmates. One of them was Randolph Turpin, the ship's cook, and the only black sailor on board. I remember him tipping a pan of soup over a sailor who had made a derogatory remark about the colour of his skin. After the war, he became a British Heavyweight Boxing Champion before tragically taking his own life. We all spent a great deal of time together and when not on duty would play 'Uckers' (Ludo) and scrub decks. Gambling was strictly forbidden. Although my quarters were in the worst part of the ship for being seasick, the Forecastle, I never was sick, although I saw many who were. One leading seaman was so seasick he was put back on shore for fear of him dying.

One of the last tasks the *Zephyr* completed was to escort President Truman's ship up the channel when Truman was coming over for the Potsdam conference. It stayed in my memory because Margaret Truman, the president's daughter, was waving to the sailors from the bridge.

HMS *Zephyr*. (*Courtesy of Alistair Wilson*)

After the war, I was sent to 'Laughing Waters', a road house with a small lake close to Cobham Hall in Gravesend, Kent, for 'quiet, relaxing time'. I was later sent to the Ashley Ainsley Hospital in Edinburgh for a short time to be treated for what would nowadays be recognised as Post Traumatic Stress.

I then joined the light fleet aircraft carrier HMS *Ocean* (68), which was going down to the Mediterranean on trials, and ending up in Palestine. I considered Malta as my home port during this time. One of the tasks they performed was dumping all the obsolete Grumman Hellcat aircraft over the side in the Bay of Biscay.

After serving on the *Ocean*, I left the Royal Navy and joined the Merchant Navy for a short time before returning home and working on the steam trawlers for a time before working out of Port Seton on the smaller fishing boats. I then built up a successful fishmongers business in the early 1980s, and ran it for around ten years before selling it on. With all the leisure time I could want at my disposal, I took up golf, but after I broke my hip, I had to slow down.

Alexander Wilson and Alistair Wilson (son), 8 July 2013.

Peter Wright
HMS *Achates*

Lieutenant (E) Peter Alfred Wright was born in Rochford, Essex, in 1910, the son of Henry William and Julia Margaret Wright, and was the eldest of three boys. Henry Wright was the manager of a foundry in Aldgate, the family living in Wanstead when Peter was born, and later moving to 97, Ramuz Drive, Westcliff-on-Sea.

Peter, like many who were on Survivors Leave and preparing for Christmas with his family, would naturally have been disappointed to receive a telegram detailing a forty-eight hour recall to war on 17 December 1942.

Since the end of November, Peter, and the rest of the crew, had left A-class destroyer HMS *Achates* (H12) docked in Gourock, on the Clyde Estuary, to enjoy some well-deserved leave. Now he was considering catching the night train to Liverpool or Newcastle, and then on to North West Scotland to join the fleet bound to protect the merchant convoys headed to Russia. His wife, Madge, and his three year old daughter, Anne, would see him reluctantly leave and return to war. Unbeknown to him, he was leaving another as well; his unborn son, who would be named after him.

His status as the only married officer in the wardroom on HMS *Achates* had earned him the responsibility of vetting all the prospective girlfriends, and his verdicts were always amusing and often libellous, but nonetheless were awaited with keen interest—a reflection made by his old commander, First Lieutenant Loftus Edward Peyton-Jones, in his memoirs in 1993.

The Achates

On 25 July 1941, HMS *Achates*, under command of Lieutenant-commander Viscount Jocelyn, RN, was taking up her position off the Seydisfjord, Iceland, as part of the screen of the carriers which were preparing to launch an air attack during the Kirkenes-Petsamo offensive, when she hit a mine; the explosion blew off everything forward of 'B' gun-deck. The entire fo'c'sle, 'A' gun, mess decks, accommodation for half the ship's company who were asleep at the time of the explosion.

She remained afloat, but sixty-three lives were lost and a further twenty-five suffered injuries. The *Achates* was towed by her sister ship HMS *Anthony* (40), to Seydisfjord for vital repairs before sailing back to the River Tyne where she was fully repaired, and converted for use as an escort destroyer—work which would take eight months to complete.

She was lying up at Swan Hunters yard in Newcastle, where she had been transformed from a wreck into a sleek destroyer, capable of achieving speeds of thirty five knots, and was fitted with the usual armoury including two 4.7-inch guns and four depth charge throwers.

Her new crew were drafted in from all areas of the country including many from Essex and Kent in particular. They were also from all walks of life; one was a forty eight-year-old publican from Colchester.

First Lieutenant Loftus Edward Peyton-Jones arrived in Newcastle to report for duty to find that only three other officers had been appointed to the ship, one of whom was the Chief Engineer, Peter Wright.

Peter was overseeing the 'Articising' of the ship for the cold climates, and escorted Peyton-Jones around his new ship, moving between the noise of drilling, riveting and the flashes of welding lights. The First Lieutenant seemed less than impressed and commented that the ship looked rather depressing. Peter assured him that the work was up to schedule, and would be completed in time for her re-commissioning on 9 April.

Peter Wright. (*Courtesy of Michael Wright*)

Little could they have known at this point that by the end of the year, the friendship they would form would help to save countless lives and their brave actions would lead to Hitler decommissioning almost the entire German naval surface fleet.

Convoy PQ-16

A month later, following her working up at Loch Ewe, and submarine sweeping in the Minch (a channel between the Isle of Lewis and the Scottish mainland), HMS *Achates* was ready for her next call of duty. The crew were all present, and of the officers, only three were 'straight stripers'—regular Navy officers. The rest were Royal Navy Reserves. She joined the Clyde Special Escort Group at Gourock, where, on 21 May 1942, orders were received to proceed to Seydisfjord, Iceland, to join convoy PQ-16 bound for Russia.

After four days at sea protecting the convoy, the first U-boat was identified and later that same evening, the first air attack developed. After a fairly unsuccessfully synchronised effort from German bombers and torpedo planes, only one of the merchant ships was disabled, and was subsequently towed back to Iceland.

From then on, U-boats were being spotted patrolling regularly, feeding information about the position of the convoy to German naval command to co-ordinate further attacks by the Luftwaffe. On one occasion, the *Achates* had to take evasive action as two torpedo tracks were spotted heading for the port bow, and to everyone's relief, they missed.

On 27 May, the convoy came under heavy air attack; the 'Stuka' dive-bombers targeting the merchant ships, and scoring a number of hits and many near misses. Fountains of water erupted around the targets and great pillars of smoke told the grim tale of damage sustained. The stricken ships dropped out of line and fell astern, some to be abandoned by their crews as they and their cargoes went to the bottom. Six ships were lost on the convoy. That night the weather drew in and a mist descended on the convoy, making further attacks near impossible. There were sporadic air attacks over the next two days, but no further damage to the convoy was sustained, and it arrived at the Kola Inlet on 30 May.

A few weeks later, HMS *Achates* was ordered home with some senior Russian army officers. She left unescorted, taking a more northerly course and picked up a passage through an iceberg-strewn Arctic Sea that formed the edge of the Polar Cap. First Lieutenant Peyton-Jones recalled that in a jovial attempt to make the Russian officers feel welcome and to 'Russianise' themselves, the officers of the *Achates* decided to rename themselves; Peyton-Jones becoming 'Uno Lectenski Peytonovitch Joneski', whilst Peter Wright became 'Peterov Wrightnokov'. This apparently made the national press.

HMS *Achates* in July 1939. (*Author's Collection*)

Towards the end of the voyage, however, the admiralty ordered the *Achates* to redirect towards the outward convoy PQ-17. The admiralty was panicking after receiving reports of imminent attack from heavy German surface ships (which proved later to be false) and ordered the convoy to scatter. In the event, and just before the *Achates* arrived, the convoy had been attacked by U-boats and aircraft; only eleven out of thirty four ships survived to reach their destination. Due to the disastrous losses, there were no further convoys to Russia until September.

The first indication that there would be a change of scenery for the crew of HMS *Achates* was the arrival on board of bales of tropical uniform. Their destination was Gibraltar, and after a day at sea, it became apparent that they were part of convoy bound for the offensive operation that was the 'Allied Landings of North Africa'. The news served to raise the spirits of the crew; after three years of mainly defensive operations, the allies were finally on the offensive. In total, 350 merchant ships, over 200 warships, and 1,000 aircraft were involved.

The passage went undetected by U-boats, and the warmer weather and calm seas led to a much more relaxed atmosphere on board HMS *Achates*. While much of the convoy headed for Gibraltar to refuel and prepare for the African Assault, the *Achates* continued to escort carriers that were carrying Hurricanes and Spitfires to replenish the Garrison at Malta.

It was during this duty that the *Achates* came into contact with her first U-boat. After spotting a submarine placing itself horizontally to the fleet in preparation for attack, the *Achates* altered course and gave chase, setting a full set of depth charges. After returning to the area there was no evidence of an explosion but there was noted 'a strong smell of diesel in the area'.

The crew enjoyed a short break after their journey back to Gibraltar, and on 6 November 1942, they set sail with a huge armada of warships to patrol the North African coast for threat of U-boat attacks, and four days later, the mission was declared a success.

On 31 December 1942, HMS *Achates* was escorting convoy JW-51B in the Barents Sea with two light cruisers: *HMS Jamaica* and HMS *Sheffield*, and four O-class destroyers: HMS *Orwell, Oribi, Obedient*, and *Obdurate*, when the convoy came under attack of a German force comprising heavy cruisers *Lützow, Admiral Hipper* and six Z-class destroyers.

In the prevailing twilight of those latitudes, the fighting was rather confused. HMS *Achates* was hit by unidentified opponents from 0930 hrs, and then, from 1130 hrs, the *Admiral Hipper* landed several salvoes on her. The heavy shells, exploding on impact; deadly splinters cut holes into the hull and the port side was riddled with openings, many below the water line.

As Loftus Peyton-Jones made his way to the bridge, he experienced the horrific scene of stepping over the wounded or dead in the passageways. An immediate problem was that the ship's lighting had been off since the last explosion had destroyed much of the electrics. Peter Wright had rigged up some emergency

HMS *Achates* lying severely damaged in Seydisfjord on the east coast of Iceland. She hit a mine on her way from Scapa Flow to Iceland, en route to Norway and Finland. (*Courtesy of Peter Nicol*)

lighting to assist the ship's doctor, MacFarlane, in seeing to the wounded, and additionally to aid his own task of somehow stopping the inevitable flooding. The survival of the boat was reliant on quick effective repair parties, and this responsibility was given to Peter to co-ordinate.

The most critical job for the repair parties was to plug the holes, which varied from an inch to a foot in size. From the larger holes the water was flowing as a solid stream. Ironically the work was slowed as the men had to pull away the installation attached to the steel plating of the hull that had been fitted to help insulate the ship in the freezing Arctic conditions. The worst of the flooding was in the mess deck and an electric pump was set up in an attempt to deal with this. Not long afterwards, however, the pump was seen not to be really effective, and the decision was made to close the hatches and shore up the bulkheads, which in turn closed the mess deck altogether. At this point the ship was now starting to list to port with the added weight of flooding.

In the memoirs of Loftus Peyton-Jones, he recalled that Peter Wright appeared on the bridge to report the damage to his new captain, which was not encouraging. The No. 2 boiler room was flooded and three more of the lower deck compartments were filling up with water.

Peter then informed his captain that a shell had also torn a gaping hole in the ship's side before exploding in the seamen's bathroom, killing many of the crew.

Peyton-Jones contemplated his options, trying to think of anything he could do to help Peter Wright in his fight to control the flooding but did not at that stage regard the position as critical as it had in fact become.

Peter reported to Peyton-Jones that although the fight was still going on, it was no longer possible to maintain steam in No. 1 boiler, the only one left. Using the battered box lamp, Peyton-Jones signalled to the trawler *Northern Gem*, that the ship was out of control, and to stand by.

The list to port became critical, and as Peyton-Jones came to terms with the reality of the situation, he ordered the men to prepare the lifeboats and rafts for launching, but the *Achates* started a slow roll onto her port side; those on deck were forced to clamber onto the side of the ship. She was now completely on her beams ends and water was gushing into her funnels, ventilator outlets, doors and hatches. She was dying.

The *Achates* slowly went further over until she was floating completely bottom up; her rudders and propellers in the air. Men slid down her side and into the water, her keel now pointing to the heavens. They were in dire peril as they started to swim towards the *Northern Gem* in the freezing water.

The *Achates* sank about 135 nautical miles east-south-east of Bear Island, taking 112 men to the bottom with her, including my grandfather, Peter Wright. Eighty-one survivors were picked up from the freezing water.

Michael Wright, 26 July 2013.

The *Franche Comte*

The 9,314-ton MV/Tanker *Franche Comte* was built as the Dutch *Loosdrecht*, and in 1939 was renamed *Franche-Comté* for the Société Française de Transports Pétrolièrs (SFTP), Paris. In 1940, she was taken over by Britain and renamed *Franche Comte* by the Ministry of War Transport. On 16 March 1941, she was torpedoed by U-99 (Otto Kretschmer) while on convoy HX-112.

Leonard George Hutt 4th Engineer

Leonard 'Len' Hutt was born in Fulham, London, on 4 July 1916, the son of Harry and Dorothy, and was one of six children; five boys and one girl. During the war his parents and his sister Audrey lived in Shepherd's Bush. Of his brothers, Harry served in the Royal Engineers in Iceland and then Italy, Frank served in the RASC (Home Forces and then later in North Africa and Italy). Dennis served in the RASC in north-west Europe; James in the REME in the Middle East (Egypt).

Len began his service with the Merchant Navy on 15 April 1939, and served continuously until 3 January 1943, which is when records indicate that he left the sea and served in the army. However, on 18 April 1944, he was back at sea and serving on the single-screw steel oil tanker SS *Pass of Ballater*, which took part in convoy ETC-5 (thirty six vessels including their escort), which left Southend-on-Sea, Essex, on 9 June 1944, and arrived at Seine Bay, France, two days later. The ETC series of convoys ran between June and November, and was the reverse of the FTM series.

Len recounted an incident involving an attack on the tanker *Franche Comte* in March 1941 while sailing in Convoy HX-112 during which they were torpedoed by U-99 (commanded by Otto Kretschmer). This turned out to have been one of the German captain's last actions, as on the following day he was himself attacked and forced to the surface before sinking although Kretschmer and all but three of his crew survived.

Franche Comte. (Courtesy of Graham Hutt)

I had been at sea for two-and-a-half years, working up from 6th Engineer on the MV *British Valour* from 13 December 1939, to 5th Engineer on the MS *Rosewood* until August 1940.

In March 1941, I was serving as 4th Engineer on board the Motor Vessel *Franche Comte*, which was one of the biggest tankers afloat in those days. It had been captured from the Germans when France fell and was sailing under the British flag, and was manned by a crew of about forty hands with seven engineers, all of whom were English with the exception of the Chief Engineer who was a Frenchman.

After a few days out of England, we knew we were going south because it was getting very warm, so at least we were not in the North Atlantic where all the action was. We kept going south and we all thought it was the Middle East we were bound for, but we must have turned left because we were heading for South America. We finally arrived at our heading port, Trinidad, to take on 17,000 tons of oil. We were all praying it was not high octane and our luck held; crude oil was our cargo and we all knew that crude took some time before it ignited.

We were made very welcome by the people in Trinidad and a lot of Yanks wanted to buy us drinks but we were warned against spies and such like. We loaded up and made our way out again, this time we knew we had to join a convoy. Two days out, we met up with the convoy en route to the UK.

We knew we were in for a hot time in the Atlantic but in those days things did not scare me easily and I don't know whether I was stupid or just brave—I will never know and don't want to anyway. I told my assistant the 7th Engineer not to walk about with his hands in his pockets. I said to him if we get hit he would want his two hands to grab hold of something. How true this advice would turn out to be.

At 2330 hrs on 14 March, during an attack on the convoy by enemy submarines, the *Franche Comte* was struck by shell fire that holed her in the No. 1 Port Tank; the damage caused being a shell hole through plating about four feet above water line. Luckily no cargo was being carried in this tank so nothing was lost. It was afterwards ascertained that the shot that struck us was fired by the MV *Auris*.

However, three ships had been lost from the convoy and we were told there was a Wolf pack of U-boats around. They used to hunt in packs and attack a convoy all at the same time. I suppose that gave our escort vessels a headache because while they were attacking one U-boat, another would be going in and doing the damage, and so on. This went on for three nights we were all keeping our fingers crossed.

On the fourth night (16 March) it happened. I had just taken over the 0000 hrs—0400 hrs watch in the engine room and had the 7th Engineer with me when at around 0030 hrs, I got a message from the bridge to jump up the revs (that means go a bit faster). I could not increase speed unless ordered from the Chief Engineer, but as I could not contact him. I increased speed on my own back

Pages from Leonard Hutt's Discharge book (*Courtesy of Graham Hutt*)

anyway, and we were going full out when I felt and heard a tremendous explosion and immediately realised that the ship had been torpedoed.

I don't know where it had hit us but I was bloody glad it was not in the engine room or I would not be writing this now.

The firemen cleared out of the Engine Room but I remained there with the 7th Engineer. As soon as the explosion occurred I stopped the engines, as I thought that was the proper thing to do. I had only stopped them for a few seconds, when the engines were rung to 'stop' from the bridge. My next thought was to turn the boiler off (as I have said before I don't know if I was stupid or brave).

I remained standing by for two or three minutes when somebody shouted down to the Engine room telling us to come up. I immediately went up on to the deck. At this time it was pitch dark, and there was a good swell running and the weather was fairly fine. The *Franche Comte's* cargo of boiler oil was well alight. She had been torpedoed forward on the starboard side and it looked as if the whole ship was on fire from the bridge to the forecastle head and explosions were occurring which were very loud and which we thought were other torpedoes hitting the ship.

I saw that the crew had already started to get away from the ship. One boat was in fact full up and was leaving the ship. The second boat had about seventeen men in it and the only people remaining on the ship were the captain and the mate (who were on the bridge), the Donkey-man and me. As soon as I got on deck, the captain asked me if I would go below again and shut off the condenser as the ship was discharging water from the starboard side which would have made the lowering of the starboard lifeboat dangerous. I immediately went below with the Donkey-man and shut off the condenser so that no water was going over the side of the ship.

I went back to the deck and by this time only the captain was left there; everyone else was in the lifeboats. The captain told me to get into the boat and he immediately followed me. To get into the boat we had to get down a ladder, as the boat was now in the water.

As soon as we were on board, the boat left the side of the ship. Where there was only the black of night was now lit by our burning ship and others. I remember a dark object coming towards us and only then was I really scared. I thought it was a German U-boat coming to spray us with fire or take us aboard as prisoners. I don't know which would have been the worse but it turned out to be a British destroyer. We rowed towards it and were picked up. Out came the rum, and one chap gave me a cupful which I gulped it down but could not hold it, and up it came. It must have been the shock coming out.

The crew went aft into the men's quarters of the destroyer and the officers went into the ward room. The destroyer immediately set off to chase the U-boat that had been attacking the convoy.

We were only down below about five minutes when word reached us that our ship was still afloat and although she appeared to be settling down and she was well down by the head, listing to starboard badly, somebody suggested going back to it. I was not feeling very well as I was suffering from the shock but I and other officers volunteered to try and go back. The captain of the destroyer gave us three minutes to get off his ship, so we went back to the lifeboat with volunteers including me, our captain and chief engineer.

We went up on deck and twelve of us, including the captain, got into one of our own life boats and were towed by the destroyer towards the *Franche Comte*. It was now a moonlight night and we could see fairly well. The ship was still on fire forward and flames were coming out of the forward tanks. She seemed to be settling down further by the head and she was creaking very badly. We stood off about ten to fifteen yards from the starboard side and the captain said he did not think it was advisable to try and go on board and we agreed with him.

Then we saw an armed trawler. I believe that arrangements had been made for this Trawler to stand by in case we got on board again, but I do not know this for a fact. When we realised that we could not get on board our ship, we rowed towards the trawler and were taken on board and we remained there until about 0830 hrs, with the trawler standing by the *Franche Comte*.

At this time we decided to try and board her once again and we all got into our own boats and rowed to her and boarded. The fire was out. She was well down by the head and the fire had been put out by the seas breaking over her. We all climbed aboard and, believe it or not, the ship's cat was waiting for us. He was the only one who never abandoned ship. The engines of the ship are aft and it looked to me as if the propeller was out of the water. I went down into the Engine Room. It was dry and appeared to be in order.

As well as the twelve men from the *Franche Comte*, we had six volunteers from another ship. These men were all survivors who had been rescued by HMS *Bluebell* from a vessel that had been torpedoed. Once on board, some of the volunteers helped us to get up steam, which took about ninety minutes to two hours to achieve. The captain asked if we were ready, and the Second Engineer asked me to turn the engines over. I went to the controls and carried out my orders and the engines worked satisfactorily and soon we were under way. By now it was somewhere between 0930 hrs and 1000 hrs.

The weather was fine and clear and there was not much sea. The chief engineer did not take a watch on the journey back, so the second, fourth and fifth engineers and I took six hour watches right round the clock.

The ship was so much down by the head that the oil, particularly in the crank case, ran forward and the pressure was too great for the doors of the crank case to hold it and every hour we had to keep blocking up the cracks round the door and notwithstanding this, oil was spurting all over the engine room and the conditions under which we had to work were dreadful.

Owing to the list on the ship, we steamed slowly (at six knots) and it took two days to cover the six hundred miles back to Scotland. HMS *Bluebell* stood by us all the way back, and we were met by a couple of Sunderland flying boats. We had lost 3,000 tons of oil through the hole the torpedo made, but still had 14,000 tons on board.

We arrived at Rothesay on Friday, 21 March. Tugs had moved towards us and tried to hook on, but the fellows on the deck turned them away; adamant that we would make it alongside by ourselves. Safely alongside, we were hailed as heroes; toasted everywhere we went. Even the schools were bringing their children along to look us over. Three cheers for Captain Church and his brave men. Well I was one of them so I must have been brave, not stupid.

The Captain's report of 26 March 1941 stated that the torpedo had caused heavy and serious damage in the No. 2 Tank, No. 1 Tank, Forward Pump room and No. 3 Tank.

On being picked up (by the destroyer), I immediately went to the bridge to advise the commander of my wish to remain by my vessel until I was satisfied that she was unsalvageable. He told me that he would do so as soon as he had returned to the convoy. When he came back to the lifeboats I ordered the crew to return with me, but I was met with a complete refusal by all the lower ratings. I then called for volunteers to go with me and am pleased to give the following names of those who immediately responded :–

J. J. Spring	Chief Officer
J. Timmes	2nd Officer
G. Rowlandson	3rd Officer
F. Le Roux	Chief Engineer
W. Marshall	2nd Engineer
L. Hutt	4th Engineer
J. G. I. Williams	5th Engineer
F. Pashley	Chief Steward
T. Martin	1st Radio Officer
D. Seymour	2nd Radio Officer
H. Davies	3rd Radio Officer

Patrick O'Sullivan Chief Officer

Patrick Percival O'Sullivan was born in 1911 in the Devonport District of Devon. He was 20 years old when he joined the Merchant Navy.

I was the Chief Officer of the British Steam Tanker HMS *Venetia*, which was carrying over 7,000 tons of maize while a part of the homeward-bound (from Halifax) convoy HX-112. On 16 March 1941, in a position which I estimated to be some 300 miles to the north-westward of the Butt of Lewis in the Outer Hebrides, the *Venetia* was torpedoed and sunk by the German U-boat U-99.

I was rescued with some other members of the crew around two hours later (around midnight) by the British corvette HMS *Bluebell* (K80).

Other vessels had been torpedoed about the same time, amongst them the Norwegian Motor Tankers *Ferm, Beduin,* and *Korshamn* and the Ministry of War Transport Tanker *Franche Comte.*

Early in the morning of the 17 March, there was a call on board for volunteers to attempt the salvage of the *Franche Comte.* Captain Church, the Master of the vessel, and some of his officers (both deck and engine-room), were in a lifeboat to which they had taken after their ship was torpedoed, and the call for volunteers had come from him.

I learned afterwards that all of the *Franche Comte*'s crew had been rescued, but had declined to leave the naval vessel (I believe a destroyer) on to which they had been taken. Captain Church had refused to leave his vessel, had insisted on remaining in the lifeboat and was calling for volunteers because he wanted to go back on board.

I volunteered for the job and I got Messrs. Pillett and Plummer, Able Seamen from the *Venetia* who were also on board the *Bluebell,* to agree to accompany me, together with a Norwegian sailor called Andersen, who came from the *Ferm.*

Very shortly after I had volunteered to go, Mr David Evans, who had been the Third Engineer on the *Venetia*, asked me if he could take my place. He said he wanted to because he was not married and I was, but I told him that I was going and I suggested that he came along too, which he agreed to do.

A request then came for volunteers from the naval men; a gunner was needed to give the *Franche Comte* aerial protection, but nobody offered. Finally an order came from the *Bluebell* for Mr Paul Redgrave to go, and that made up our party of six—myself and the two ABs, Andersen, Mr Evans the Engineer, and the naval gunner.

Without further delay we got into the *Franche Comte*'s lifeboat, where we found Captain Church, his Chief Officer, his Second and Third Officers, his Chief Engineer and two or three Junior Engineers, some Radio Officers and the Chief Steward.

Captain Church asked me to take charge of the men who came from other ships than the *Franche Comte* and I agreed to do so.

It was a pitch dark night; there was a moderate confused swell, which a big steamer would not feel but which made the lifeboat lively, and it was hazy with no wind to speak of.

The *Bluebell* then took the lifeboat in tow and we proceeded towards the *Franche Comte*, the glow from whose fire we saw, of course, long before getting near her.

When we were near enough to see what she looked like, the sight was a terrifying one and the work of salvage appeared to be completely hopeless: for in the night she appeared to be a mass of flames from her bridge right forward to where her forecastle head rose from the forward well-deck.

The fire was particularly fierce on her port side, and in addition, it was plain that her structure had been badly damaged by the torpedo and even in that moderate swell the strain caused by the lack of some of her structure from the bridge to the forecastle, coupled with the heat of the fire, was causing the vessel to make great noises: the bursting of rivets, buckling of plates and frames, in addition of course to the roar of the fire. It looked as if the vessel might at any time explode.

I said to Captain Church that I thought it would be wise not to attempt to board while it was still pitch dark but to wait for sufficient daylight to enable us to see what kind of a job it was that we were proposing to tackle, and Captain Church agreed.

HMS *Bluebell* could not wait, and after ascertaining from us that it would be all right for her to do so, she left our lifeboat with us in it, floating some three hundred yards away from to the *Franche Comte*, and went away. We did not go any closer because of the danger that the vessel, as the fire spread, might capsize in our direction, and there was the further danger of blazing oil spreading over the surface of the water.

A naval trawler, whose name I think was either the *Northland Star* or the *Northland Light*, came alongside us during the night and offered to take our lifeboat up on her davit falls and enable us to spend the hours before day came on the trawler's deck rather than in our lifeboat. We agreed and this was done and then we stood by until first daylight at about 0800 hrs, which enabled us to attempt the job. We all got back into the lifeboat, and proceeded to the Franche Comte to board her.

By good fortune the fire had been contained among only some of her forward tanks, and by the time we went on board was tending to burn itself out, although columns of black smoke and some flames were still coming from the vessel's forward end.

So far as I could subsequently ascertain, the torpedo, which had hit her forward on the port side, had either demolished or fired the oil cargo in six of the vessel's tanks, namely Nos 1, 2 and 3 port and midship tanks. Between her thwart-ship bulkheads the *Franche Comte*'s cargo tanks were sub-divided into three, so that you had No. 1 port, No. 1 midship, and No. 1 starboard, the same with No. 2, 3 and so forth.

As I recollect it, Nos 1, 2 and 3 sets of tanks lay forward of the bridge, the others aft—in the space between the bridge and the engine-room, which as usual in a tanker was right astern. The damage had been done, therefore to the three tanks on the port side forward of the bridge and to the next three inboard of those: while the tanks called Nos 1, 2 and 3 on the starboard side were either not so badly damaged or not damaged at all.

It wasn't possible to do much in the way of inspecting these tanks. The damage caused by both the torpedo and the fire had lead to a very dangerous weakening of the ship's forward structure, and when we started to get under way, the deck plating on what remained of the forward well-deck was buckling and straining dangerously, Every now and then rivets, burst by the strain, shot into the air. However, as far we could see, there was still oil in the three tanks on the starboard side, so we decided to get the engine going again and do our best to navigate.

In the meantime, the trawler who had taken us on board overnight (16/17 March) had gone away and HMS *Bluebell* returned.

We got the *Franche Comte* under way before midday on 17 March. The *Bluebell* was back by this time; and she accompanied us, but at no time gave us a tow all the time until we entered into the safety of Rothesay Bay in the River Clyde, which we did on 21 March 1941, at about 1430 hrs.

During the voyage of 500 miles or thereabouts from the position where we boarded her till the time she got to Rothesay Bay, the navigation of the *Franche Comte* was difficult and slow.

The condition of her forecastle, or rather the weakening of the structure between the forecastle and the rest of the ship, made it impossible, of course, to navigate at any speed; our average was about four knots. In addition, the hole on her port side tended to throw her bows off: so that most of the time we had to navigate with the helm hard over: and this brought extra strain on the very few men who were responsible for the navigation of the vessel.

The engine-room staff was, of course, greatly undermanned, allowing very little time for rest. The same was just as true—if not more—about the deck. The *Franche Comte*'s navigating officers kept their usual watches; but those of us who volunteered from the *Venetia* (including Mr Anderson) had to act as reliefs, sailors, helmsmen, and generally to do everything that was required with perhaps four hours on and two hours off, or two hours on and two hours off, throughout the whole time.

Indeed, Mr Pillett was so exhausted towards the end of the voyage that when an emergency arose in the Clyde and he was at the wheel, he fainted. He was in any event not a very strong man; the emergency was a combination of a sudden failure of the telemotor steering (due, I think, to the stain it had been subjected to owing to continued navigation with the helm hard over) and a fusing of the electric lights.

She was yawing badly the whole way. Early on during the voyage the lifeboat, which we had tied up with a brand-new boat's fall astern of the *Franche Comte*, was swung adrift and we lost her during one of the yaws. It was not possible to get her on deck or into the davits because one of the effects of the torpedoing had damaged the return lines of the deck steam service, rendering it impossible to use any of the steam gear on deck.

There was no other lifeboat on board the Franche Comte, and if rough weather had come up, I have no doubt at all in my mind that she would have been unable to weather it.

The services to the *Franche Comte* lasted for a period of approximately five days and nights. During the time the steering gear failed when we were going up the Clyde, which was on the night of 20 March; she was going round in circles, and part of the arc of that circle lay over the minefield.

During the voyage the *Bluebell* came alongside us because she had run short of stores; this occurred at 1400 hrs on 19 March. At that time another naval gunner was ordered on board us. Several times during the tow the *Bluebell* was dropping depth charges and taking other anti-submarine action.

After anchoring, I remained on board the *Franche Comte* until the following Tuesday, 25 March, when I was relieved by order of the Ministry of War Transport; I went to the office of the *Venetia*'s owners, to whom I made a report of the loss of my own vessel and the salvage of the *Franche Comte*.

Captain Church received, I understand, the OBE for his services; I received a mention in Dispatches.

Patrick went on to serve on the frigate HMS *Bann* from 22 March 1943 until October 1944.

Francis Rowland Pashley, Chief Steward

I was serving as Chief Steward on board the *Franche Comte* when she was torpedoed. When she was actually struck, I was walking aft along the flying bridge. The first I knew was the shudder on the ship, and the flash of the explosion, and then oil began to fall all around, and she burst into flames.

I was going to put provisions in the lifeboats when the Master going told me to go to the starboard lifeboat. Once loaded, we cast off.

I was one of the volunteer crew who went back on board the ship, and we set off to do this in the early morning with one boat. When we came up alongside her port side however, it was decided we should not then board her, after some discussion between the Master and the Officers. We then boarded the trawler to await daylight.

We boarded the ship at 0900 hrs and I came home with her. I was the only one from my department who had volunteered, and I carried on myself until we arrived in Rothesay, the Radio Officers and others giving me a hand as might be necessary with the additional work which was thrown on me.

F. R. Pashley, 29 August 1941.

Gordon Rowlandson, 3rd Officer

I was Third Officer on board the *Franche Comte*, and was on board her at the time she was torpedoed. My watch that night was from 2000 hrs until midnight, when I was on the bridge as Officer of the watch, with a man at the wheel and a man on the lookout.

The night was dark but clear, and a safe night for navigating. We knew submarines were about, and at 2355 hrs that night, without any warning, the vessel was struck with a torpedo on the port side. The first I knew of it was seeing a violent flash, and then hearing a swishing noise and immediately afterwards oil began to fall and the ship burst into flames about abreast of the foremast on the port side.

The effect of the torpedo was that it tore a huge opening in the ship's side, and burst the deck in two around the centre, throwing a large volume of oil into the air. The whole of the front of the ship was instantaneously enveloped in flames, and there was nothing to be seen ahead at all. The flames from the hole in her side were reaching the bridge, which also caught fire with the oil which had fallen on it as a result of the explosion.

The Master came on the bridge at once. I was on the starboard wing, which even at that time was very uncomfortable with heat and smoke. The master said to me, 'Where has she been struck?', and I replied, 'on the port side in way of No. 2 tank'. I had judged this from the point at which I had seen the flash. The Master left me without saying anything further—where he went I don't know—and I was driven off the bridge at once. I tried to go down the ladder on the starboard side, but could not do so for the flames there, and I had to jump from the bridge onto the deck through the flames, and make my way aft. The deck was covered with oil.

I went into my room and got some things, and then made my way aft along the fore and aft bridge to the lifeboats, which were on our quarter. The mid-ship lifeboat on the port side was damaged.

I got into the boat on the port side with the Chief Officer. At that time I had no conversation with the Master, and did not know what had been arranged, but when we reached the water and we had all got into the boat, the painter was cut and we stood off. The reason the painter was cut was that we were lying right under the ship's counter, and with the sea breaking on board we were all being covered with oil on the water coming from the wound in her side.

We approached her at 0200 hrs the following morning, all in one boat as a volunteer crew. We went along her port side to see what she was like, and to arrive at a decision as to whether we should board her then as we had intended to do when we came up to her. At that time her foredeck had the seas breaking over it, and although the fire was burning out, she looked highly dangerous, and we were all of the one opinion namely, that it would be unsafe to board her in the darkness when we could not see really definitely what her condition was, and that we should stand by till daybreak. From what we could see of her, it looked as if she might go at any minute.

We all said to one another, 'Well what do you think of going on board?' We were all agreed that it would be unwise in the circumstances to board her. The Master was of that opinion also. I boarded her with the others later that morning at 0900 hrs and brought her in.

I have heard the statement of the Second Officer, and subject to what I say above, I entirely agree with what he has said.

John Richard Weston Timms, 2nd Officer

I was the Second Officer on board the *Franche Comte* at Cardiff. The *Franche Comte* was a single screw oil driven motor ship that was built in 1936 in Denmark, and was previously a French ship but was taken over and was being run by the Ministry of War Transport. She was 483.9 feet in length and grossed 9,314 tons.

In February 1941, we sailed from Trinidad bound for the United Kingdom. On the night of 16 March 1941, we were proceeding off the south of Iceland, about 700 miles from the United Kingdom, in a convoy of about fifty ships, and were the fourth ship in the third column counting from the port side convoy. The night was very dark, but clear, with a moderate wind and some swell and we were steaming without lights.

At around 2355 hrs, while Third Officer Rowlandson was on watch, the vessel was torpedoed; struck on the port side forward in-way of No. 2 tank. We were loaded with about 14,000 tons of fuel oil for the Admiralty. The result of the torpedoing was that it blew part of the side completely out of the ship and part of the deck from the aft end of No. 1 tank to and including the pump room.

The oil was blown in considerable volume over the ship and the result was that fire immediately broke out and the ship began to settle forward. Flames were leaping out from the side and whatever oil had fallen on the ship it was burning. The foredeck was all ablaze as was also the front of the bridge and the bridge itself and upper works which were all covered with oil.

Looking to the way she was settling and the extent of the fire, none of us had any doubt that she was going to founder there and then. There was no order given from the Master so far as I am aware regarding leaving the ship, but the vessel was in such a state with fire, and with the damage on her side, everyone thought she was going to founder and naturally went to the lifeboats.

I was in the saloon at the time with the Master. He went to the Bridge and when I saw what it was like went to my boat. I could not leave the saloon in the ordinary way because of the fire raging outside and left it to go to the boat by going down to another deck and outside by the Master's accommodation.

Two of our lifeboats were aft. There was also one on our port side but it had been damaged by the explosion and I went to the starboard lifeboat at the stern. The vessel was then well down by the head, by the angle walking along the deck to the lifeboat. Having satisfied ourselves that everybody was there the boats were lowered into the water. I was in the boat with the Master, and the Chief Officer was in the other.

The Master and the Officers had some discussion as to whether we should remain where we were or whether we should clear away from her altogether in case, in the condition in which she was in she would serve as a beacon to another submarine and that another torpedo might be delivered at the stern involving ourselves, as well, and it was decided that we should cast off and stand by clear of her until day-break to see how she was and if anything could be done with her. We could not in any event lie alongside her as the sea was coming on board and we were being covered with oil. It was extremely difficult to see what damage she had sustained in the darkness. The fire was still blazing from the tear in her side as well as from her deck and bridge. The whole sea was lit up for miles with the blaze.

The position is that we all left the vessel thinking she was bound to founder but at the same time to stand by in case at daylight we might be able to save her.

Whilst standing by, a submarine chaser came alongside. She had been one of the escorting ships. The commanding officer ordered us to board his vessel, and after speaking with the Master, came to the wardroom where all the Officers were.

He said that he thought the ship was salvageable and asked if anyone was willing to go on board with him to try and take her in. J. J. Spring, Chief Officer, myself, G. Rowlandson, Third Officer, F. Le Roux Chief Engineer, W. Marshall, Second Engineer, L. Hutt, Fourth Engineer, J. Williams, Fifth Engineer, F. Pashley, Chief Steward, T. Martin, First Radio Officer, D. Seymour, Second Radio Officer and H. Davies, Third Radio Officer, all volunteered.

I went forward with the Third officer to get some of the Firemen and seamen to volunteer but none of them would do so. The submarine chaser then took us to one of the lifeboats which we boarded. We attempted to row back to our own vessel but could not do so because of the wind and sea and insufficient pulling power. A corvette which had arrived was instructed by the chaser to stand by and she proceeded to go after the convoy.

The corvette came alongside and we asked her whether she could give us any men. She had some members of the crew of another ship on board and six of these men volunteered and joined us in the lifeboat. We had a second lifeboat in tow, but we let it go. She towed us part of the way towards our own ship and we rowed the rest and came alongside her about 0200 hrs. We came up on the port side. At this time the fire was out on her side and forward deck as the water was then washing over it, but the bridge was still burning although the fire was dying down. There was a good deal of noise from her also with her plates grinding as she worked in the sea-way. Having taken a good look at her we all thought she was still settling and was bound to go and we decided to stand off and not board her until daylight when her condition could be better seen. I cannot say there was any conversation between the Master and the Officers with regard to re-boarding her.

The decision not to re-board her was a decision arrived at by us all saying so after seeing and hearing her and exchanging views. We all thought that it was unsafe to go on board her. Nobody suggested that we should go on board her and no one objected.

If the Master says he was prepared to board her and we were unwilling to board her I cannot agree with him. I am quite satisfied that he was of the same mind as us at that time, that it was unsafe to board her.

We, accordingly, lay off to wait until daylight but an armed trawler came alongside and we boarded her. I do not know where the corvette was. She had disappeared. The trawler stood by until daylight, and at 0900 hrs we boarded the lifeboat again, having decided to go on board. At that time her foredeck from the forecastle to the bridge was awash with the seas breaking over it. There was an enormous tear in her port side and the deck was burst to about amidships in way of it. She was standing about upright. The fire in the bridge was out. The heavy fuel oil does not burn so violently as a lighter oil, and the result was that the bridge was standing fairly well intact although substantially burned.

On looking at her then it was apparent that No. 1 port tank and No. 1 centre, No. 2 port and No. 2 centre, and the pump room were all open to the sea with No. 3 port tank as well.

We examined her and we came to the conclusion that we might be able to get her in if the weather held. At that time there was a considerable south westerly swell but no sea, with a light wind. We raised steam on her and at 1125 hrs we put her under way at a very slow speed. There were on board myself and the other officers I have mentioned and six of the crew of the other torpedoed ship, eighteen against her normal compliment of forty-five. We towed the lifeboat astern for a bit but it was swamped later and we thereafter had no lifeboats.

The corvette which had been detailed to stand by and which we had lost for a time was standing by when we proceeded with her and she preceded us. Our compasses were out of order with the explosion and the corvette gave us the course. We followed the course she gave us for some three days and when we came within striking distance of land she then told us what to do again. The weather freshened on the afternoon, about 1600 hrs on 20 March to a gale. Until then the deck on the starboard side in way of the damage on the port side had been level, but when the wind freshened she was pitching and rolling and the deck began to buckle on the starboard side in way of the damage. We had been coming along at a speed of about four to five knots, but adjusting this on the revolutions of the engines to whatever the conditions might be and not by the engine room telegraph.

We eased her down to begin with but as she still continued to buckle we increased the speed again in an attempt to get her in as quickly as possible. We thought there was serious risk of her breaking altogether if left any longer in bad weather and that to drive her faster was the lesser risk.

The weather continued bad into the evening when it again moderated and we brought her into the Clyde and put her in Rothesay Bay on 21 March between 1400 hrs and 1500 hrs. The vessel was down by the head and sheering badly all the way and was difficult to handle. The deck was considerably buckled by the time we got there.

All the way back none of us were really ever off watch being always at hand in case we were wanted in daytime, although at night we turned in if we thought conditions were no worse than they had been through the day.

My view is that had the vessel not been picked up and brought in as promptly as she was, she would have broken her back, and become a total loss. I don't think she would have lived long in weather much worse than we had on 20 March. The wind was blowing a gale of force about eight, with a rough sea and a heavy westerly swell, but I think that had she been left in an open sea with any sea running at all she could not have stood up to it looking to the enormous tear there was on her side and the consequent weakening of her around that area.

Graham Hutt, June 2013.

List of Arctic Convoys

1941

Outbound		Homebound	
Dervish	departed Hvalfjord, Iceland August 21; arrived Archangel, Russia, August 31		
PQ 1	departed Hvalfjord September 29; arrived Archangel October 11	QP 1	departed Archangel September 28; arrived Scapa Flow, Scotland October 10
PQ 2	departed Liverpool, England, October 13; arrived Archangel October 30		
PQ 3	departed Hvalfjord November 9; arrived Archangel November 22	QP 2	departed Archangel November 3; arrived Kirkwall, Scotland November 17
PQ 4	departed Hvalfjord November 17; arrived Archangel November 28		
PQ 5	departed Hvalfjord November 27; arrived Archangel December 13	QP 3	departed Archangel November 27; dispersed, arrived December 3
PQ 6	departed Hvalfjord December 8; arrived Murmansk, Russia December 20		
PQ 7a	departed Hvalfjord December 26; arrived Murmansk January 12, 1942	QP 4	departed Archangel December 29; dispersed, arrived January 9

PQ 7b	departed Hvalfjord December 31; arrived Murmansk January 11		

1942

Outbound		Homebound	
PQ 8	departed Hvalfjord January 8; arrived Archangel January 17	QP 5	departed Murmansk January 13; dispersed, arrived January 19
Combined PQ 9 and PQ 10	departed Reykjavík, Iceland February 1; arrived Murmansk February 10	QP 6	departed Murmansk January 24; dispersed, arrived January 28
PQ 11	departed Loch Ewe, Scotland February 7; departed Kirkwall February 14; arrived Murmansk February 22	QP 7	departed Murmansk February 12; dispersed, arrived February 15
PQ 12	departed Reykjavík March 1; arrived Murmansk March 12	QP 8	departed Murmansk March 1; arrived Reykjavík March 11
PQ 13	departed Reykjavík March 20; arrived Murmansk March 31	QP 9	departed Kola Inlet, Russia March 21; arrived Reykjavík April 3
PQ 14	departed Oban, Scotland March 26; arrived Murmansk April 19	QP 10	departed Kola Inlet April 10; arrived Reykjavík April 21
PQ 15	departed Oban April 10; arrived Murmansk May 5	QP 11	departed Murmansk April 28; arrived Reykjavík May 7
PQ 16	departed Reykjavík May 21; arrived Murmansk May 30	QP 12	departed Kola Inlet May 21; arrived Reykjavík May 29

Outbound		Homebound	
PQ 17	departed Reykjavik June 27; dispersed, arrived July 4	QP 13	departed Arkhangelsk June 26; arrived Reykjavík July 7
	(August sailing postponed)		(August sailing postponed)
PQ 18	departed Loch Ewe September 2; arrived Archangel September 21: first convoy with aircraft carrier escort (HMS *Avenger*)	QP 14	departed Archangel September 13; arrived Loch Ewe September 26
	(PQ cycle terminated)	QP 15	departed Kola Inlet November 17; arrived Loch Ewe November 30
Operation FB	sailings by independent unescorted ships		(QP cycle terminated)
JW 51A	departed Liverpool December 15; arrived Kola Inlet December 25		
JW 51B	departed Liverpool December 22; arrived Kola Inlet January 4, 1943	RA 51	departed Kola Inlet December 30; arrived Loch Ewe January 11

1943

Outbound		**Homebound**	
JW 52	departed Liverpool January 17; arrived Kola Inlet January 27	RA 52	departed Kola Inlet January 29; arrived Loch Ewe February 9
JW 53	departed Liverpool February 15; arrived Kola Inlet February 27	RA 53	departed Kola Inlet March 1; arrived Loch Ewe March 14
	(cycle postponed through summer)		(cycle postponed through summer)
JW 54A	departed Liverpool November 15; arrived Kola Inlet November 24	RA 54A	departed Kola Inlet November 1; arrived Loch Ewe November 14

JW 54B	departed Liverpool November 22; arrived Archangel December 3	RA 54B	departed Archangel November 26; arrived Loch Ewe December 9
JW 55A	departed Liverpool December 12; arrived Archangel December 22	RA 55A	departed Kola Inlet December 22; arrived Loch Ewe January 1, 1944
JW 55B	departed Liverpool December 20; arrived Archangel December 30	RA 55B	departed Kola Inlet December 31; arrived Loch Ewe January 8

1944

Outbound		Homebound	
JW 56A	departed Liverpool January 12; arrived Archangel January 28		
JW 56B	departed Liverpool January 22; arrived Kola Inlet February 1	RA 56	departed Kola Inlet February 3; arrived Loch Ewe February 11
JW 57	departed Liverpool February 20; arrived Kola Inlet February 28	RA 57	departed Kola Inlet March 2; arrived Loch Ewe March 10
JW 58	departed Liverpool March 27; arrived Kola Inlet April 4	RA 58	departed Kola Inlet April 7; arrived Loch Ewe April 14
	(escorts only to Murmansk)	RA 59	departed Kola Inlet April 28; arrived Loch Ewe May 6
	(cycle postponed through summer)		(cycle postponed through summer)
JW 59	departed Liverpool August 15; arrived Kola Inlet August 25	RA 59A	departed Kola Inlet August 28; arrived Loch Ewe September 5

JW 60	departed Liverpool September 15; arrived Kola Inlet September 23	RA 60	departed Kola Inlet September 28; arrived Loch Ewe October 5
JW 61	departed Liverpool October 20; arrived Kola Inlet September 28	RA 61	departed Kola Inlet November 2; arrived Loch Ewe November 9
JW 61A	departed Liverpool October 31; arrived Murmansk November 6	RA 61A	departed Kola Inlet November 11; arrived Loch Ewe November 17
JW 62	departed Loch Ewe November 29; arrived Kola Inlet December 7	RA 62	departed Kola Inlet December 10; arrived Loch Ewe December 19
JW 63	departed Loch Ewe December 30; arrived Kola Inlet January 8, 1945	RA 63	departed Kola Inlet January 11; arrived Loch Ewe January 21

1945

Outbound		**Homebound**	
JW 64	departed Clyde, Scotland February 3; arrived Kola Inlet February 15	RA 64	departed Kola Inlet February 17; arrived Loch Ewe February 28
JW 65	departed Clyde March 11; arrived Kola Inlet March 21	RA 65	departed Kola Inlet March 23; arrived Loch Ewe April 1
JW 66	departed Clyde April 16; arrived Kola Inlet April 25	RA 66	departed Kola Inlet April 29; arrived Clyde May 8
JW 67	departed Clyde May 12; arrived Kola Inlet May 20	RA 67	departed Kola Inlet May 23; arrived Clyde May 30

Glossary

ASDIC comes from the Anti-Submarine Detection Investigation Committee, and was the primary underwater detection device that located objects submerged in water by echolocation, and was used by Allied escorts throughout the war

ATS Auxiliary Territorial Service for women who acted as drivers, worked in mess halls, acted a cleaners, and they worked on anti-aircraft guns; aircraft tracking, and fusing shells.

Beaufort Scale is an empirical measure that relates wind speed to observed conditions at sea or on land

Bevin Boys were young British men chosen at random, and conscripted to work in the coal mines of the United Kingdom, from December 1943 until 1948

CAM (ship) Catapult Armed Merchantman

Carley Raft or Carley Float was an oval-shaped lightweight reversible life-raft comprising of a frame of copper or steel tubing which was surrounded by a canvas covering over a cork-like material, and would remain afloat even if punctured

Civvies are civilian clothes as opposed to a uniform

CO Commanding Officer

Dan layers were usually small trawlers, fitted for the purpose of laying dans, which were marker buoys which consists of a long pole moored to the seabed and fitted to float vertically, usually with a coded flag at the top.

Donkeyman was the nickname given to people on ships whose duties included maintaining the boilers

Drake's Prayer The official form for the National Day of Prayer in 1941 printed the prayer by Sir Francis Drake was based on the words of a letter written in 1587: 'There must be a begynnyng of any great matter, but the contenewing unto the end untyll it be thoroughly ffynyshed yeldes the trew glory'. The prayer became popularly known as Drake's Prayer.

DSO Distinguished Service Order (Military decoration of the United Kingdom)

FAT Torpedo The standard German Navy torpedo which ran a wandering course with regular 180-degree turns

Foxer was the codename for a British built acoustic decoy. It consisted of one or two noise making devices towed several hundred metres behind the ship, and seduced the simple guidance mechanisms of acoustic torpedoes away from the rear of the ship into a circling pattern around the noise maker until the torpedo ran out of fuel

Gnat Torpedo German Navy acoustic torpedo. It employed passive acoustic homing to find its target, becoming active after a straight run of 400 metres

Gun Turret Ships of the Royal Navy had four gun turrets; 'A' Gun was at the front of the ship (and on big ships were always manned by Marines), and 'B' Gun was behind but mounted higher on a plinth. 'X' Gun was at the rear of the ship on a plinth and 'Y' Gun was aft of that at deck level. On a gun there is a Gun Layer, a Gun Trainer, and a person to fire the gun as well as several persons to supply and load the ammunition. The Layer moves the gun on one direction, and the Trainer moves the gun to get the range

Haka is a traditional ancestral war cry, dance or challenge from the Māori people of New Zealand. *It* was made familiar worldwide by the *All Blacks* rugby team who perform a haka before their matches

Hawser is a nautical term for a thick cable or rope used for mooring or towing a *ship*

Hedgehog was an anti-submarine device used to supplement the depth charges. The weapon fired a number of small spigot mortar bombs from spiked fittings, which exploded on contact, rather than using a time or depth fuse as depth charges did. It was named for the way the rows of empty spigots resembled the spines of a hedgehog

HMS His Majesty's Ship—the prefix given to ships (and shore establishments) of the Royal Navy.

HMS Unicorn/Cressy was a reserve ship that was launched in 1824, and from 1873 served as a training ship for the Tay. She remained unrigged and had a roof which covered her entire upper deck. She is now the World's last intact warship from the days of sail, one of the six oldest ships in the world and Scotland's only representative of the sailing navy.

Korvettenkapitän German Corvette Captain

Lend-Lease was a unique phenomenon in the history of the Second World War: under extreme conditions, countries with different systems of government—the USA, Great Britain, the USSR and Canada—succeeded in reaching an accord and pooling their efforts toward victory over German Nazism.

LDV Local Defence Volunteers

Liberty Ships were cargo ships of British concept that were adapted and built in the United States during the Second World War. They were cheap and quick to build, and came to symbolise US wartime industrial output

LST (Landing Ship, Tank) is the military designation for naval vessels created during World War II to support amphibious operations by carrying significant quantities of vehicles, cargo, and landing troops directly onto an unimproved shore

Measured Mile (St Abb's Head) Four Admiralty Distance Poles lie on the southern coast of the Firth of Forth, on rough ground and cliffs to the west of St Abb's Head. It was on the basis of these trials that the owners decided whether or not the ships (newly built or re-engined) were up to specification and agreed to accept them

NAAFI The Navy, Army and Air Force Institute is an organisation created by the Government in 1921 to run recreational establishments needed by the British Armed Forces

OGPU was the early security and political police (and was responsible for the creation of the Gulag system) of the Soviet Union and a forerunner of the more widely known Committee for State Security, the KGB

PLUTO The Pipe Line Under The Ocean operation provided a reliable supply of petrol for the advancing Allied forces following the D-Day landings; the largest amphibious landing in history, and the planners realised that any loss of momentum could jeopardise the whole operation as German forces would have time to regroup and counter-attack

Pompey The nickname for Portsmouth, although there is no definitive answer as to why

Primus stove A pressurized-burner kerosene (paraffin) stove

RAF Royal Air Force

RAAF Royal Australian Air Force

RASC Royal Army Service Corps

RE Royal Engineers

REME Royal Electrical and Mechanical Engineers

RNAS Royal Naval Air Service

RNVR Royal Naval Volunteer Reserve. The Royal Naval Volunteer Reserve was comprised of civilian volunteers who weren't professional seamen.

RNZNVR *Royal New Zealand Naval Volunteer Reserve*

Rear Admiral is a naval commissioned officer rank above that of a Commodore and Captain, and below that of a Vice-Admiral

RNLI Royal National Lifeboat Institution

Sea Bees From the abbreviation of Construction Battalions (CB's), which were created by the United States Navy after the attack on Pearl Harbor when the use of civilian labour in war zones became impractical.

Sten Gun A submachine gun of simple design and low production cost. STEN is an acronym from the names of the weapon's chief designers, Major Reginald V Shepherd and Harold Turpin, and **EN** for Enfield (the small arms factory where the gun was commissioned).

Stone Frigate is a nickname for a naval establishment on land

WRAF Women's Royal Air Force, which was reformed as the Women's Auxiliary Air Force for the 1939-45. The term Auxiliary had been chosen to indicate that women volunteers were not fully part of the RAF

WRNS Women's Royal Naval Service. Also referred to as the Wrens

The Russian Arctic Convoy
Museum Project

The importance of highlighting the legacy of the Second World War Russian Arctic Convoys is central to the project plans for a Russian Arctic Convoy Museum on the shores of Loch Ewe, in Aultbea, Wester Ross, Scotland. Loch Ewe was where almost half of the convoys to Russia began their perilous journeys between 1941 and 1945. Over 3,000 men lost their lives on the convoys and 104 ships were sunk.

The Arctic Convoys of the Second World War were Britain's means of sending vital supplies and war materials to Northern Russia (then part of the Soviet Union). Protected by Royal Navy warships, merchant vessels sailed from British ports to the harbours of Archangel and Murmansk. Although hazardous, this was the shortest route by which Britain could supply Russia. Keeping as far north as possible to keep out of range of the German U-boats and aircraft, the convoys hugged the limit of the ice. Because of this necessity, most of the convoys ran throughout the coldest winter months when poor visibility would give them as much cover as possible. For Prime Minister Winston Churchill, these supplies were a vital demonstration of Allied solidarity. He called the Arctic Convoys 'the worst journey in the world'.

The Museum Project is a key part in the Aultbea Regeneration Plan, together with a new Community Centre, to help bring much needed employment and income potential to the area whose community gave so much to the war effort in this North West Highland anchorage for the Arctic Convoys. The aim of the project is to create a lasting legacy to all those who took part in the acts of heroism and extreme physical endurance that were the Second World War Arctic Convoys. We hope to achieve this within the lifetime of the few remaining veterans.

For more information about the project and how to donate to the project, go to www.russianarcticconvoymuseum.co.uk. The Museum Group in Wester Ross hold an annual WWII and Arctic Convoys Week in early May each year, where there are a wide range of expert speakers on the subject of the Arctic Convoys. Scottish Charity No: SCO42286

Russian Arctic Convoy Museum Logo.

Index

German Ships